A DREAMSPEAKER CRUISING GUI

Revised Fourth Edition

Desolation Sound & the Discovery Islands

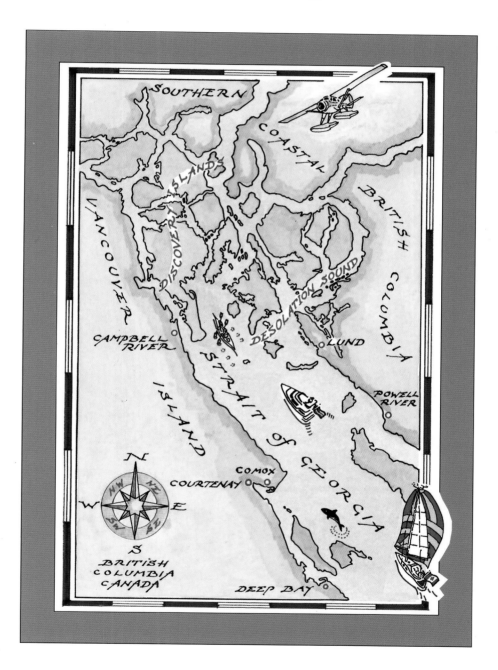

ANNE & LAURENCE YEADON-JONES

HARBOUR PUBLISHING

www.harbourpublishing.com

Featured Destinations

TABLE OF CONTENTS

125°W

Cover: Laura Cove, Desolation Sound Marine Park.

Text copyright © 2000, 2011, 2017 by Anne Yeadon-Jones and Laurence Yeadon-Jones

Photographs and illustrations copyright © Laurence Yeadon-Jones (except where otherwise noted).

4 5 6 7 8 — 21 20 19 18 17

Harbour Publishing Co. Ltd.
P.O. Box 219
Madeira Park, BC V0N 2H0
www.harbourpublishing.com

Project editor Peter A. Robson
Composition by Mary White

Printed in China by Prolong Press

Harbour Publishing acknowledges the support of the Canada Council for the Arts, which last year invested $153 million to bring the arts to Canadians throughout the country. We also gratefully acknowledge financial support from the Government of Canada through the Canada Book Fund and from the Province of British Columbia through the BC Arts Council and the Book Publishing Tax Credit.

Library and Archives Canada Cataloguing in Publication

Yeadon-Jones, Anne, author
  Desolation Sound & the Discovery Islands / Anne & Laurence Yeadon-Jones. — Revised fourth edition.

(A Dreamspeaker cruising guide ; volume 2)
Includes bibliographical references and index.
ISBN 978-1-55017-790-9 (paperback)

    1. *Dreamspeaker* (Yacht). 2. Boats and boating—British Columbia—Desolation Sound—Guidebooks. 3. Boats and boating—British Columbia—Discovery Passage—Guidebooks. 4. Desolation Sound (B.C.)—Guidebooks. 5. Discovery Passage (B.C.)—Guidebooks. I. Yeadon-Jones, Laurence, author II. Title. III. Title: Desolation Sound and the Discovery Islands. IV. Series: Yeadon-Jones, Anne. Dreamspeaker cruising guide ; v. 2.

GV776.15.B7Y3233 2016   797.109711'3   C2016-906982-6

WE WOULD LIKE TO HEAR FROM YOU!
We hope you enjoy using Volume 2 of *A Dreamspeaker Cruising Guide*. We welcome your comments, suggestions, corrections and any ideas about what you would like to see in future editions of the guide. Please drop us a line at info@harbourpublishing.com or info@dreamspeakerguides.com.

Caution: This book is meant to provide experienced boaters with cruising information about the waters covered. The suggestions offered are not all-inclusive and, due to the possibility of differences of interpretation, oversights and factual errors, none of the information contained in this book is warranted to be accurate or appropriate for any purpose other than the pursuit of great adventuring and memorable voyages.
A Dreamspeaker Cruising Guide should be viewed as a guide only and not as a substitute for official government charts, tide and current tables, coast pilots, sailing directions and local notices to boaters. Excerpts from charts are for passage planning only and are not to be used for navigation. Shoreline plans are not to scale and are not to be used for navigation. The publisher and authors cannot accept any responsibility for misadventure resulting from the use of this guide and can accept no liability for damages incurred.

FOREWORD

The sheer magnificence of the geography of the Desolation Sound and Discovery Islands area cannot be truly appreciated without exploring it first-hand. Canadian Hydrographic Service (CHS) field surveyors, frequently wearied with years of experience in remote, scenic locations, and many others earning their livelihood on or near the water never fail to be moved by travels in this region.

In any voyage by sea, preparation and planning are key to a successful outcome. From a navigation standpoint, official CHS charts and other nautical publications are required to safely reach one's desired destination. In addition to these official publications, many enthusiastic explorers, boaters and kayakers will seek further knowledge of their destinations through other literature. *Desolation Sound & the Discovery Islands*, part of the *Dreamspeaker Cruising Guide* series, is the perfect follow-up to the first informative and successful book in the series (*The Gulf Islands & Vancouver Island, Sooke to Nanaimo*) and is an excellent source of additional, vital information on this beautiful cruising ground.

Through hand-drawn shoreline plans, photographs and written descriptions of this exceptionally beautiful and abundant region, Anne and Laurence Yeadon-Jones once again pass on their extensive boating knowledge and experience in an easy and effective style. This colourful, sturdy book is a well-organized and handy reference that provides a full suite of pertinent information, from the charts required to get you to your destination, to safe anchorages, to the restaurants and shops to explore once you've arrived. Local knowledge, insights and tips contained within this cruising guide can all play a crucial role in making any journey both safe and enjoyable.

This second volume of *A Dreamspeaker Cruising Guide* complements the official CHS charts and publications and will undoubtedly have a reassuring presence near the helm for all cruisers and coastal explorers travelling in the area.

George Eaton
Former Director, Hydrography
Canadian Hydrographic Service, Pacific Region

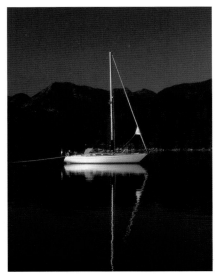

Dreamspeaker *in Desolation Sound.*

SPECIAL THANKS TO:

The team at Corilair—Mike Farrell, Bill Dutch and Pat Hadikin—who generously helped connect the *Dreamspeaker* team with all the coastal communities. 1-888-287-8366, www.corilair.com.

GRATEFUL APPRECIATION TO OUR INDUSTRY SUPPORT:

HUB International Insurance Brokers, specialist marine insurance, www.hubmarine.ca.

C-Tow, marine assistance network, www.c-tow.ca.

Beta Marine Canada, powering *Dreamspeaker*'s explorations, www.betamarinecanada.com.

Helly Hansen, for providing lifestyle and sailing gear to the *Dreamspeaker* team, www.hellyhansen.com.

ACKNOWLEDGEMENTS

We would like to thank the team at the Canadian Hydrographic Service, Pacific Region, for their input and contributions; Murray Archdekin for his keen attention to detail; Lynn Ove Mortensen for her photographic contributions; Ted Kramer and Vicki Haberi, BC Provincial Parks and Comox–Strathcona Regional District Parks; Duart Snow, former editor of *Pacific Yachting*; Al Wood, Lund Water Taxi; all the coastal people who generously gave us their time; the staff at Harbour Publishing; and finally, our family and friends, for their patience and enthusiastic support.

DREAMSPEAKER type SHE 36

Length overall	37'
Length on water	27'
Beam	10.6'
Draft	6.6'
Height above water	50.0'

AUTHORS' SAILBOAT

Dreamspeaker is a 36-foot SHE, a fibreglass sloop designed by Sparkman and Stephens and built by South Hants Engineering, UK, in 1979. She has a fin keel, draws 6.5 feet and sails like a dream. *Tink*, our faithful dinghy, is a 10-foot Tinker RIB, designed and hand-built by Henshaw Inflatables, UK. The oarlocks and wooden oars make for smooth, easy rowing. Sadly, the design has been discontinued.

To Jim, Ruby, Tilly and Vera, for inspiring us.

Entrance to Laura Cove in magnificent Desolation Sound

Chapter 1
DESOLATION SOUND & THE DISCOVERY ISLANDS

"The mountains grew higher and higher, and gossiped together across our heads. And somewhere down at their feet, on that narrow ribbon of water, our boat with the white sails flew swiftly along, completely dwarfed by its surroundings."

Muriel Wylie Blanchet, The Curve of Time

DESOLATION SOUND & THE DISCOVERY ISLANDS

Quadra/Cortes inter-island ferry.

CUSTOMS

The ports of entry covered by this guide for recreational boaters entering Canadian waters are located in Campbell River at the Coast Marina and the Discovery Harbour Marina. Contact Canada Customs toll free at 1-888-226-7277. The following are the main ports of entry in waters south of this guide: Victoria, Sidney, Bedwell Harbour, Nanaimo, White Rock, Steveston and Vancouver.

SEWAGE PUMP-OUT LOCATIONS

Comox Harbour Public Wharf – Page 15
Deep Bay Public Wharf – Page 29
Westview Public Wharf – Page 41
Lund Harbour Public Wharf – Page 49
Campbell River Public Wharf – Page 169

Note: "No Sewage Discharge" applies to all destinations in this guide.

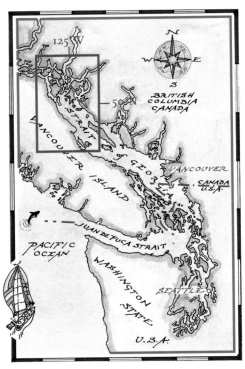

The cruising waters of Desolation Sound and the Discovery Islands.

In Volume 2 of *A Dreamspeaker Cruising Guide*, we focus on the cruising waters of Desolation Sound and the Discovery Islands. This seductive maze of interconnecting waterways also encompasses large tracts of accessible wilderness, and although the more adventurous boater and kayaker will be challenged by hazardous tidal rapids, the reward will be a rare opportunity to observe wildlife at close quarters. We introduce you to a wealth of protected anchorages, hideaway picnic stops, tranquil marine parks, excellent marinas and convenient public wharfs; we also show you where to hike, beachcomb, dig clams at leisure or indulge in some warm-water swimming and freshwater bathing. Provisioning stops are numerous and range from large urban centres to charming island stores. Those willing to venture off the beaten track may be rewarded with majestic fjords, cascading waterfalls, snow-capped mountains and, best of all, a moment to enjoy the quiet and solitude.

Although sport fishing was once the mainstay of this area, yacht charters and ecotourism are fast becoming major attractions, and traditional fishing lodges now welcome boaters to enjoy their cozy facilities and hearty home cooking. The warmer, more popular cruising months are July and August, although weather from mid-May to June and during September is often idyllic, with the lack of crowds making up for a drop in temperatures.

The cruising waters in the Northern Strait of Georgia are bordered by four very accessible urban rendezvous centres that provide easy connections by land, sea and air to Vancouver, Victoria and Seattle. The bustling towns of Powell River on the mainland, Courtenay, Comox and Campbell River on Vancouver Island's eastern shoreline serve as convenient gateways to all island destinations.

To help protect and preserve the sensitive ecosystems of these shorelines and islands, we encourage boaters to keep unnecessary wake and noise to a minimum, pack out all garbage and be aware of "no sewage discharge" for all destinations. Private-property boundaries are often unfenced and should be respected at all times. The summer season is short, and local enterprises really appreciate the patronage of visiting boaters, who will be rewarded with good service, local knowledge and insights into island life.

The threat of our peaceful waterways becoming noisy highways in the busy summer months is very real, and the delicate balance of these unspoiled cruising grounds lies in the hands of every boater and kayaker who comes to enjoy the rugged beauty of British Columbia's coastal waters.

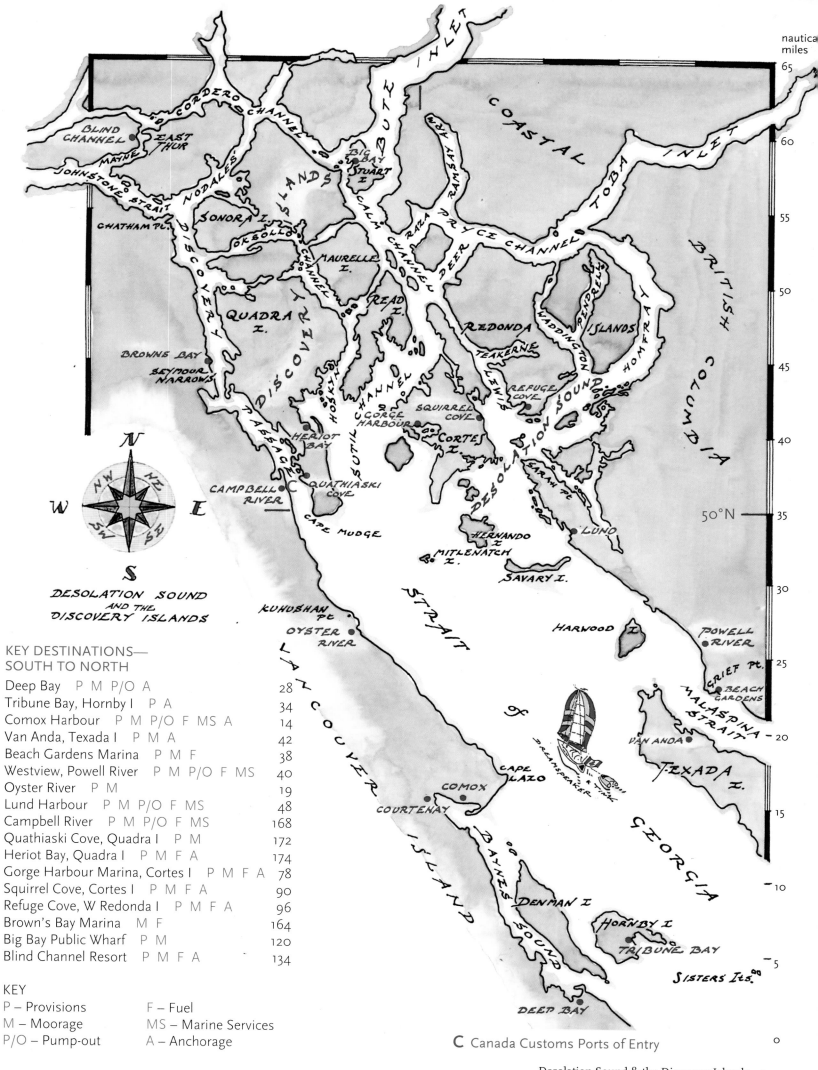

nautical miles

65

60

COASTAL

BRITISH COLUMBIA

55

TOBA INLET

50

BUTE INLET

CORDERO CHANNEL

BLIND CHANNEL

EAST THUR

MAYNE

NODALE'S

JOHNSTONE STRAIT

CHATHAM PT.

SONORA I.

OKSOLLO

MAURELLE I.

CALM CHANNEL

RAMSAY

RAZA

DEER

PRYCE CHANNEL

PENDRELL

ISLANDS

WADDINGTON

HOMFRAY

QUADRA I.

READ I.

REDONDA

TEAKERNE

LEWIS

REFUGE COVE

DESOLATION SOUND

BROWNS BAY

SEYMOUR NARROWS

HOSKIN

SUTIL CHANNEL

GORGE HARBOUR

SQUIRREL COVE

SARAH PT.

PASSAGE

HERIOT BAY

CORTES I.

CAMPBELL RIVER

QUATHIASKI COVE

C

LUND

HERNANDO I.

MITLENATCH I.

50°N

35

CAPE MUDGE

SAVARY I.

30

HARWOOD I.

POWELL RIVER

KUHUSHAN PT.

OYSTER RIVER

STRAIT

GRIEF Pt.

BEACH GARDENS

MALASPINA STRAIT

20

LANCOUVER

of

VAN ANDA

DESOLATION SOUND
AND THE DISCOVERY ISLANDS

**KEY DESTINATIONS—
SOUTH TO NORTH**

Deep Bay	P M P/O A	28
Tribune Bay, Hornby I	P A	34
Comox Harbour	P M P/O F MS A	14
Van Anda, Texada I	P M A	42
Beach Gardens Marina	P M F	38
Westview, Powell River	P M P/O F MS	40
Oyster River	P M	19
Lund Harbour	P M P/O F MS	48
Campbell River	P M P/O F MS	168
Quathiaski Cove, Quadra I	P M	172
Heriot Bay, Quadra I	P M F A	174
Gorge Harbour Marina, Cortes I	P M F A	78
Squirrel Cove, Cortes I	P M F A	90
Refuge Cove, W Redonda I	P M F A	96
Brown's Bay Marina	M F	164
Big Bay Public Wharf	P M	120
Blind Channel Resort	P M F A	134

KEY

P – Provisions   F – Fuel

M – Moorage   MS – Marine Services

P/O – Pump-out   A – Anchorage

GEORGIA

TEXADA I.

CAPE LAZO

DREAMSPEAKER & TINK

COMOX

COURTENAY

15

BAYNES SOUND

DENMAN I.

10

HORNBY I.

TRIBUNE BAY

5

SISTERS Its.

DEEP BAY

C Canada Customs Ports of Entry

0

WEATHER & WIND

Strong wind warning, Strait of Georgia. Winds 20–30 knots.

WEATHER A well-trained and experienced weather eye is a great asset, but a diligent weather ear regularly tuned to the marine forecasts will keep you well informed.

MARINE FORECASTS and warnings are available as continuous marine broadcasts on the following VHF channels and frequencies: WX1: 162.55; WX2: 162.40; WX3: 162.475; and 21B: 161.65. Alternatively, phone the following continuous marine weather recordings:

Vancouver:	604-666-3655
Comox:	250-339-0748
Alert Bay:	250-974-5305

For further information on weather products and services, visit Environment Canada at www.weatheroffice. ec.gc.ca.

ENVIRONMENT CANADA WEST COAST WEATHER PUBLICATIONS

Mariner's Guide: West Coast Marine Weather Services
Marine Weather Hazards Manual— West Coast: A Guide to Local Forecasts and Conditions
The Wind Came All Ways, by Owen Lange

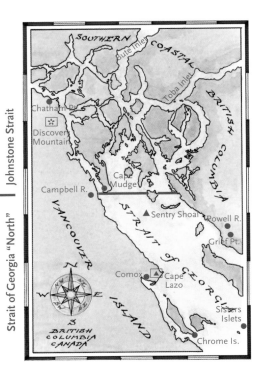

● Marine Weather Reporting Station

▲ Marine Weather Buoy

❋ 21B 161.65 MHz

▲ WXI 162.55 MHz

MARINE WARNINGS:

Strong Wind Warning	20–33 knots
Gale Warning	34–47 knots
Storm Warning	48–63 knots
Hurricane Force Wind Warning	64 knots or more

WEATHER in the summer months, from mid-June to mid-September, is influenced by the arrival of the Pacific high-pressure systems. As the pressure builds and anchors itself over the coast, sunshine and light winds are often the norm. Summer mean maximum temperatures vary from 19°C (66°F) in the north to 22°C (72°F) in Desolation Sound. The prevailing summer winds are westerlies, being strongest as the high-pressure ridge approaches. As the land warms, afternoon southerly or southwesterly sea breezes develop and penetrate into the channels of Desolation Sound and become inflow/up-inlet winds. As the land cools, overnight outflow/down-inlet winds often rattle the rigging of boats at anchor in the early morning hours. The forecast for southeasterly winds generally means the return to unsettled, rainy weather. The coast has a few idiosyncratic "local weather hazards," which we describe at the beginning of each chapter.

However, from November to April, the "raincoast," as the region is known, is very cold, wet and windy, weather not at all conducive to the pleasantries of messing about in boats.

SUMMER WINDS (Courtesy of Environment Canada)

JOHNSTONE STRAIT: Westerly winds that begin as a 15–20-knot sea breeze in Queen Charlotte Strait during the afternoon gradually increase as they move into Johnstone Strait. These winds often reach 25–30 knots off Chatham Point by late evening. Even stronger winds may occur just to the west of Chatham Point. The westerly winds usually become light during the early morning hours.

STRAIT OF GEORGIA "NORTH": Northwesterly winds of 10–15 knots (occasionally 20 knots) spread down the strait during the early morning hours. Beginning near Campbell River at a little after midnight, these winds usually stop near Nanaimo but occasionally reach all the way down to the Vancouver area. The northwesterlies generally become light during the early afternoon.

MARINE FORECAST ISSUE TIMES: 0400, 1030, 1600 and 2130. Issue times remain the same throughout the year.

WAVES, TIDES & CURRENTS

TIDE AND CURRENT TABLES provide essential navigational information and must be acquired prior to venturing into these waters. A working knowledge of tides and currents, and their interplay with the wind, is especially important in this region.

Each chapter begins with Volume 5 or 6 of the *Canadian Tide and Current Tables* referenced. Tides (reference port and secondary ports) and currents (reference station and secondary stations) are followed by a note describing any local tidal peculiarities or currents that may occur within the boundaries covered by the chapter.

OFFICIAL PUBLICATIONS

Refer to *Canadian Tide and Current Tables, Volume 5: Juan de Fuca Strait and Strait of Georgia and Volume 6: Discovery Passage and the West Coast of Vancouver Island.*

Hazardous tidal rapids clearly visible in Seymour Narrows.

WAVES: Hazardous wave action in this region develops as a result of the wind interacting with the tidal current. In general, conditions can be very dangerous when the wind opposes the current. It's best to travel when the winds are in the same direction as the current. The "strong wind warning" means just that: winds forecast at between 20 and 30 knots can be hazardous to small craft. The seas that subsequently develop can become treacherous in a wind-against-current situation.

TIDES (the vertical movement of water): Due to the meeting of the two flooding streams, the tidal range (rise and fall of the water) is large, with a maximum range of over 5.5 m (18 ft) in Prideaux Haven. The boundary between the two volumes is a line drawn through the southeastern end of the Discovery Islands to the mainland. The line is just north of the convergence of the northerly flowing flood tide (Volume 5) and the southerly flowing flood tide (Volume 6). The actual convergence is more complex, shifting due to weather, wind and freshwater-runoff conditions.

CURRENTS (the horizontal movement of water): The tidal rise and fall results in currents flooding into and ebbing out of the Strait of Georgia. The currents in the Northern Strait of Georgia rarely exceed 2 knots, but they can increase wave height dramatically in a wind-against-current situation. Currents in the Desolation Sound region are minimal, allowing the surface water temperature to rise substantially. Stronger currents exist in the channels, passages and narrows that make up the waterways between the Discovery Islands and Vancouver Island. Where the channels narrow, the currents accelerate to produce exceedingly hazardous tidal rapids, which should only be negotiated at times of slack water.

CAUTIONARY NOTE: Times of slack water (turns) at the rapids may differ significantly from the times of shore-side high and low water. It's of paramount importance to be able to read and interpolate the tide and current tables accurately.

Tides   •   Reference Port
Currents   ■   Reference Station
Direction   ➔   **Flood Tide**

CHARTS & NAUTICAL PUBLICATIONS

Never rely on Neptune for guidance. Use only CHS charts and publications.

We have carefully designed this cruising guide to work in conjunction with the Canadian Hydrographic Service (CHS) charts and publications, and above each destination we have referenced the appropriate charts.

In almost all cases, operators of ships and boats are required to have official, up-to-date charts and publications on board that cover the area they are navigating. For the few exceptions, see the chart carriage requirements in the Charts and Nautical Publications Regulations, 1995, of the Canada Shipping Act. Charts can be referenced from the *Pacific Coast Catalogue, Nautical Charts and Related Publications*, edited by the CHS and available free of charge at any chart dealer.

Individual charts are the primary tools used by professional mariners and recreational boaters, and those listed below cover the entire area included in this book (Volume 2): Charts: 3311, 3312, 3513, 3527, 3536, 3537, 3538, 3539, 3540, 3541, 3542, 3543, 3555 and 3559.

The Cruising Atlas (Chart 3312) is especially useful for Volume 2, as it covers Desolation Sound and the Discovery Islands and has been designed with the recreational boater in mind. This comprehensive navigational resource gives extensive supplementary information, extracts from *Sailing Directions* (see Nautical Publications section, below) and provides approach photographs to certain anchorages and passages. All charts referenced are metric editions.

ELECTRONIC CHARTS

Electronic charts are either raster (direct electronic scans of the paper charts) or vector (where charts are presented in an electronic graphic schematic manner). We recommend the use of raster charts, as they match the paper charts. Most manufacturers of charting software are licensed to use CHS chart data in their digital products. While CHS does not sell charts directly to the public, it distributes through a very large dealer network. Monthly updates to the charts are included with a licence. For more information, visit www.charts.gc.ca.

APPROACH WAYPOINTS

Approach waypoints are marked on the hand-drawn charts and give latitude and longitude positions based on NAD 83 and shown in degrees, minutes and decimals of a minute. They are located in deep water, at positions from which the illustrated features will be readily discernible in daylight.

PUBLICATIONS

We recommend the following publications to accompany your copy of Volume 2 of *A Dreamspeaker Cruising Guide*. For further reading, consult the Selected Reading list on page 180.

NAUTICAL PUBLICATIONS, CHS

Canadian Tide and Current Tables, Volume 5: Juan de Fuca Strait and Strait of Georgia.
Canadian Tide and Current Tables, Volume 6: Discovery Passage and the West Coast of Vancouver Island.
Catalogue of Nautical Charts and Related Publications: Pacific Coast 2.
Sailing Directions: British Columbia Coast (South Portion).
Symbols and Abbreviations Used on Canadian Charts: Chart 1.

WEATHER PUBLICATIONS, ENVIRONMENT CANADA

Marine Weather Hazards Manual – West Coast: A Guide to Local Forecasts and Conditions.
Mariner's Guide: West Coast Marine Weather Services.

BOATING SAFETY PUBLICATIONS, CANADIAN COAST GUARD

The Canadian Aids to Navigation System: Marine Navigation Services Directorate.
List of Lights, Buoys and Fog Signals: Pacific Coast.
Protecting British Columbia's Aquatic Environment: A Boater's Guide.

EMERGENCY PROCEDURES & HOW TO USE THIS BOOK

THE CANADIAN COAST GUARD is an organization whose primary role of search and rescue is supported by the following roles: maintaining the Aids to Navigation, operating the Office of Safe Boating and, in association with Environment Canada, the Marine Weather Forecast. For a copy of the *Safe Boating Guide*, call 1-800-267-6687. For search and rescue, call

Telephone   1-800-567-5111
Cellular (SAR)   727
VHF Channel   16
Worldwide Emergency Phone
                   01-250-363-2333

If in doubt, call 911

EMERGENCY RADIO PROCEDURES

MAYDAY: For *immediate danger* to life or vessel.

PAN-PAN: For *urgency* but no immediate danger to life or vessel.

For MAYDAY or PAN-PAN, transmit the following on VHF channel 16 or 2182 khz.

1. MAYDAY, MAYDAY, MAYDAY (or PAN-PAN, PAN-PAN, PAN-PAN), this is [vessel name and radio call sign].

2. State your position and the nature of the distress.

3. State the number of people on board and describe the vessel (length, make / type, colour, power, registration number).

NOTE: If the distress is not life threatening, the Coast Guard will put out a general call to boaters in your area for assistance. A tow at sea by a commercial operator can be expensive. Check that your insurance policy adequately covers a marine tow.

HOW TO USE THIS BOOK

This sample layout identifies the various features of this cruising guide that will help you to reach your destination safely, and give you plenty of information.

Chapter & featured destination reference

Chapter legend

Destination locator

* Approach waypoint latitude & longitude

Tips on best approach & anchorages

Cautionary note

Depth contour (approximate position). Depths reduced to lowest normal tide (zero tide)

Solid black line indicates high-water mark

Green area indicates land above high-water mark

Sepia area indicates shoreline that covers & uncovers with the tide

Blue area indicates shallower water

White area indicates deeper water that is safe for navigation

* Asterisk indicates approximate position of approach waypoint

Boats at anchor

Red broken line indicates a safe approach course

Aerial approach or ambient photograph

HW: high water
LW: low water

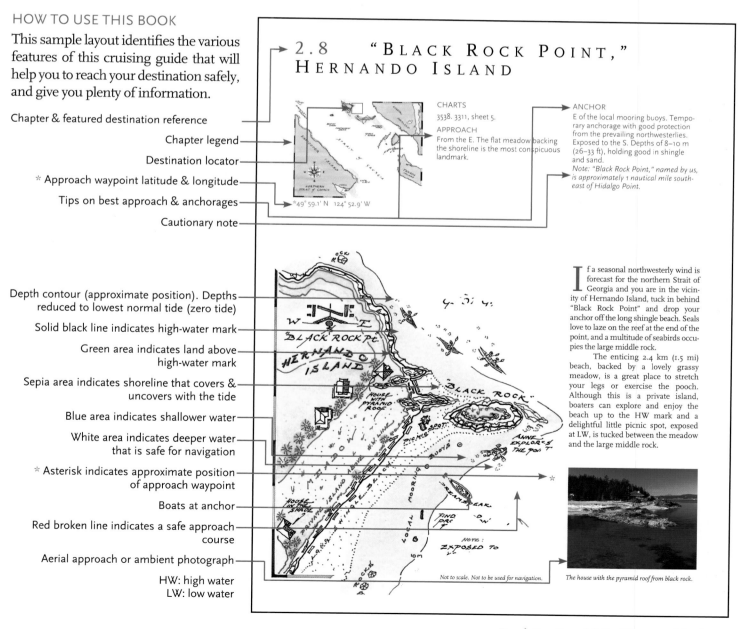

2.8   "BLACK ROCK POINT," HERNANDO ISLAND

CHARTS
3538. 3311, sheet 5.

APPROACH
From the E. The flat meadow backing the shoreline is the most conspicuous landmark.

*49° 59.1' N 124° 52.9' W

ANCHOR
E of the local mooring buoys. Temporary anchorage with good protection from the prevailing northwesterlies. Exposed to the S. Depths of 8–10 m (26–33 ft), holding good in shingle and sand.
Note: "Black Rock Point," named by us, is approximately 1 nautical mile southeast of Hidalgo Point.

If a seasonal northwesterly wind is forecast for the northern Strait of Georgia and you are in the vicinity of Hernando Island, tuck in behind "Black Rock Point" and drop your anchor off the long shingle beach. Seals love to laze on the reef at the end of the point, and a multitude of seabirds occupies the large middle rock.

The enticing 2.4 km (1.5 mi) beach, backed by a lovely grassy meadow, is a great place to stretch your legs or exercise the pooch. Although this is a private island, boaters can explore and enjoy the beach up to the HW mark and a delightful little picnic spot, exposed at LW, is tucked between the meadow and the large middle rock.

Not to scale. Not to be used for navigation.

The house with the pyramid roof from black rock.

PASSAGES NORTH

MAJOR MARINE CENTRES & ANCHORAGES

We recommend getting a copy of *Vol. 3: Vancouver, Howe Sound and the Sunshine Coast*, which illustrates this area in detail and describes the major marine centres and anchorages the cruising boater will find between *Vol. 1: The Gulf Islands & Vancouver Island* and this volume (2).

SUNSHINE COAST: Departing Vancouver

1. Snug Cove: moorage
2. Gibsons: moorage, fuel, anchorage
3. Plumper Cove Marine Park: anchorage
4. Smuggler Cove Marine Park: anchorage
5. Secret Cove: moorage, fuel, anchorage
6. Pender Harbour: moorage, fuel, anchorage
7. Hardy Island Marine Park: anchorage
8. Powell River, Chapter 4. Westview 4.1: moorage, fuel; Beach Gardens 4.3: moorage, fuel

Passages North – – – – – – – –
Ferry Routes – – – – – – – –

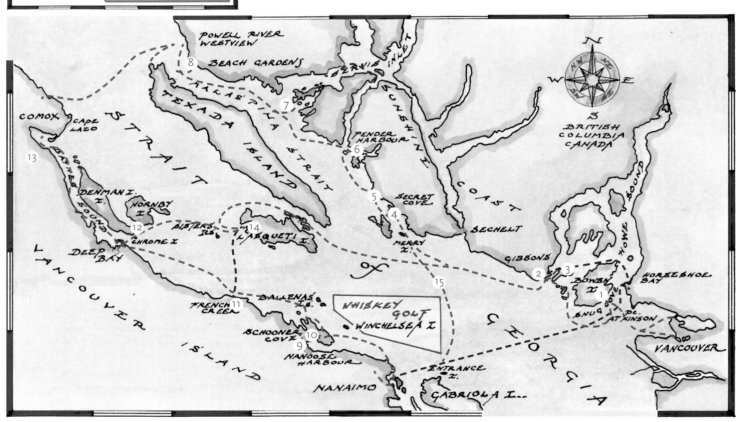

VANCOUVER ISLAND: Departing Nanaimo (Volume 1 of *A Dreamspeaker Cruising Guide*)

9. Nanoose Harbour: anchorage
10. Schooner Cove: moorage, fuel
11. French Creek: moorage, fuel
12. Baynes Sound, Chapter 3. Ford Cove 3.4: moorage, anchorage; Deep Bay 3.1: moorage, anchorage

13. Northern Strait of Georgia, Chapter 2. Comox 2.2: moorage, anchorage
14. As a midway crossing stopover, Lasqueti Island has good anchorage in False Bay
15. Sailors' route directly to the Sunshine Coast.

Area "Whiskey Golf" is a Torpedo Testing Range; when active, it's a no-go zone for all craft. Listen for notice to shipping as part of the continuous marine weather forecast or call Winchelsea Control at 1-888-221-1011 or contact them on VHF channel 10 (for information on safe transit). They also monitor channel 16.

Chapter 2
NORTHERN STRAIT OF GEORGIA

Optimists off Comox Harbour with the Comox Glacier in the background.

Hot Chocolates in Courtenay, with many flavours of handmade chocolates.

Chapter 2
NORTHERN STRAIT OF GEORGIA

TIDES

Canadian Tide and Current Tables, Volume 5
Reference Port: Point Atkinson
Secondary Ports: Comox, Mitlenatch Island
Note: Travelling N to the Discovery Islands, you will also require Volume 6 of the Canadian Tide and Current Tables.

CURRENTS

No specific reference or secondary stations cover this chapter.

WEATHER

Area: Strait of Georgia (northern half)
Reporting Stations: Comox, Cape Lazo, Cape Mudge, Sentry Shoal (S of Mitlenatch)

Note: Northwesterly winds prevail in the summer, and winds of 10–15 knots are common. They spread down the strait during the early morning hours, beginning near Cape Mudge a little after midnight. Occasionally, strong southeasterly winds may also be encountered.

CAUTIONARY NOTES

Take caution regarding the current and sea conditions under SE winds near Cape Mudge. Listen for and take heed of the small-craft warning. This stretch of sea is no kids' playground. These warnings are issued beginning in April and continuing until November 11. Warnings are broadcast when winds are expected to rise to 20–30 knots, creating potentially dangerous conditions.

On your journey north to Desolation Sound and the Discovery Islands, you will have to cross the 40 km (25 mi) of open water that lie north of Cape Lazo. If the forecast is for anything stronger than a moderate wind, it would be advisable to break your journey up and spend a day or two relaxing in sheltered Comox Harbour.

Take the opportunity to venture inland and discover the beautiful Comox Valley—gateway to Strathcona Park, British Columbia's oldest provincial park. Here hiking trails link Forbidden Plateau with Comox Glacier and the Mount Washington Resort. This fertile valley also grows an abundance of organic produce, sold at local farm stands or weekly farmers' markets.

Comox is also conveniently situated for visitors wishing to charter a boat or meet up with family and friends before the big hop north. Easy connections can be made by air, float plane, bus or car from Vancouver, Victoria and Seattle. The Powell River/Comox ferry terminal is also located nearby.

The charming "old town" of Courtenay is a delight to explore and offers an eclectic mix of shops, art galleries and restaurants, while the Courtenay River estuary affords a fascinating variety of bird life, easily viewed by kayak or dinghy.

After rounding Cape Lazo, you might wonder if a convenient stopping-off point is available on the long coastal stretch north. The well-managed marina and resort at Oyster River comes as a pleasant surprise and provides sheltered moorage, hot showers and a small sandy beach.

In settled weather, don't miss the opportunity to visit some of the lovely islands lying in the northern strait. Grassy Mitlenatch Island, a provincial nature park, is far more accessible than it first appears, offering relatively sheltered day anchorage and a chance to observe its protected seabird colonies and abundant wildflowers in the spring months.

Savary Island is perfect for an energetic, fun day out. Pack a picnic lunch and kayak, hike, bike and explore the beautiful white sandy beaches. You can anchor off in settled weather or just hop onto the water taxi in Lund.

Finally, lounge with the seals at "Black Rock Point" on Hernando Island, where a long shingle beach beckons you to stretch those sea-weary legs.

FEATURED DESTINATIONS

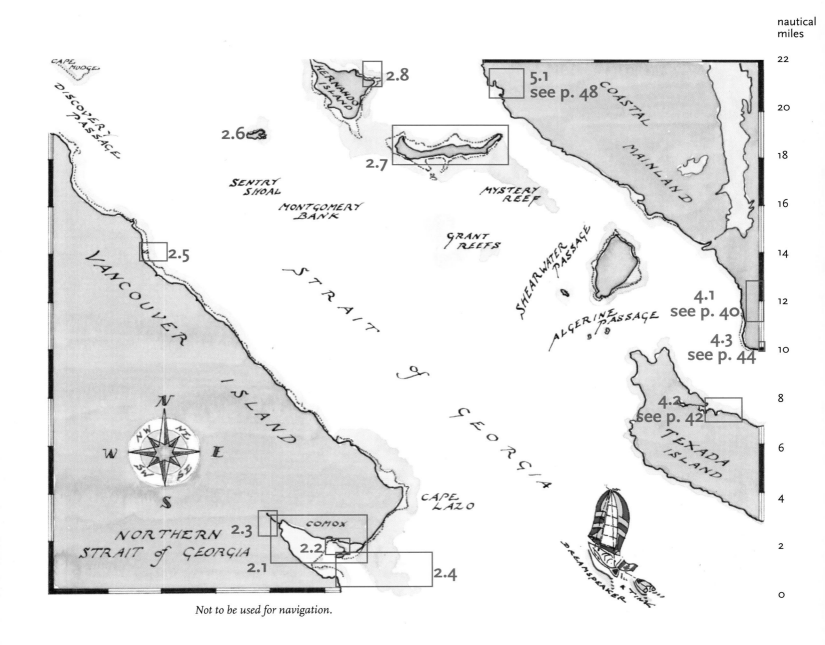

nautical
miles

5.1
see p. 48

4.1
see p. 40

4.3
see p. 44

4.2
see p. 42

Not to be used for navigation.

Sailing in Comox Harbour with the Comox Glacier as backdrop.

See 2.3, page 16.

COURTENAY RIVER & SLOUGH

CHART 3527.

Although Courtenay River is navigable from Comox Harbour to the public wharf at Courtenay Slough (max. 1.8 m [6 ft] at LW), it is more than just a casual undertaking for the recreational boater and entails (1) crossing the river's drying mud flats on a suitable tide via a channel marked by day beacons and ranges and (2) timing your passage into the slough as close to high tide as possible, because sufficient depth is needed to clear the bar just inside the entrance.

Note: ! Light
Range lights are in position atop the daymarks leading to the Courtenay River.

Local advice and guidance are highly recommended. Prior to your trip, contact the harbour manager at COMOX VALLEY HARBOUR AUTHORITY, 250-339-6041, to secure moorage and to arrange the lifting of the 17th Street Bridge. Note that the marina north of the Courtenay Airpark has a boat launch but no visitor moorage. A float for temporary moorage is available for boats waiting for the 17th Street Bridge to be lifted.

Comox Harbour, located below the majestic Comox Glacier on Vancouver Island's eastern coast, offers sheltered anchorage, a public wharf and expanded marina facilities. It is a key provisioning stop and a convenient base for boaters wishing to explore the delights of downtown Courtenay or the beauty of Comox Valley. (For Comox town and marinas, see page 14.)

Goose Spit, on the harbour's eastern side, provides protected anchorage and serves as the HMCS *Quadra* Cadet Training Camp. The clean and lovely sandy beaches surrounding the spit are for public day use. Fires are prohibited.

The Courtenay River offers access to downtown Courtenay, with moorage at the public wharf at the slough, although this is not a straightforward undertaking for the recreational boater (see page 16). A fun alternative is to explore the river and slough by kayak or dinghy and observe the fascinating variety of bird life. The slough has been enhanced with a river walk and viewpoint, an interpretive route, native plant gardens and a park pavilion. For kayak rentals call COMOX VALLEY KAYAKS at 1-888-545-5595. (For downtown Courtenay, see page 16.)

COURTENAY RIVER & SLOUGH, VANCOUVER ISLAND

COMOX HARBOUR

CHART 3527.

APPROACH

From the SE, out of Baynes Sound. The most obvious landmark is the starboard-hand light (red) on Goose Spit. Enter Comox Harbour by rounding the tip of the spit.

ANCHOR

Good all-weather protection can be found behind Goose Spit between the boats on mooring buoys or off and to the W of the breakwaters as indicated in depths of 5–15 m (16–49 ft). Holding good in sand and mud.

Note: Anchoring between HMCS Quadra and boats on mooring buoys is not recommended because you can foul your anchor with old log-booming debris.

The "Lagoon" (local name) is a shoal draft-boat anchorage not recommended for the visitor because the channel is very shallow and requires local guidance. A great place, however, to explore by kayak or paddle board.

PUBLIC WHARF, MARINAS, BOAT LAUNCH & FUEL

See 2.2, page 14.

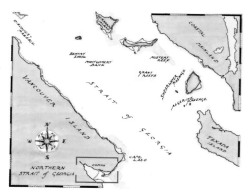

✿ 49° 39.6' N   124° 55.8' W

Approaching Goose Spit.

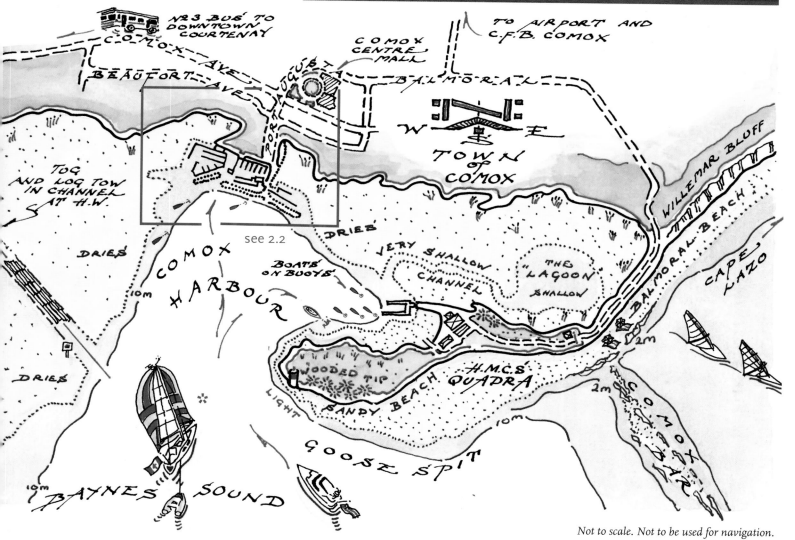

Not to scale. Not to be used for navigation.

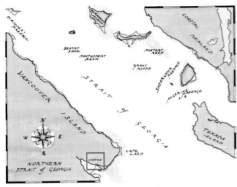

✱ 49° 40.1' N   124° 55.8' W

The entrance to the public wharf, east.

Indulge yourself with fresh fish and chips.

The Town of Comox has a distinct maritime flavour.

Nestled below the majestic Beaufort Mountains and the dazzling Comox Glacier on Vancouver Island's eastern coast, the town of Comox is a delight to visit and a convenient base for boaters wishing to explore Desolation Sound.

The historic town of Comox lies on a ridge overlooking the harbour, and the shoreside trail above the marina connects to the boardwalk and view pavilions built above the long stone breakwater. Freshly caught fish and shrimp can be bought directly from local fish boats tied up at the public wharf. THE BLACK-FIN PUB sits back from the harbour with a glorious view of the anchorage and the sun setting over the Comox glacier.

Downtown Comox provides an excellent choice of restaurants, cafés and bistros. Some favourites include TWISTED DISHES CAFÉ (tasty breakfast and lunch menu), MARTINE'S BISTRO (great food, cozy atmosphere) and TOSCANO'S MEDITERRANEAN GRILL (fresh pasta dishes). COMOX CENTRE MALL, a short walk from the public wharf and marina, is open seven days a week and houses a supermarket (customer service will call COMOX TAXI if you need a ride back), pharmacy, bank and a BC Liquor Store. The bus to Courtenay (a loop route) stops outside the mall.

You can spend a few pleasant hours shopping along Comox Avenue and browsing in the shops and gift stores. DUDUZA BED AND BATH stocks a tempting collection of duvet covers and sheets, and the CAROSEL FASHIONS consignment store offers a unique range of clothing, hats and shoes. BLUE HERON BOOKS has a large selection of international and local books, plus boating guides, and stocks official CHS charts. Treat yourself to a homemade gelato or sorbetto at BENINO GELATO. They have 24 flavours to choose from and their freshly made panini and wraps are delicious.

SIMON'S CYCLES rents bikes and there are numerous park trails to be hiked and biked. Just a short walk from Comox Harbour, you can play a round of golf at the COMOX GOLF CLUB. Nearby FILBERG HERITAGE LODGE AND PARK serves lunch and traditional afternoon tea overlooking sweeping green lawns and Comox Harbour. The park and its extended gardens cover nine acres of beautifully landscaped grounds with a stream running through a natural ravine—they also host the annual Filberg Festival on the BC Day long weekend, featuring the province's finest artists and artisans.

CHART 3527.

APPROACH

From the S, having cleared the tip of Goose Spit. The stone breakwater with the silhouette of the town of Comox behind it is the most prominent landmark.

ANCHOR

Good all-weather protection can be found behind Goose Spit between the boats on mooring buoys or off and to the W of the breakwaters, as indicated in depths of 5–15 m (16–49 ft). Holding good in sand and mud.

PUBLIC WHARF

The COMOX VALLEY HARBOUR AUTHOR-ITY, 250-339-6041, VHF 66A. Two-hour courtesy tie-up and extensive visitor moorage on "D" dock. Power up to 50 amps, water, free Wi-Fi, a complimentary computer and phone, and shower and laundry facilities. Pump-out on "G" dock.

MARINAS

COMOX VALLEY MARINA, 250-339-2930, VHF 66A, has visitor moorage, shower and laundry facilities and a designated dinghy dock. The municipal town marina is for local resident craft.

BOAT LAUNCH

At the foot of Wilcox Road.

FUEL DOCK

GAS 'N' GO MARINE has gasoline, diesel, water and ice and offers visitor moorage at their marina when available—call ahead, 250-339-4664.

Note: The public wharf and marina complex, with its mix of pleasure and commercial craft, makes for a busy place in the summer months.

Note: WILLS MARINE SUPPLY is well reputed and will provide any marine and chandlery services—delivery to your boat is prompt and courteous. Call 250-941-7373.

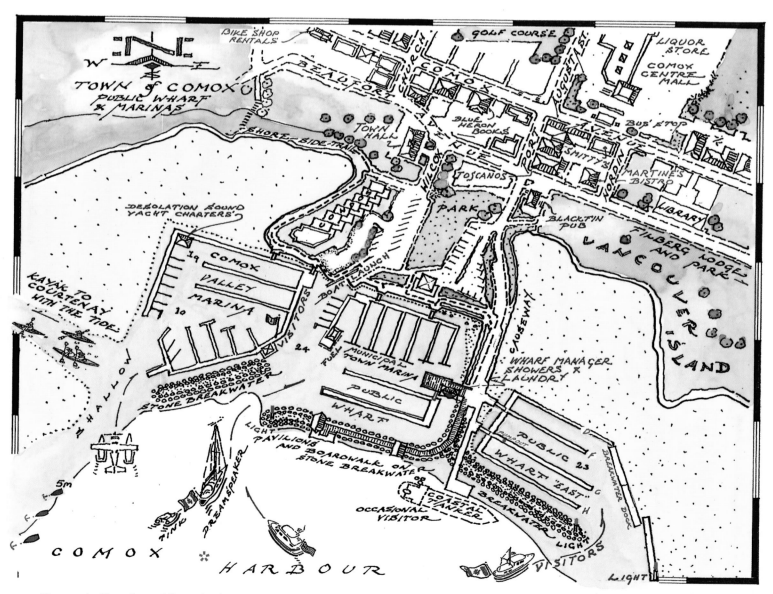

Not to scale. Not to be used for navigation.

2.3 DOWNTOWN COURTENAY, VANCOUVER ISLAND

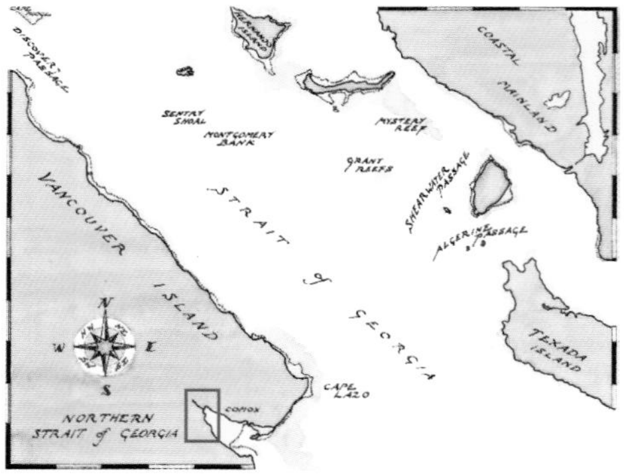

49° 41.2' N 124° 59.4' W

CHART 3527.

APPROACH

Once you have cleared the lifting bridge by prior arrangement, you will reach Courtenay Slough, located a short way upstream of the river on the northeast bank. Just inside the entrance lies a bar that dries 2.4 m (7.8 ft) at local chart datum, and inside the bar there is a minimum depth of 1.8 m (6 ft). The public wharf consists of 210 m (690 ft) of float space that extends from the head of the slough. Both power and water are available. (See 2.1, page 12, for navigation details.)

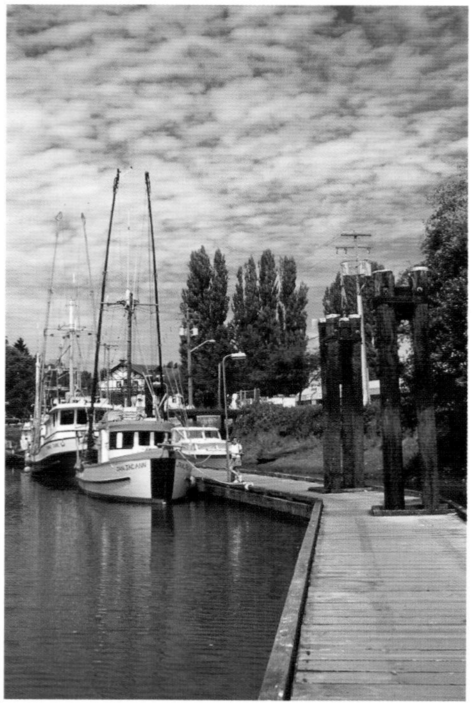

The Courtenay Slough.

The city of Courtenay developed during the late 1800s along the banks of virtually the only navigable river on Vancouver Island. The easiest way to visit the "old town" is to hop on a bus outside the Comox Centre Mall and enjoy the scenic route to Cliff Avenue and the hub of downtown Courtenay on 4th, 5th and 6th streets. Here you will find hanging baskets bursting with flowers and a wonderful variety of shops, bookstores, art galleries, restaurants, cafés and thrift stores to explore.

Discover the city's Elasmosaur (12 m [39.4 ft] long) at the COURTENAY AND DISTRICT MUSEUM, visit THE COMOX VALLEY CENTRE FOR THE ARTS, whose gift store contains a wonderful selection of handcrafted works, or take in a performance at the renovated SID WILLIAMS THEATRE, central Vancouver Island's major performance centre.

HOT CHOCOLATES on 5th Street hand-make their chocolates and truffles. They also carry Italian gelato and sorbetto and their artisan bakery is not to be missed. The CAPPUCCINO GRANDE CAFÉ serves delicious soups and sandwiches and RAWTHENTIC EATERY produces raw juice, salads, desserts and smoothies that are out of this world! Pop into the LAUGHING OYSTER BOOK SHOP and pick up one or two of their 10,000 in-stock titles.

Don't miss NATURAL PASTURES CHEESE COMPANY on McPhee, where you have fifteen handmade artisan cheeses to choose from. EDIBLE ISLAND WHOLE FOODS MARKET on 6th Street keeps fresh, local and organic produce; it's a great place to stock up on specialty foods or to pick up a picnic lunch. If you have the time, stroll along Beckensell Avenue to Riverside Lane to LOCALS RESTAURANT, located in the OLD HOUSE. Dine in casual elegance and enjoy "food from the heart of the island." The restaurant is open for lunch, dinner and weekend brunch.

Downtown Courtenay hosts the popular COMOX VALLEY FARMERS' MARKET (summer only) every Wednesday on 5th Avenue. Open from 9 a.m. to 12:30 p.m., this market is bursting with local and organic products including meats, fish and poultry, berries, eggs, honey and baked goods.

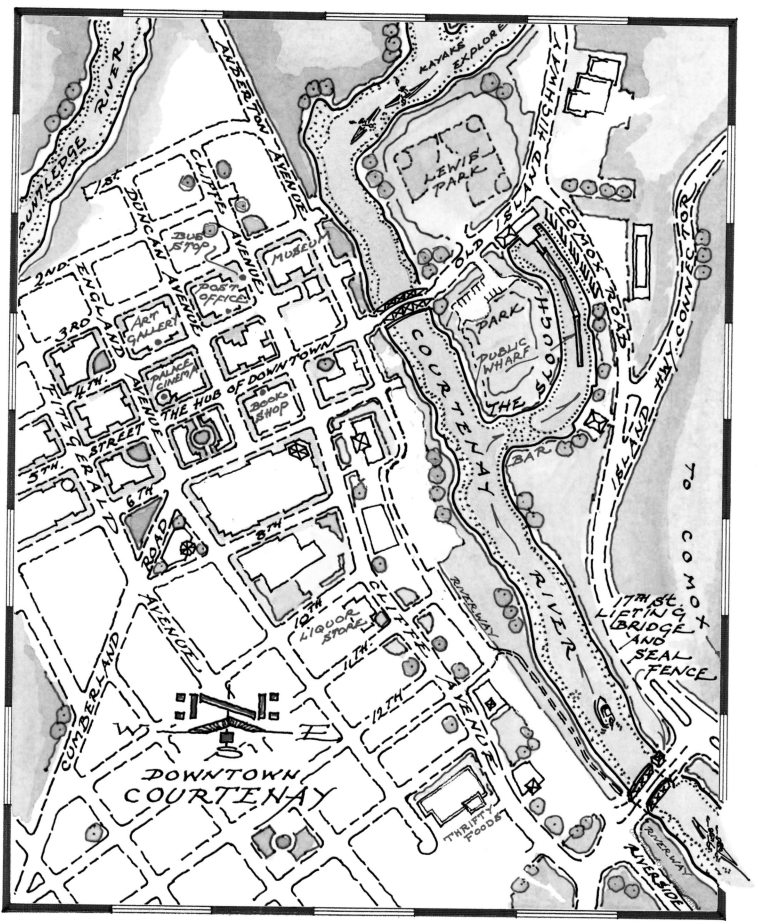

Not to scale. Not to be used for navigation.

2.4 Comox Bar, Vancouver Island

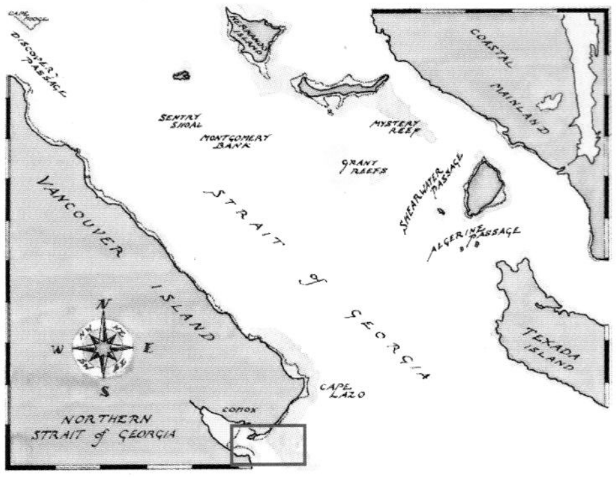

✲ 1) 49° 39.7' N 124° 51.3' W Strait of Georgia

✲ 2) 49° 38.6' N 124° 52.8' W Baynes Sound

CHART 3527.

APPROACH

FROM THE STRAIT OF GEORGIA: The outer starboard-hand buoy (red), P54, has a bell, light and radar reflector. The transit bearing of 222° true indicates the track across the bar in line with the onshore ranges (leading marks). A course made good of 200° magnetic should carry you to the next buoys and hence across the bar.

FROM BAYNES SOUND: The outer starboard-hand buoy (red), P50, is unlit and conical. The ranges (leading marks) are obscured by houses and trees until you are virtually on the transit bearing of 222° true on the stern. A course made good of 020° magnetic should carry you to the next buoy and hence across the bar.

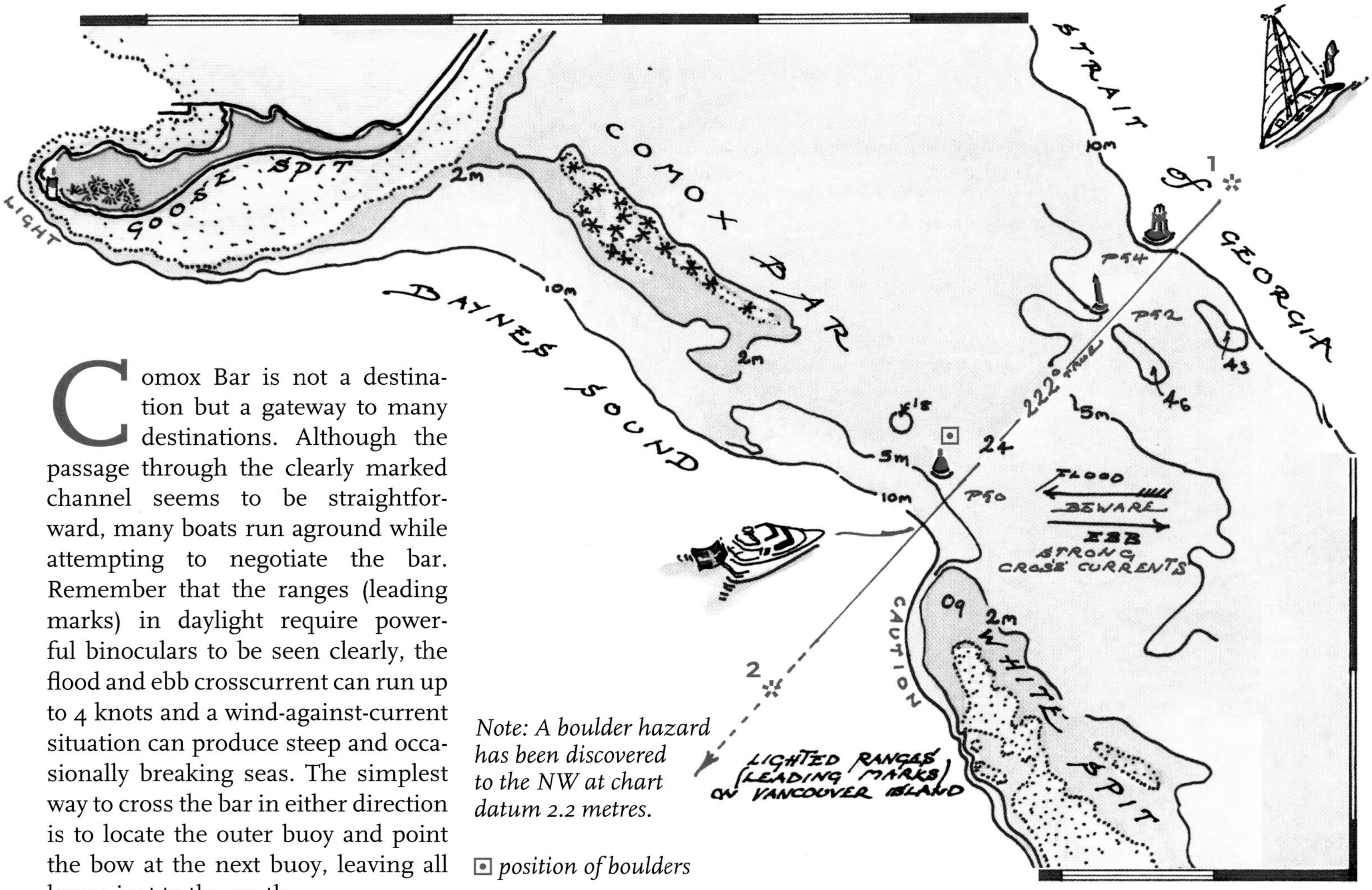

Comox Bar is not a destination but a gateway to many destinations. Although the passage through the clearly marked channel seems to be straightforward, many boats run aground while attempting to negotiate the bar. Remember that the ranges (leading marks) in daylight require powerful binoculars to be seen clearly, the flood and ebb crosscurrent can run up to 4 knots and a wind-against-current situation can produce steep and occasionally breaking seas. The simplest way to cross the bar in either direction is to locate the outer buoy and point the bow at the next buoy, leaving all buoys just to the north.

Note: A boulder hazard has been discovered to the NW at chart datum 2.2 metres.

⊡ *position of boulders*

Not to scale. Not to be used for navigation.

CHART 3513.

APPROACH

Having lined up the pilings well out to sea, approach with extreme caution. From the E the channel to the marina is dredged to 0.6 m (2 ft) and lies just to the S of the river mouth, which has a bank of shingle extending 0.3 nautical miles from the shoreline. The channel is approximately 450 m (1,476 ft) long, very narrow and not entirely straight. It is best to negotiate the channel prior to HW, when the banks are still visible. The seaward end of the channel

is marked by two piles. Enter between them and follow the remaining pilings in, on a 1.8 m (6 ft) plus tide.

MARINA

PACIFIC PLAYGROUNDS INTERNATIONAL offers visitor moorage for boats up to 11 m (36 ft) long. Power, water and free Wi-Fi on the docks. Call 1-877-239-5600.

BOAT LAUNCH

Private, at the marina.

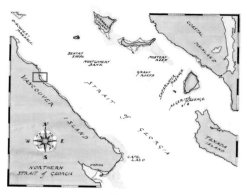

✽ 49° 52.2' N   125° 6.2' W

I f you need to break up your journey while voyaging north, pop into OYSTER RIVER PACIFIC PLAYGROUNDS MARINA, on Vancouver Island's eastern coast. Primarily a fishing and family resort, it also offers sheltered moorage for boats up to 11 m (36 ft) long. Power, water, showers and laundry facilities are provided, and kids have their own fishing dock. The convenience store stocks ice, basic groceries, books, charts, fishing licences, tackle and hardware, and has an on-site freezing facility. A clean sandy beach, heated swimming pool and tennis courts are also available at this pleasant stopover.

Approach to Pacific Playgrounds Marina.

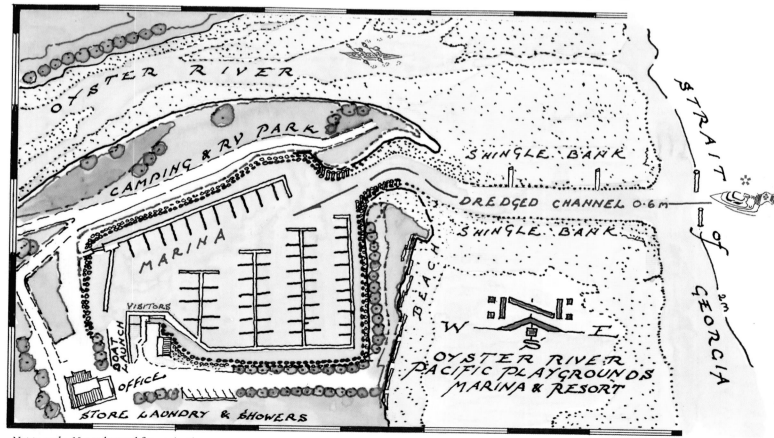

Not to scale. Not to be used for navigation.

2.6 Mitlenatch Island Provincial Nature Park

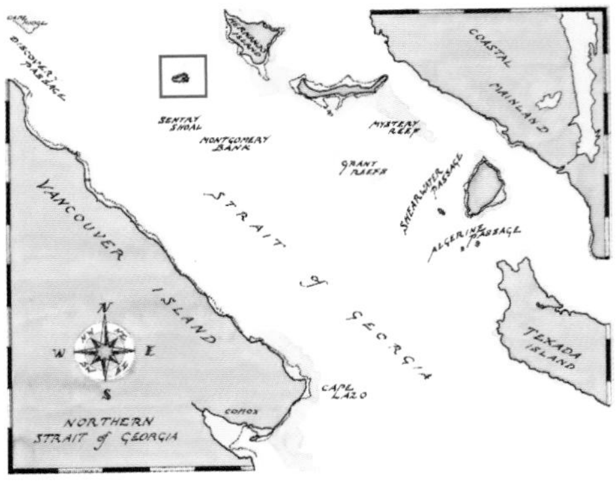

49° 56.8' N 124° 59.6' W

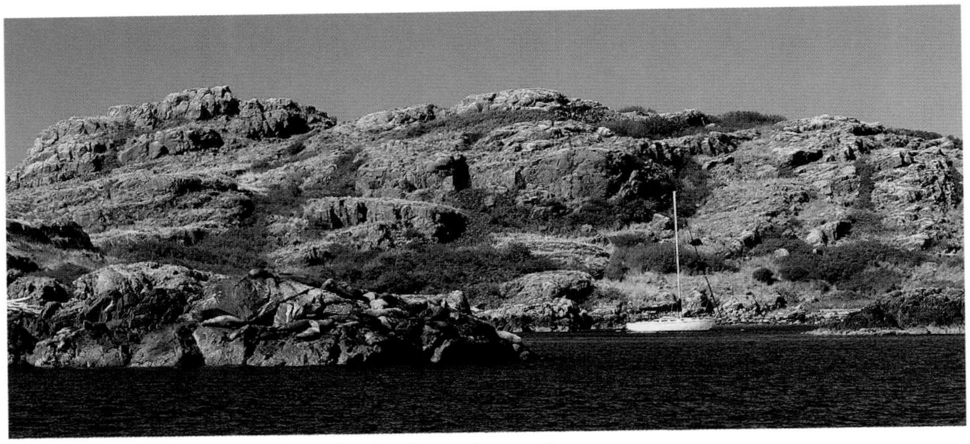

At anchor in Camp Bay, Mitlenatch Island, a unique setting.

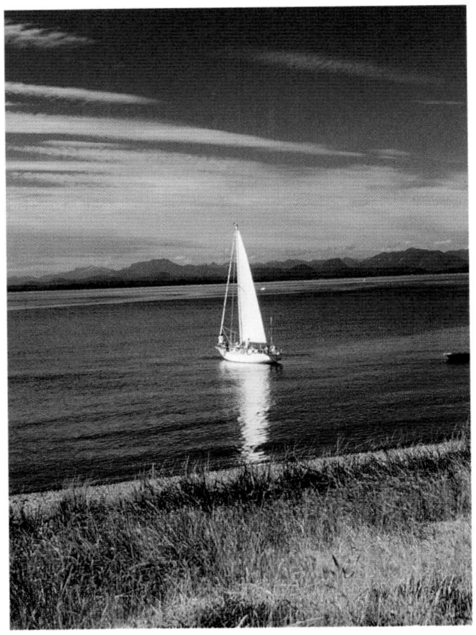

"Northwest Bay" and a tranquil Strait of Georgia.

Mitlenatch Island, low-lying and isolated at the southern entrance to Desolation Sound, is far more accessible than it first appears. The island is home to hundreds of harbour seals and, in the early spring, migratory Steller's and California sea lions bark and grunt from their basking rocks. Recreational boaters are welcome to visit the protected seabird colony as long as pets are kept on board, park rules are observed and nesting birds are not disturbed. The park boundary extends 300 m (1,000 ft) out from the shore, and all sedentary marine life—including abalones, oysters, scallops and sea cucumbers—are fully protected within this zone. Collecting is not permitted at Mitlenatch Island.

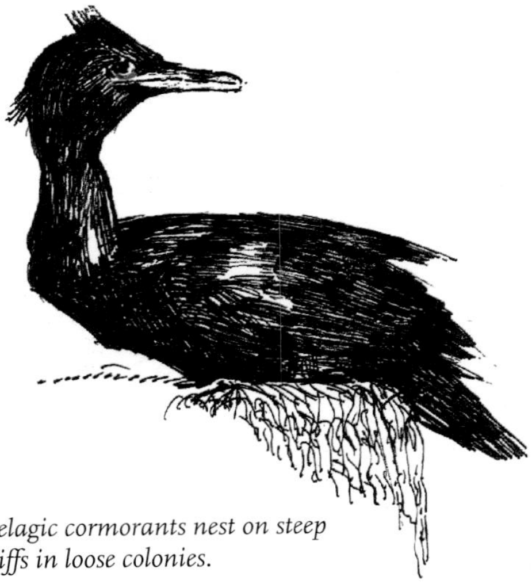

Pelagic cormorants nest on steep cliffs in loose colonies.

Anchorages on both the east and west sides of the island offer relatively sheltered protection from either northwest or southeast winds. If you are anchoring in Camp Bay, be sure to visit the friendly warden's cabin, where a volunteer naturalist will be happy to answer any questions. An informative brochure on the island's history and its protected seabirds and marine life is available from the information shelters.

"Northwest Bay" has a beautiful shingle beach with easy access to the island's designated trails and wooden observation blind on East Hill. From here, the patient observer can view the glaucous-winged gull's family life, including its fascinating feeding ritual.

Spring and summer flowers abound on Mitlenatch Island from late April onward. Since the island is home to the largest seabird colony in the Strait of Georgia, visitors should also be prepared for a high level of noise.

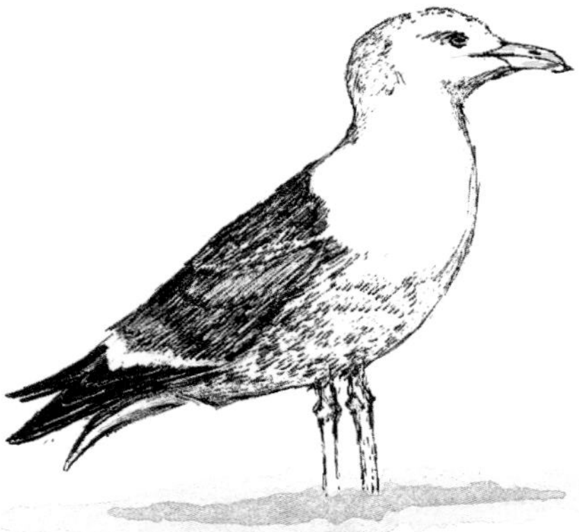

Over 3,000 pairs of glaucous-winged gulls choose to nest on Mitlenatch Island.

CHART 3538.

APPROACH

CAMP BAY: From the SE at LW with caution. The passage to the inner anchorage is fringed to the N with rocks and a reef.

ANCHOR

CAMP BAY: Temporary anchorage giving protection from prevailing northwesterlies. For two to three small boats in depths of 1.8–3 m (6–10 ft), over mixed bottom of mud, sand, shell and grass with moderate holding.

Note: Alternative temporary anchorage may be found off Northwest Bay in settled conditions or when seeking protection from a southeasterly.

Mitlenatch is home to 12 species of starfish.

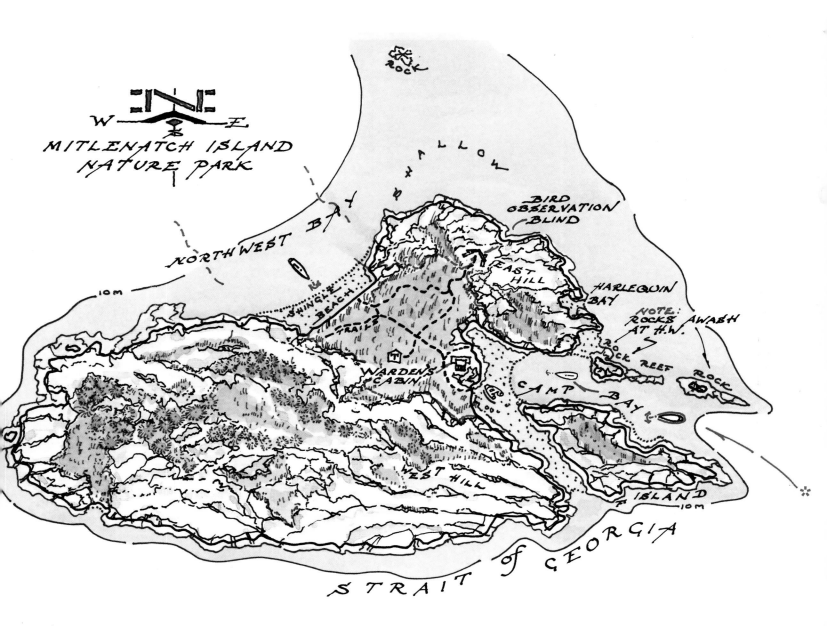

Not to scale. Not to be used for navigation.

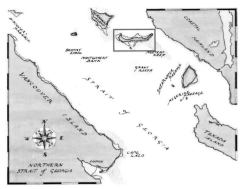

✿ 49° 57.1' N   124° 46.7' W

Flotilla at anchor off Mace Point.

When viewed from the air, it seems that Savary Island and its beautiful white sandy beaches were towed from an archipelago in the South Pacific—perhaps by an old sea captain homesick for his West Coast roots.

Even though the island lacks an all-weather anchorage, good temporary holding is available east of the public wharf, where wooden boardwalks protect the fragile beaches from further erosion. The island is a great place to visit for a fun day out and can easily be accessed by water taxi from Lund (see page 48). Kayakers can explore the wonders of Stradiotti and Mystery Reefs, and there are wooded trails for hiking, unpaved roads for biking and a lovely expanse of beach on the southern shore to be enjoyed. After a short uphill walk from the public wharf you will find bike and scooter rentals, RIGGERS RESTAURANT and THE GENERAL STORE. This popular family restaurant and pub is the hub of the community, serving tasty pub-style fare and offering shaded outdoor seating on the patio and in the back garden. The General Store keeps a small selection of provisioning basics, fresh and frozen produce and a variety of ice-cream flavours. Please pack out all garbage—there is a bin for refundable bottles and cans at the dock.

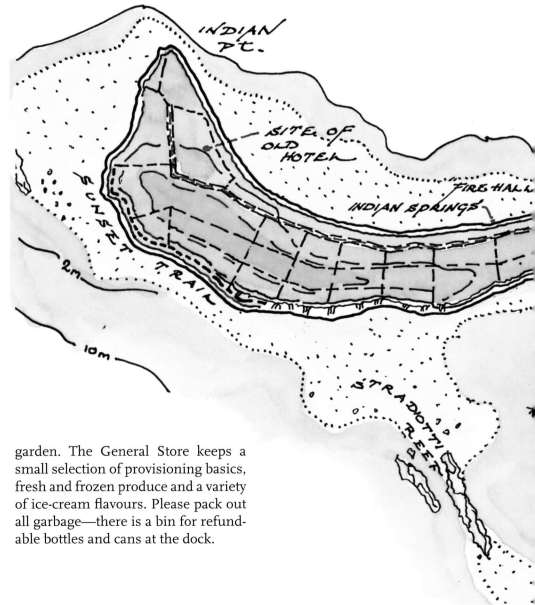

CHARTS 3538. 3311, sheet 5.

APPROACH

KEEFER BAY: From the NE, the jetty connecting the public wharf to the shore is the most noticeable landmark.

ANCHOR

Temporary anchorage to the E of the public wharf and N of the boats on buoys in settled weather. Alternatively, if a northwesterly is blowing, tuck into the south of Mace Point. In depths of 4–8 m (13–26 ft), holding good in sand.

PUBLIC WHARF

Water taxi and local boat facility only. Best to row your dinghy ashore.

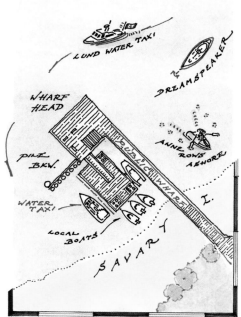

Detail: Public wharf.

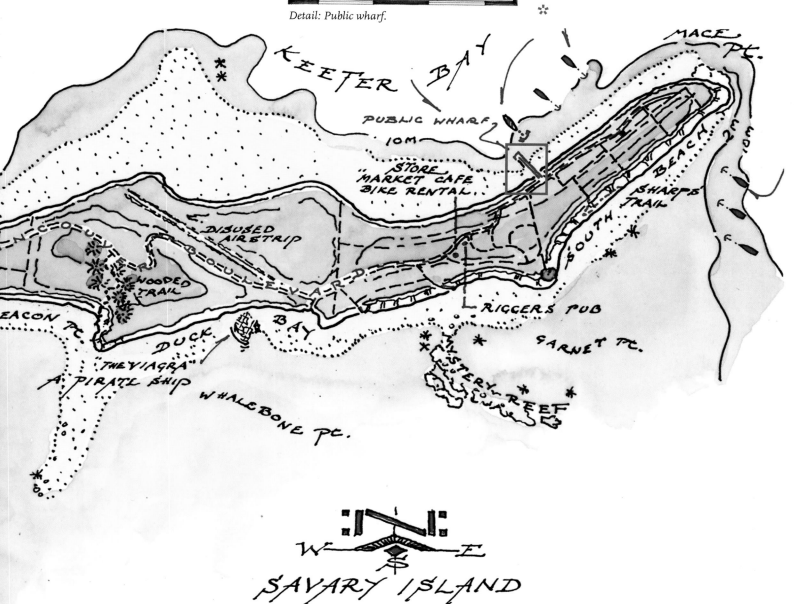

Not to scale. Not to be used for navigation.

2.8 "BLACK ROCK POINT," HERNANDO ISLAND

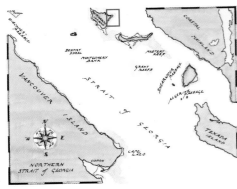

✲ 49° 59.1' N   124° 52.9' W

CHARTS
3538. 3311, sheet 5.

APPROACH
From the E. The flat meadow backing the shoreline is the most visible landmark.

ANCHOR
SE of the local private mooring buoys. Temporary anchorage with good protection from the prevailing north-westerlies. Exposed to the S. Depths of 8–10 m (26–33 ft), holding good in shingle and sand.

Note: The anchorage we dubbed "Black Rock Point" is approximately 1 nautical mile southeast of Hidalgo Point.

If a seasonal northwesterly wind is forecast for the northern Strait of Georgia and you are in the vicinity of Hernando Island, tuck in behind "Black Rock Point" and drop your anchor off the long shingle beach, southeast of the private buoys. Seals love to lounge on the reef at the end of the point, and a multitude of seabirds occupy the large middle rock.

The enticing 2.4 km (1.5 mi) beach, backed by a lovely grassy meadow, is a great place to stretch your legs. Although this is a private island, boaters can explore and enjoy the beach up to the high-water mark.

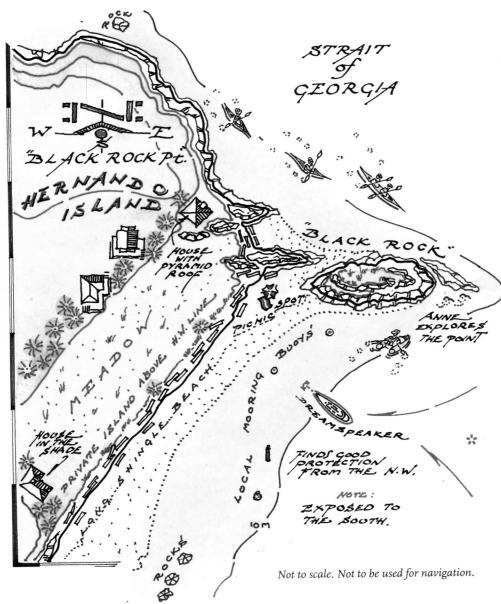

Not to scale. Not to be used for navigation.

The house with the pyramid roof, from "Black Rock."

Chapter 3
BAYNES
SOUND

The Chrome Island lighthouse stands guard at the southern entrance to Baynes Sound.

Paddle boarders enjoy Tribune Bay.

Chapter 3
BAYNES SOUND

TIDES

Canadian Tide and Current Tables, Volume 5
Reference Port: Point Atkinson
Secondary Ports: Hornby Island, Denman Island

CURRENTS

Although there is no reference station, tidal currents attain 2–3 knots out of the southern entrance to Baynes Sound.

WEATHER

Area: Strait of Georgia (northern half)
Reporting Stations: Sisters Islets, Chrome Island

See CAUTIONARY NOTES below.

CAUTIONARY NOTES

At the southern entrance to Baynes Sound, an ebb tide creates rough seas when a strong southeasterly wind is blowing.

Strong southwesterly winds, known locally as "Qualicums," can build to 30–40 knots on summer afternoons. These winds extend from Qualicum Beach on Vancouver Island to the northern tip of Lasqueti Island and affect the southern shores of Hornby Island.

Both conditions present potentially hazardous conditions for small craft navigating these waters.

Baynes Sound, the sheltered neck of water sandwiched between the shores of Vancouver and Denman Islands, is a welcome sight to the weary boater battling north from Nanaimo against prevailing summer northwesterlies. Also included in this chapter are breezy Lambert Channel and the rocky shores of Denman and Hornby Islands.

The colourful Chrome Island light, at the southeast end of Denman Island, welcomes you into Baynes Sound. Be sure to keep well clear of the sand-and-mud spit off Mapleguard Point. Once you've cleared the point, it's safe to tuck into Deep Bay for the night. Although the public wharf and marina are filled with local boats, a fully stocked general store, licensed café and hot showers are available and a walk along the sandy spit offers spectacular views up Baynes Sound.

The waters of Baynes Sound are well known for their variety of quality oysters, which can be sampled at local restaurants. The Baynes Sound Connector ferry from Buckley Bay has a scheduled service to Denman Island. Tie up at the public wharf south of the terminal and pop into Denman village (a five-minute walk from the dock), provision at the charming General Store, breakfast at the bistro or shop and enjoy a relaxed lunch at the Hardware Emporium.

Sandy Island Marine Park and its beautiful, clean beaches are located at the northern tip of Denman Island, and at low water you can beachcomb for 4 km (2.5 mi), from White Spit south to Longbeak Point and the anchorage in Henry Bay.

Hornby Island has an all-weather protected anchorage in Ford Cove and is famous for its mile-long stretch of fine white sand at Tribune Bay, where you can spend a few blissful days relaxing on the beach and enjoying the warm water. There are also grassy bluffs to be hiked, winding roads to be biked and rocky islets to explore. Hornby is a friendly island filled with an eclectic mix of talented artisans who welcome visitors to their workshops and galleries.

FEATURED DESTINATIONS

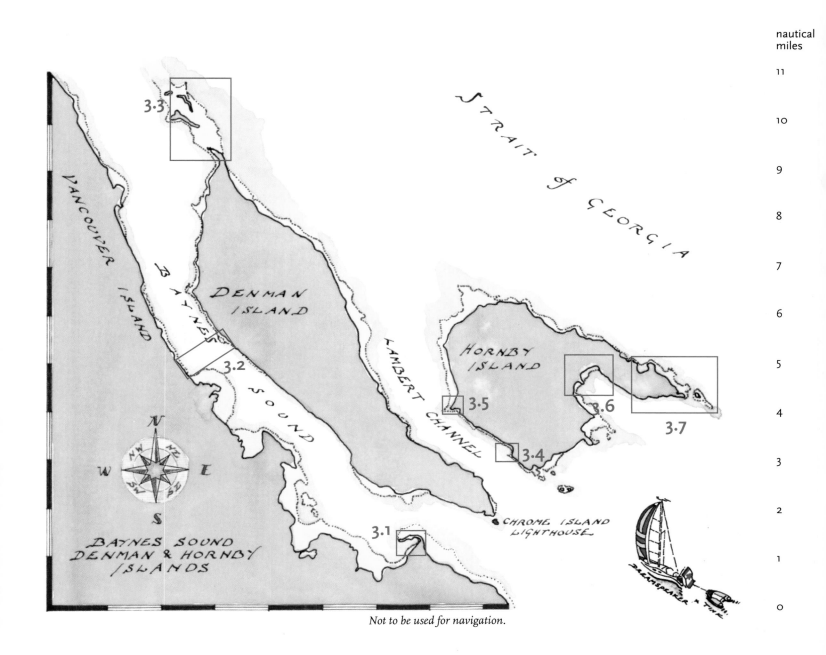

Not to be used for navigation.

3.1 Deep Bay, Vancouver Island

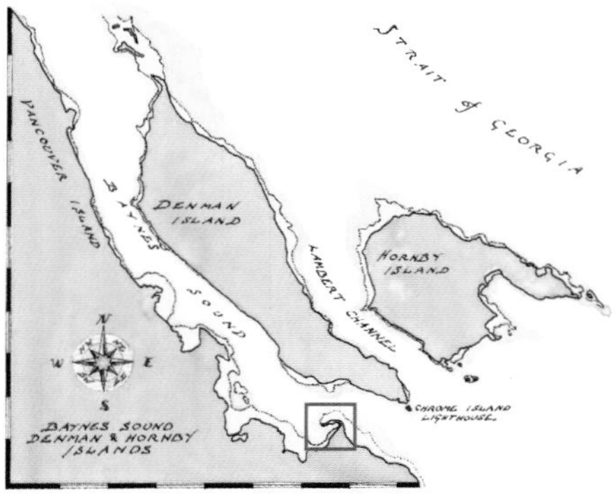

49° 28.0' N 124° 44.3' W

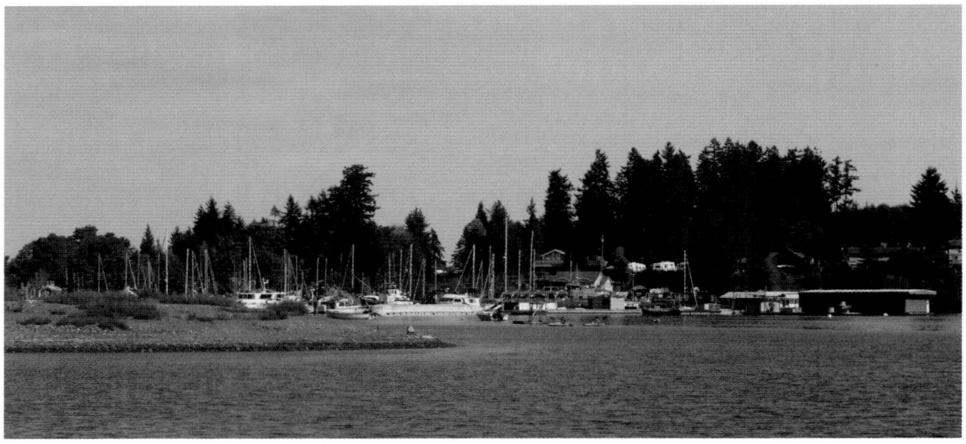

The approach to Deep Bay.

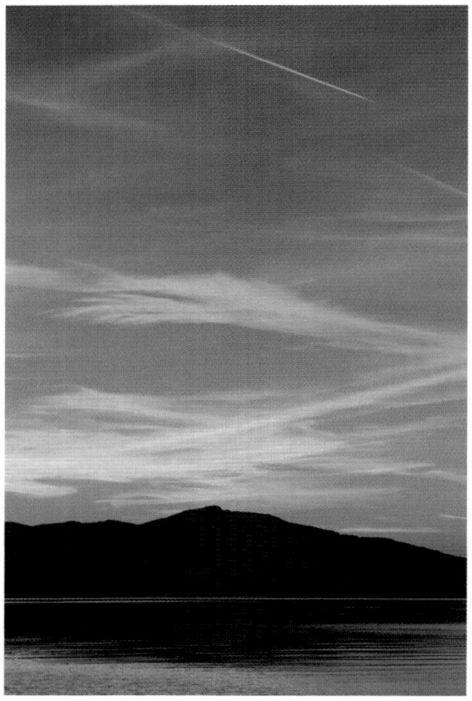

Baynes Sound sunset from Deep Bay.

If you get caught out by the sudden onset of a southerly or "Qualicum" wind, pop into Deep Bay, the safest natural anchorage between Nanaimo and Comox. The bay also offers spectacular views up Baynes Sound.

Moorage at the public wharf is plentiful but occupied by commercial and local boats, so be prepared to raft up if necessary. Power and water are available, and shower and laundry facilities are located at SHIP AND SHORE MARINE. Here you will also find a small general store with a licensed café and a campground with RV and tenting spots and a non-tidal boat ramp.

The café serves breakfast, lunch and dinner, and patio picnic tables enable you to enjoy their popular fish and chips and burger platters along with the view. This is also the perfect spot for kayakers to set up camp while exploring southern Baynes Sound. When the local fish boats come home with their catch, don't miss the opportunity to purchase freshly caught shrimp.

DEEP BAY MARINA welcomes visitors but has limited transient moorage, so be sure to call ahead. The marina is also home to the DEEP BAY YACHT CLUB.

A finger-like natural spit protects Deep Bay from virtually all winds and, although most of the spit is private, there is public access to the lovely sandy beach along Mapleguard Point—the best place to stretch your legs with a leisurely sunset walk.

Note: At the time of writing, the wharf manager at Deep Bay Harbour Authority informed us that over the next two years the wharfs will be undergoing construction. As these are primarily commercial wharfs, no extra visitor moorage will be added.

CHARTS 3527 & 3513.

APPROACH

From the NW; the most obvious landmark is the Deep Bay light amid the white sands and bush of Mapleguard Point.

Note: Extensive sand flats extend northward from Mapleguard Point; leave both port-hand (green) buoys, P39 and P41, to the S if approaching Baynes Sound from the E.

ANCHOR

Good protection from southeasterly winds may be found SW of the breakwater in variable depths of 4–10 m (13–33 ft), holding good in mud.

PUBLIC WHARF

Managed by Deep Bay Harbour Authority, the wharfs are filled with commercial and local boats and rafting is the norm. Visitor moorage when available, call ahead 250-757-9331. Power and water on the docks. Pumpout located at the loading zone.

MARINA

Deep Bay Marina is essentially for local boats. Visitor moorage when available, call ahead 250-830-8589.

BOAT LAUNCH

Private, operated by Ship and Shore Marine.

FUEL

Tidal fuel float adjacent to launch ramp—gas only—call Ship and Shore Marine, 250-757-8399.

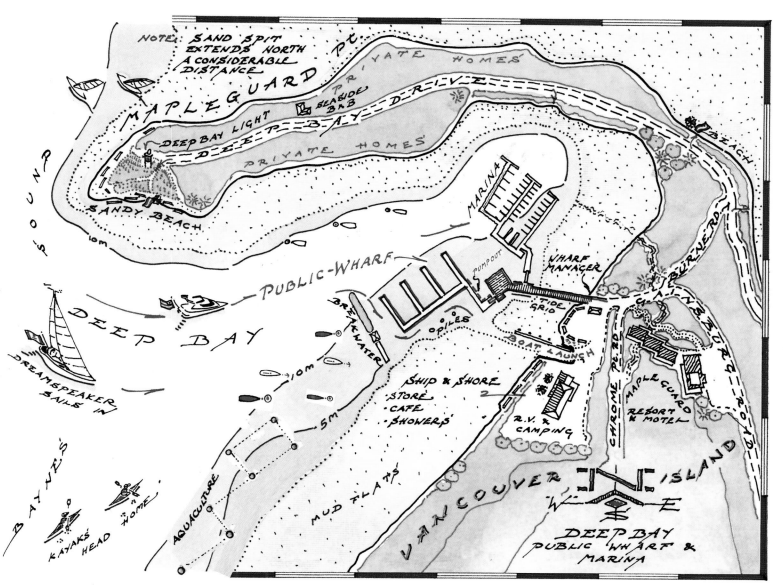

Not to scale. Not to be used for navigation.

3.2 BAYNES SOUND CONNECTOR, BAYNES SOUND

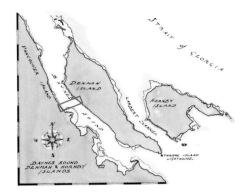

With BC Ferries cable ferry in service, there are green and red transit light operations in Baynes Sound.
The transit lights inform boaters when the Baynes Sound Connector is in transit and when it is safe to cross the channel. BC Ferries urges all marine traffic either operating or transiting in the area to be aware of these changes, as well as the Navigation Act's Ferry Cable Regulations. *SOR/86-1026—No person in charge of a vessel shall navigate the vessel across a ferry cable when the red lights are illuminated at the onshore terminal ends of the ferry cable.*

Transit Light Operations
Sets of red and green transit lights have been installed at both Buckley Bay and Denman West terminals to indicate when the Baynes Sound Connector is in transit.

When the lights are green, this means the cable ferry is securely docked at either terminal and it is clear for boaters to cross the channel.

Buckley Bay Terminal

When the lights are red, do not cross the channel. This indicates that the cable ferry is in transit, and the cables may not be fully submerged underwater.

Denman West Terminal

Exact location and angle of transit lights may differ from illustrations. This is for informational purposes only.

When approaching from either side of the Baynes Sound Connector, tune in to VHF channel 16. We found that when the ferry operator announced that the ferry was departing, the light changed to red and the ferry departed immediately.

The busy Denman Island public wharf is located just south of the ferry terminal. Take a short walk to charming Denman village. The DENMAN ISLAND GENERAL STORE has a post office and BC Liquor Store outlet, and it stocks locally grown fresh produce, baked goods and groceries. Enjoy a coffee or light lunch at the DENMAN ISLAND HARDWARE EMPORIUM opposite, or indulge in a tasty homemade breakfast or lunch at the DENMAN ISLAND GUESTHOUSE AND BISTRO at Earth Club Factory.

Note: For more information pertaining to the Baynes Sound Connector, including transiting information, visit bcferries.com or call 1-888-223-3779.

Denman Island public wharf.

SANDY ISLAND MARINE PARK & HENRY BAY, DENMAN ISLAND

CHART 3527.

APPROACH

Sandy Island and Henry Bay lie at the northern tip of Denman Island. Approach from Baynes Sound with caution, because the sand bank drops off dramatically.

ANCHOR

Good protection from northwesterly winds can be found off Sandy Island, but this anchorage is open to south-easterly winds. Better all-weather protection is available in Henry Bay and off Longbeak Point. Depths of 6–12 m (19.5–39 ft), holding good in sand.

Note: Longbeak Point is private and accessible for day use only; no fires permitted.

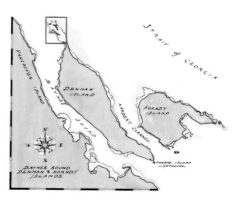

❋ 49° 36.7' N   124° 51.1' W

Dreamspeaker *basks in the sunset.*

Known locally as "Tree Island," this wonderful park also includes Seal Islets to the north and is often missed by the cruising boater. The islands are best explored at low water, and you can stretch your boat-weary legs beach-combing from the northern tip of White Spit to Longbeak Point on Denman Island. Henry Bay, just south of here, provides sheltered over-night anchorage when a southeasterly springs up.

The most popular day anchorage is on Sandy Island's southern shore. Its clean, inviting waters, white shell-and-sand beach and grassy uplands also make it a camper's paradise. Kay-akers can pitch their tents right on the beach or under the shady canopy of trees behind it.

Not to scale. Not to be used for navigation.

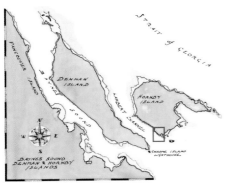

✳ 49° 29.8' N 124° 40.8' W

CHART 3527.

APPROACH

From the S. The stone breakwater and the community behind it are the most apparent landmarks. Enter E of the port-hand buoy, P37 (green).

ANCHOR

Good protection from southerly winds can be found NW of the floating breakwater and E of Maude Reef. Depths are 3–5 m (10–16 ft). Good holding in sand and mud.

PUBLIC WHARF

Extensive and managed by the Ford Cove Harbour Authority, 250-335-0003.

BOAT LAUNCH

Public. Car toppers, kayaks and canoes only. Launch for larger boats at Shingle Spit, page 33.

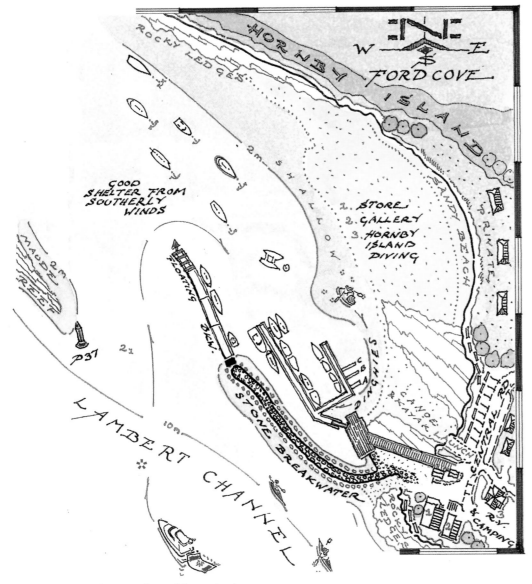

Not to scale. Not to be used for navigation.

Ford Cove, Hornby Island's only all-weather anchorage, provides more than just a bolt hole when the southeasterly and "Qualicum" winds make nearby Tribune Bay an uncomfortable and potentially dangerous anchorage.

FORD COVE MARINA LTD. operates the RV/campsite, cabins and well-stocked store, where ice, snacks, fresh and frozen produce, specialty coffee and pizza to order are available.

ARBUTUS ARTS showcases excellent works by local artists. HORNBY ISLAND DIVING offers guided dives to Flora Islet. The seasonal SEASIDE GRILL serves fish and chips and a good hamburger.

A pleasant 45-minute walk along the cliffs to Shingle Spit is possible on the lower beach trail.

Approaching the floating breakwater from Lambert Channel.

SHINGLE SPIT, HORNBY ISLAND

CHART 3527.

APPROACH

From the SW. The Denman–Hornby BC Ferries terminal is the most visible landmark.

ANCHOR

The spit provides good protection from northwesterly winds but is exposed to southerly winds blowing up Lambert Channel. Depths are 2–4 m (6.5–13 ft), and holding is moderate over a shingle bottom.

MARINA

Pub float is for patrons and shoal draft boats only. Very shallow alongside at LW.

BOAT LAUNCH

Public.

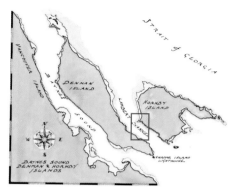

✿ 49° 30.6' N   124° 42.4' W

Shingle Spit extends into Lambert Channel and provides good protection from prevailing northwesterly winds. It is a good spot for boaters wishing to anchor and stretch their legs or indulge in a leisurely pub lunch. The Denman–Hornby ferry terminal is also located here. HORNBY ISLAND RESORT includes the THATCH PUB AND RESTAURANT and a gift shop featuring local artists and artisans. MOUNT GEOFFREY REGIONAL NATURE PARK and its network of public hiking and biking trails are easily accessible from the resort.

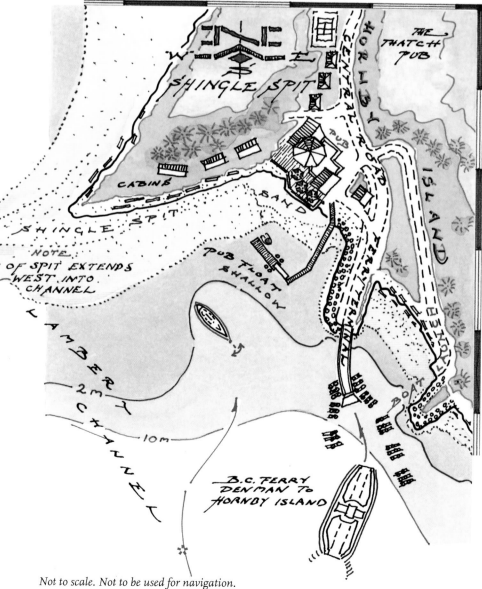

Approach to Shingle Spit.

Not to scale. Not to be used for navigation.

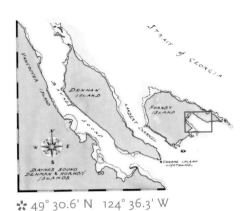

✵ 49° 30.6' N   124° 36.3' W

The bluffs at Helliwell Park. Follow the cliffs into Tribune Bay.

Most boats anchor off the beach.

Beautiful Tribune Bay is completely exposed to the south. Fortunately, the prevailing summer winds in the northern Strait of Georgia are mostly from the northwest, making safe anchorage possible for a good portion of the season. In settled weather, stay awhile kayaking, paddle boarding and enjoying the bay's mile-long sweep of fine white sand and idyllic warm-water swimming.

This magnificent stretch of clean beach is backed by TRIBUNE BAY PROVINCIAL PARK, well used by locals and visitors alike. Overnight camping is not permitted, but a wooden gazebo, picnic tables and fire rings are provided for day use. Changing cabins, toilets and a hand pump for water are located near the parking area.

Kayakers wishing to explore the delights of Hornby Island can pitch their tents adjacent to the park in the TRIBUNE BAY CAMPSITE. It offers hot showers and beach access from "Little Tribune Bay" (local name), west of Spray Point; the bay is also a popular spot for sunbathing *au naturel*.

If you enjoy a good hike, visit HELLIWELL PARK and its scenic bluff trail (see page 36), easily accessed from St. John's Point Road, north of the park. An alternative route for visitors without dogs or bikes is possible from the turnoff to High Salal. Continue along the private road until you reach Lot 16–17. From there a trail leads through private land out to the cliffs.

The CO-OP GENERAL STORE and RINGSIDE MARKET, with its eclectic mix of shops, is a 5-minute walk from the western path of Tribune Bay beach. The Co-op offers an excellent selection of bulk foods, fresh and organic produce and specialty items; the hardware and liquor store are located in the basement. It also houses the post office. The Ringside Market has an ambience all its own, with an emphasis on local arts, crafts and pottery, and is the perfect rendez-vous spot for both islanders and visitors. Relax with a latté and a freshly baked muffin while planning your bike trip—the best way to discover Hornby Island. HORNBY ISLAND OUTDOOR SPORTS/BIKESHOP is located in the market and will provide you with rental bikes, a trail map and local knowledge.

The HORNBY ISLAND SUMMER FESTIVAL, a musical extravaganza, takes place in the first week of August.

CHART 3527.

APPROACH

From the SE. The bluffs at Helliwell Park are clearly visible. Follow the cliffs into the bay.

ANCHOR

Although well protected from the NW, the anchorage affords no protection from the south. If the forecast is for strong to gale-force NW winds, the bay is an excellent anchorage. Anchor in depths of 3–6 m (10–19.5 ft). Holding good in sand.

Note: On entering or leaving Tribune Bay, clear the port-hand buoy, P35 (green), off Nash Rock.

CAUTIONARY NOTE

If the forecast indicates "Qualicum" or southerly winds, Tribune Bay will become a lee shore. Substantial swells can develop. Enter the bay only in moderate conditions.

The beach is a terrific playground.

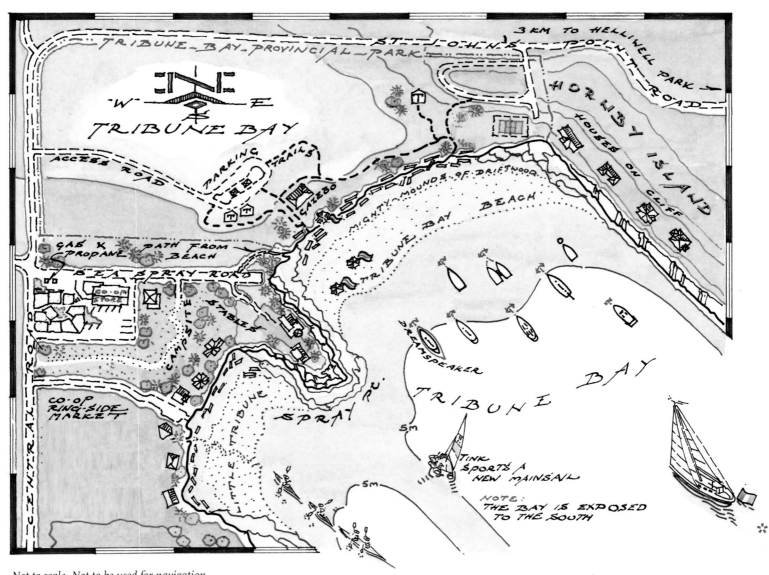

Not to scale. Not to be used for navigation.

3.7 HELLIWELL PROVINCIAL PARK & FLORA ISLET, HORNBY ISLAND

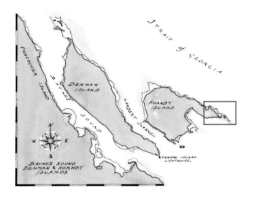

✽ 49° 30.8' N   124° 34.8' W

CHART 3527.

Notes:
(1) Helliwell Provincial Park, donated by John Helliwell and established as a park in 1966, is best visited as a day hike while your boat is anchored at Tribune Bay (see page 34) or Ford Cove (see page 32). Please stay on designated trails to protect the park's fragile areas.

(2) Flora Islet, part of Helliwell Park, is best visited by dinghy, kayak or paddle board. It is one of only two locations in the world where divers can see the near-threatened bluntnose sixgill shark, and the islet attracts scuba divers and marine biologists from around the world.

(3) The small-craft passage between St. John Point and Flora Islet should only be attempted at LW and in calm seas. Temporary anchorage is also possible here.

(4) Give the reef off the tip of Flora Islet a wide berth.

A leisurely hike in the cool of the evening to the grassy bluffs in Helliwell Provincial Park is quite an experience. The park is a must for visitors to the island, and the 5 km (3.1 mi) loop from the information shelter takes approximately 1.5 hours to complete. Alternatively, take a low-water hop, skip and jump along the sandstone ledges from Whaling Station Bay to St. John Point and join the trail back to Helliwell Park Road. Whaling Station Bay has a wonderful expanse of compacted white sand beach, only visible at low water, and public access is possible from St. John's Point Road.

Flora Islet provides several buoys for visiting divers. It is not advisable to anchor along the reef, as damage to its delicate structure is often irreparable. Helliwell Park and the islet are bursting with wildflowers in the spring.

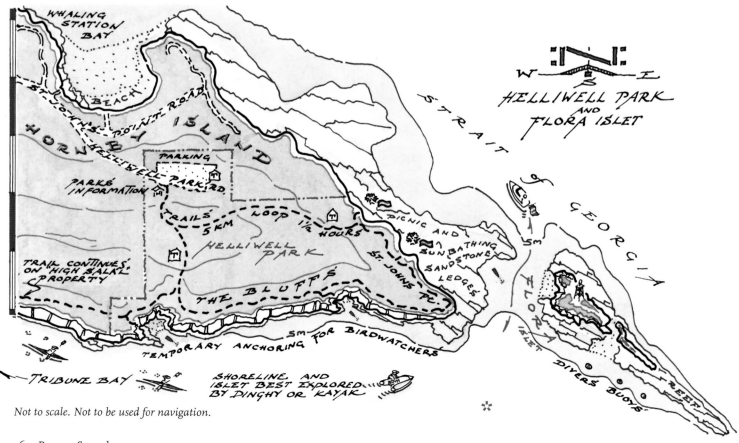

Not to scale. Not to be used for navigation.

Chapter 4
POWELL RIVER

A Texada sunset over the Sturt Bay anchorage.

The public wharf in Van Anda Cove.

Chapter 4
POWELL RIVER

TIDES

Canadian Tide and Current Tables, Volume 5
Reference Port: Point Atkinson
Secondary Ports: Powell River, Blubber Bay

CURRENTS

Note: Although there is no reference station, tidal currents attain 1–2 knots in Malaspina Strait. Beware of the potential for a wind-against-current situation.

WEATHER

Area: Strait of Georgia (northern half)
Reporting Station: Grief Point

Note: Southeasterly winds accelerate around Grief Point, giving speeds 5–10 knots higher than the area forecast (listen for the weather report from Grief Point).

CAUTIONARY NOTES

The Malaspina Strait between Grief Point and Northern Texada Island is notorious for steep seas produced by a wind-against-current situation. This is potentially dangerous to small craft.

This compact but essential chapter encompasses Powell River on the mainland shore, the northern tip of Texada Island and the northern approaches to Malaspina Strait.

The cruising boater may be lulled into a false sense of security by the calm waters in the lee of Texada Island, but should be aware that the area in the vicinity of Grief Point is renowned for its strong winds and ferocious seas—in fact, the weather proved so brutal in 1913 that it sank the union steamship *Cheslakee* off the wharf in Van Anda Cove on Texada Island.

If you do happen to be caught in the strait in unfavourable conditions, pop into BEACH GARDENS RESORT AND MARINA for the night and take advantage of their facilities. Sturt Bay and the community of Van Anda, on the northern tip of Texada Island, are steeped in history and offer visitor moorage, sheltered anchorage, a fully stocked store and a fascinating museum.

On the mainland shore, the town of Powell River is accessible by land and air, and provides the cruising boater with a convenient rendezvous and provisioning centre. Westview Harbour and its public wharf offer visitor moorage, well-managed facilities, and provide the only boat access to the district's lively downtown. The national heritage district of TOWNSITE is a wonderful example of town planning in the early 1900s.

A convenient courtesy bus to the TOWN CENTRE MALL operates in July and August. A walk along Marine Avenue is well worthwhile and offers a wide variety of restaurants, cafés, galleries and a real Italian butcher and fishmonger for provisioning.

FEATURED DESTINATIONS

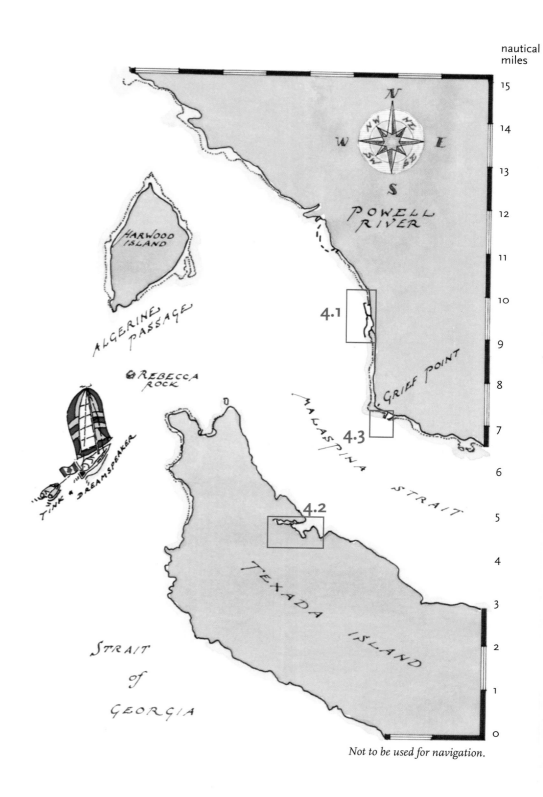

nautical
miles

Not to be used for navigation.

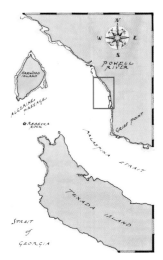

Approaching the Westview public wharf.

✸ 49° 50.0' N 124° 31.9' W

Good eateries on Marine Avenue.

Quality local produce and provisions at the Chopping Block.

Powell River built the first pulp and paper mill in Western Canada. Westview, one of the four communities that make up Powell River, offers visiting boaters moorage facilities and access to the district's lively downtown in Westview Harbour.

The welcoming and efficient public wharf, adjacent to the ferry terminal serving Texada Island and Comox, has large, clean shower and laundry facilities, and the wharf manager will be happy to pass on any local information you might need.

The best way to enjoy a day in Westview is to take a leisurely walk north up Willingdon Avenue to WILLINGDON PARK AND BEACH and browse the eclectic consignment store. Return via Marine Avenue, which offers a variety of galleries, gift stores, shops, restaurants and cafés. Provisioning couldn't be easier. The CHOPPING BLOCK—a reputable butcher, fishmonger and deli—also sells fresh local produce, specialty items and tasty picnic fare. ECOSSENTIALS, opposite, carries organic and local fresh produce, cheeses, meat and homemade sauces. DUKE'S LIQUOR STORE stocks a selection of craft beer and wine.

Recommended cafés and restaurants on Marine Avenue include LITTLE HUT CURRY, THE ALCHEMIST RESTAURANT (French Mediterranean cuisine), TREE FROG BISTRO (Western/European fusion), COSTA DEL SOL (Latin cuisine), COASTAL COOKERY (local craft beers on tap), BASE CAMP (coffee, food and art), ROCKY MOUNTAIN PIZZA & BAKERY and SNICKERS RESTAURANT with its shaded outdoor patio.

A fast and efficient way to view the town is to hop onto a local transit bus. Pick up a map at the VISITOR INFORMATION CENTRE on Joyce Avenue for a self-guided architectural tour of TOWNSITE—now a national heritage district. In July and August a courtesy shuttle bus will transport you to the TOWN CENTRE MALL from the south harbour, which houses over 50 stores, including two supermarkets and a BC Liquor Store.

Note: MARINE TRADERS, just a short walk from the docks, provides one-stop-shopping for boaters and will arrange marine services—call 604-485-4624. KOLESZAR MARINE (marine mechanics) can be found on Willingdon Avenue—call 604-485-5616.

CHARTS 3536. 3311, sheet 5.

APPROACH

The public wharf at Westview from the W. The entrance lies to the S of the ferry terminal.

ANCHOR

Day/picnic anchorage in calm, settled weather is possible off Willingdon Beach.

PUBLIC WHARF

Westview Harbour, managed by Westview Harbour Authority, lies behind a rock-mound breakwater, and has extensive visitor moorage. Call 604-485-5244, VHF channel 66A. Floats 4–11 for visiting and resident boats. Larger boats can be accommodated on Floats 10 and 11. Power, water and free Wi-Fi are available on the docks. A pump-out facility is situated on Dock 11. Shower and laundry facilities at the harbour office. Short stays of one to two hours are permitted.

MARINA

The municipal marina has no designated visitor moorage.

BOAT LAUNCH

Public, at the municipal marina. Kayaks can be launched from Willingdon Beach.

FUEL

Westview Fuels lies between floats 6 and 7—call 604-485-2867, VHF 66A. Diesel, gasoline, lubricants and ice.

Note: Extreme caution should be exercised upon entering Westview Harbour because boats may be exiting, and manoeuvring is restricted.

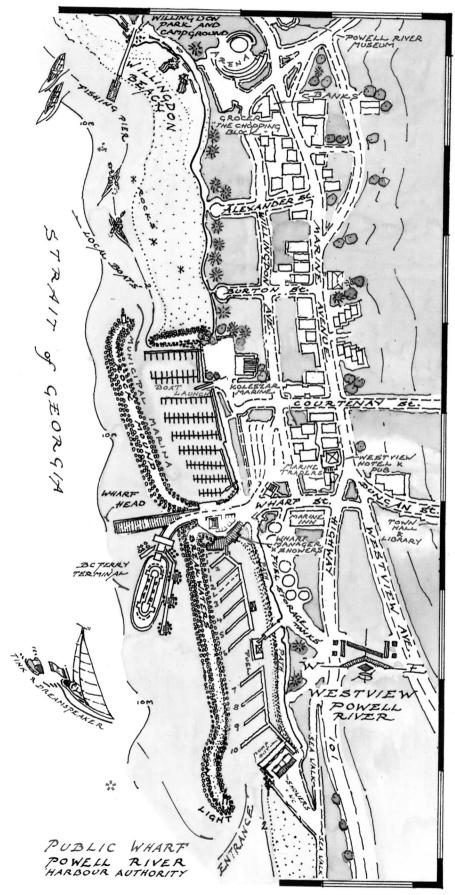

Not to scale. Not to be used for navigation.

4.2 Sturt Bay & Van Anda Cove, Northern Texada Island

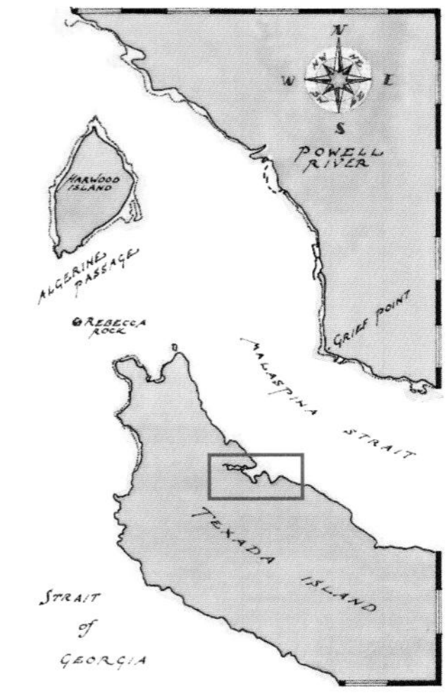

49° 45.8' N 124° 33.4' W

CHARTS 3536. 3311, sheet 5.

APPROACH

To Sturt Bay. Enter between the starboard day mark (red) off Hodgson Point and the port-hand day mark (green) that marks the tip of the reef that extends out from Ursula Rock and the breakwater.

ANCHOR

Good temporary anchorage may be found in the western corner of Sturt Bay, with good protection from northwesterly winds and moderate protection from SE winds. Depths 4–12 m (13–39 ft), holding good in mud and gravel. Be aware of some logging debris on the bottom.

Note: Hike logging road W to Blubber Bay Road, then N to old quarry swimming hole (second entrance gate).

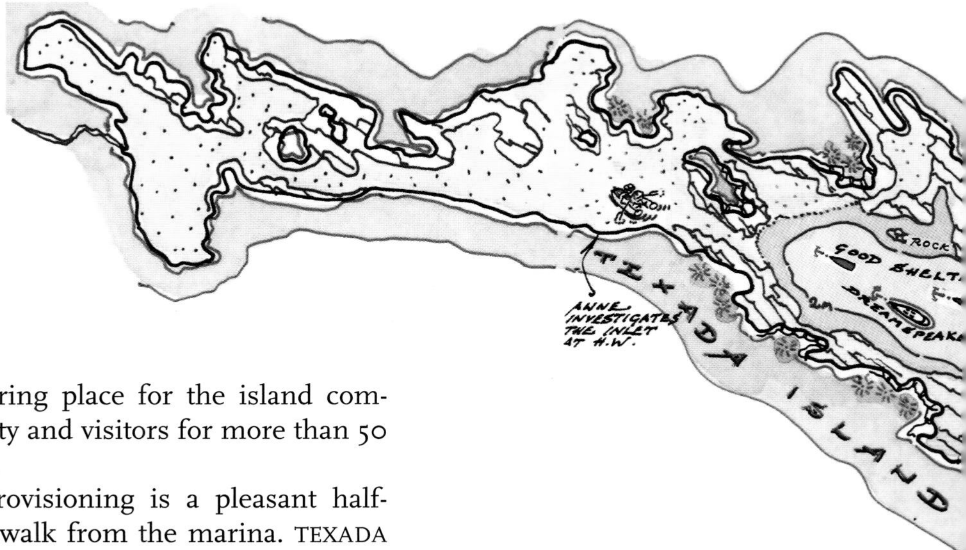

If you are up against a strong northwesterly wind or ferocious seas in Malaspina Strait, tuck into Sturt Bay (known locally as "Marble Bay"), where protected anchorage, visitor moorage and a taste of island history await you. The history of Van Anda as a boom town for prospectors and miners in the 1800s is a colourful one, kept alive by the TEXADA ISLAND HERITAGE SOCIETY.

The TEXADA BOATING CLUB welcomes visiting boaters to their marina. The designated visitor docks offer ample moorage and the friendly wharfinger will pass on necessary local information and provide you with a historic walking map of Van Anda. Anchorage off the marina is prohibited due to underwater cables, and Caesar Cove is filled with local boats. You can drop your hook in the western corner of Sturt Bay, which affords good protection from northwesterly winds. This quiet spot is surrounded by forested uplands and a diversity of birdlife.

In May 2016 the TEXADA ISLAND INN was destroyed by fire. At the time of writing, the owners are planning to rebuild the inn, which has been a gathering place for the island community and visitors for more than 50 years.

Provisioning is a pleasant half-hour walk from the marina. TEXADA MARKET has a BC Liquor Store outlet, an ATM and stocks fresh produce, ice and a good selection of groceries; they also have an excellent in-house butcher. The store is open 10 a.m. to 7 p.m. Monday to Saturday and 12 p.m. to 5 p.m. on Sundays. It's well worth visiting the TEXADA ISLAND MUSEUM on Waterman Avenue, with its wonderful collection of historic artifacts and the excellent Jack Leslie Model Ship Display.

For a change of pace, check your tide tables and dinghy or kayak to the head of Sturt Bay. A 20-minute walk along the trail and logging road will take you to Blubber Bay Road and the old quarry swimming hole. Fed by a natural spring and known locally as Hachelt Lake, a refreshing dip in the emerald green mineral waters is pure bliss; jumping off the high rocky cliffs into the lake is a favourite local pastime.

PUBLIC WHARF

In Van Anda Cove. Approach from the N. The wharf is exposed to northwesterly winds and offers little protection from the SE. A 45-foot float lies along the NE side for temporary moorage. Dinghy tie-up on the inside. A short walk to Texada Market should you need a quick provisioning stop.

MARINA

TEXADA ISLAND BOATING CLUB. Call the wharfinger at 604-414-5897. The marina has designated visitor moorage on Dock #4 (both sides) and Dock #3 on the W side. Courtesy tie-up before 2 p.m. Power and water available on the dock. Cash only (ATM at store). Ice available at the wharfinger's residence.

BOAT LAUNCH

At end of breakwater.

Approaching the breakwater in Sturt Bay.

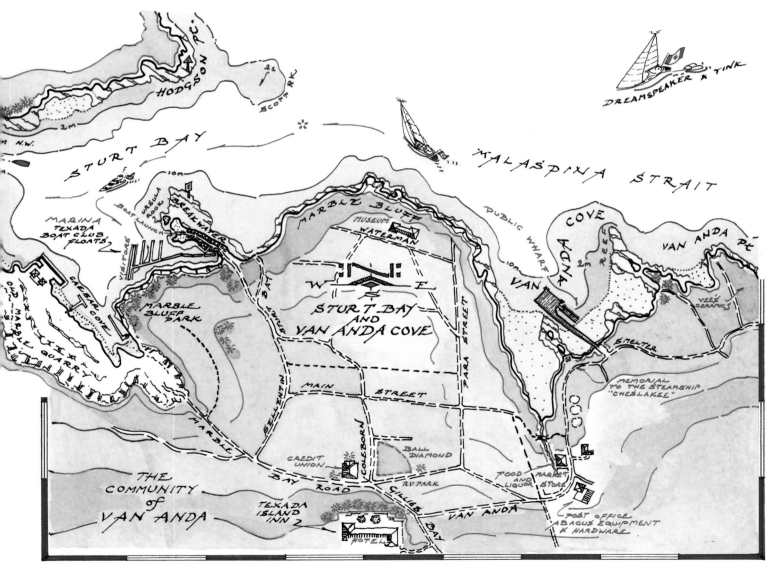

Not to scale. Not to be used for navigation.

4.3 BEACH GARDENS RESORT & MARINA, GRIEF POINT, POWELL RIVER

✿ 49° 47.9' N   124° 31.2' W

CHARTS

3513, sheet 5.

APPROACH

The marina breakwater lies approximately 0.5 nautical miles SE of Grief Point. Approach the entrance from the SW with caution.

MARINA

The marina is operated by the Beach Gardens Resort, 1-800-663-7070, VHF 66A. They welcome visitors to their moorage and resort facilities. In summer, it is advisable to reserve a berth in advance. Strong SW winds make some of the berths uncomfortable. Power, water and Wi-Fi on the docks.

BOAT LAUNCH

No paved launch, but kayaks may access the beach.

FUEL

Fuel float operated by the resort and marina. Diesel and gas mid-June to mid-September.

Note: This area is prone to log debris.

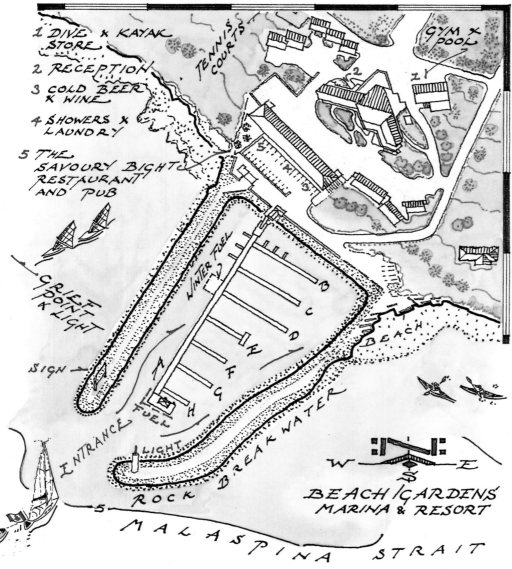

Not to scale. Not to be used for navigation.

Boaters are given a warm welcome when they tie up for the night at the Beach Gardens Resort and Marina—a full-service marina with power and water on the docks and free Wi-Fi. Just up from the docks, you will find a clean and airy laundry, a cold beer and wine store (open seven days a week) and the SAVOURY BIGHT SEASIDE RESTAURANT & PUB. They serve "Modern Pacific Cuisine" and their spacious waterfront patio, shaded by colourful umbrellas, offers expansive views out to Malaspina Strait.

The pool, shower facilities and a gym are located in the upper section of the resort and are open to marina guests. For a shopping spree in Powell River, hop on the courtesy shuttle, which will transport you to the TOWN CENTRE MALL in Westview during July and August. A small convenience store is located just a short walk from the resort.

Entrance to Beach Gardens Marina.

Chapter 5
DESOLATION SOUND

Laura Cove, the quintessential Desolation experience.

SV Raineer *snug in Laura Cove.*

Chapter 5
DESOLATION SOUND

TIDES

Canadian Tide and Current Tables, Volume 5
Reference Port: Point Atkinson
Secondary Ports: Lund, Okeover Inlet, Prideaux Haven

CURRENTS

Although there are no reference and secondary current stations, tidal currents stream through the inlets at rates of 1–2 knots. Tidal streams attain 2–4 knots in the entrance of Malaspina Inlet.

WEATHER

Although no specific reporting station covers this area, weather forecasting is a matter of extrapolation of weather forecasts for the Strait of Georgia (northern half) and Johnstone Strait.

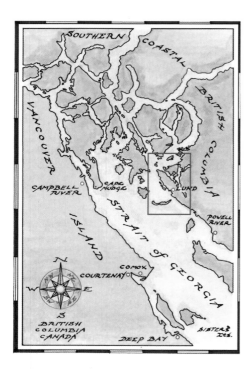

CAUTIONARY NOTES

Desolation Sound enjoys prolonged periods of light or windless days. However, on a weather change, the leading edge of the approaching system will create strong winds that tend to swirl down and through the anchorages.

The featured destinations all have their fair share of rocks, reefs and ledges that annually seek out unwary skippers. Be aware of the many isolated rocks that dot these waters even in deep channels and keep a careful lookout for Sky Pilot Rock, north of Otter Island, which dries on a 1.2 m (4 ft) tide.

T he alluring waters of Desolation Sound, named by a disenchanted Captain Vancouver in 1792, lie south of West Redonda Island. The sound's southern shore is dominated by the legendary Desolation Sound Marine Park, with its maze of deep, interconnecting inlets and cozy hideaway anchorages. To date it is the largest marine park in British Columbia, and it is treasured by boaters and kayakers as one of the most accessible tracts of wilderness almost anywhere in the world.

The park's boundaries include Gifford Peninsula, Prideaux Haven, Tenedos Bay and Grace Harbour. This extensive chapter also encompasses the far reaches of Malaspina, Okeover, Lancelot and Theodosia inlets.

Breathtaking vistas, an abundance of protected anchorages and the rare opportunity to observe wildlife at close quarters are not all that Desolation Sound Marine Park has to offer. Its geographical location also ensures mainly light summer breezes and blissfully warm water temperatures, which come as a surprise, because this stretch of water experiences one of the largest tidal ranges (5.5 m/18 ft) on the BC coast.

For some freshwater bathing, visit Unwin Lake, just a short hike from Tenedos Bay.

Those journeying by road to Desolation Sound with trailer boats or kayaks can use the boat launch in Lund. Situated at the end of Highway 101 and only a 20-minute drive from Powell River, this enterprising community offers moorage, marine facilities, a fully stocked general store and an excellent bakery. It is also the only fuelling and provisioning stop mentioned in this chapter—Refuge Cove, on West Redonda Island, being the other alternative (see 7.2).

Okeover Landing, on Malaspina Peninsula's eastern shore, is the most convenient spot to launch kayaks because it is located only about 5 km (3 mi) from the sheltered waters of Desolation Sound Marine Park. The public wharf provides visitor moorage and the barbecue-weary boater will find the LAUGHING OYSTER RESTAURANT a very pleasant surprise.

Finally, those wishing to avoid the summer crowds and experience Desolation Sound in its undisturbed glory should consider visiting this coastal jewel during late spring or early fall.

FEATURED DESTINATIONS

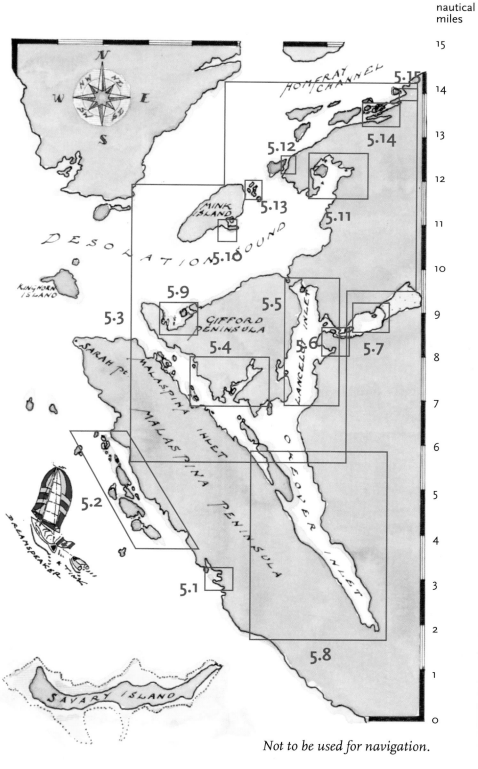

nautical miles

Not to be used for navigation.

✳ 49° 58.9' N   124° 45.9' W

The historic Lund Hotel from the hotel floats.

A variety of freshly baked bread and pastries is available at Nancy's Bakery.

The Boardwalk Restaurant is the place for fish and chips in Lund.

Highway 101 was originally known as the Pan-American Highway. It extends over 15,000 km (9,300 mi) from Puerto Montt, Chile, to Lund, British Columbia, with only a 100 km gap (the Darien Gap) between Panama and Colombia. Lund is the cruising boaters' gateway to Desolation Sound and beyond, the last "urban" stop as you head north. Lund's colourful and enterprising community will accommodate visitors arriving by sea or road, as tourism is its livelihood and the boating season is short.

Friendly Lund Harbour public wharf welcomes visiting boaters. If the docks are full, rafting is the norm, and overflow boats can tie up alongside one of the floating breakwaters.

Built in 1903, the heritage LUND HOTEL comes complete with a small marina, fuel dock, waterfront pub and restaurant, general store, post office and laundry facilities. TUG GHUM GALLERY features the works of over 40 regional artists. Products range from carvings and jewellery to handmade cards and prints as well as Debra Bevaart's renowned stone carvings. LUND GENERAL STORE is well stocked for provisioning and includes a cold beer and wine store and deli. It also carries books, cruising guides, clothing and hardware. Garbage disposal, for a fee, is available on the wharfhead above the fuel dock.

Famed for its oversized, melt-in-the-mouth cinnamon buns, freshly baked pastries, exotic pizza and excellent bread, NANCY'S BAKERY includes an extensive bakery and café and the best Wi-Fi connection. The building's West Coast design blends into the uplands and there is plenty of indoor and outdoor patio seating overlooking the harbour. The upper deck houses TERRACENTRIC COASTAL ADVENTURES and POLLEN SWEATERS, which produces quality washable wool sweaters and stocks a selection of hand-chosen books.

A stroll along the shoreside path will take you to SASSYMACKS, a must-stop for delicious handmade ice cream in the summer, and SPIRALMONKEY BEAD COMPANY with Yvonne's colourful display of Bali sarongs and selection of unique beads and jewellery. Seat yourself on the shaded deck of the BOARD-WALK RESTAURANT and enjoy a platter of fish and chips or a seafood special; sunsets from here are magnificent.

CHARTS 3538. 3311, sheet 5.

APPROACH

From the W, the most prominent landmark being the black-and-white structure of the Lund Hotel, which lies back from the wharfhead.

PUBLIC WHARF

Enter Lund Harbour close to the ends of the floating breakwater. Call when outside the breakwater—604-483-4711, VHF channel 73. In the busy summer months, be prepared to raft up or use the inside of the floating breakwater (no power or water). Wi-Fi and a pump-out facility available on the main docks. Shower and washroom facilities adjacent to the harbour office. One-hour courtesy tie-up.

MARINA

The Lund Hotel & Marina, 604-414-0474. Limited moorage. The floats are exposed to westerly swells and the wakes of passing boats.

FUEL

The fuel float operated by the Lund Hotel is located N of the public wharf.

BOAT LAUNCH

Public, opposite the public wharf.

Note: Finn Cove, just N of Lund, will provide emergency sheltered anchorage at the head of the cove.

Notes: Jack's Boat Yard in Finn Cove has a 60-ton Travelift and can haul out sailboats, 604-483-3566. They also offer storage. The only two lift facilities in the area covered in this guide are at Jack's Boat Yard and Ocean Pacific Marine in Campbell River (see page 168).

Lund Automotive & Outboard on Lund Highway provides mechanical and electrical services and supplies, 604-483-4612. Haulout to 30 feet. They offer long-term trailer parking in secure lots.

Lund Water Taxi provides scheduled daily services to Savary Island—reservations required (see page 22). Individual trips and delivery of parts can also be arranged—call 604-483-9749.

At the time of writing, the Lund Hotel has plans to enhance the hotel and waterfront facilities.

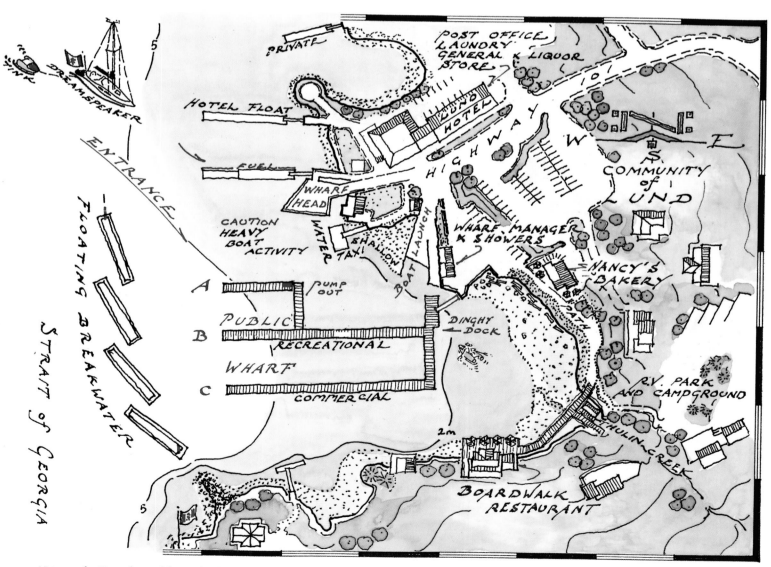

Not to scale. Not to be used for navigation.

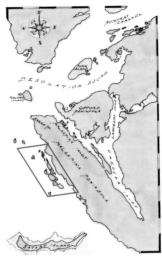

✤ 50° 0.7' N 124° 48.5' W

Peace and quiet in the Copeland Islands Marine Park.

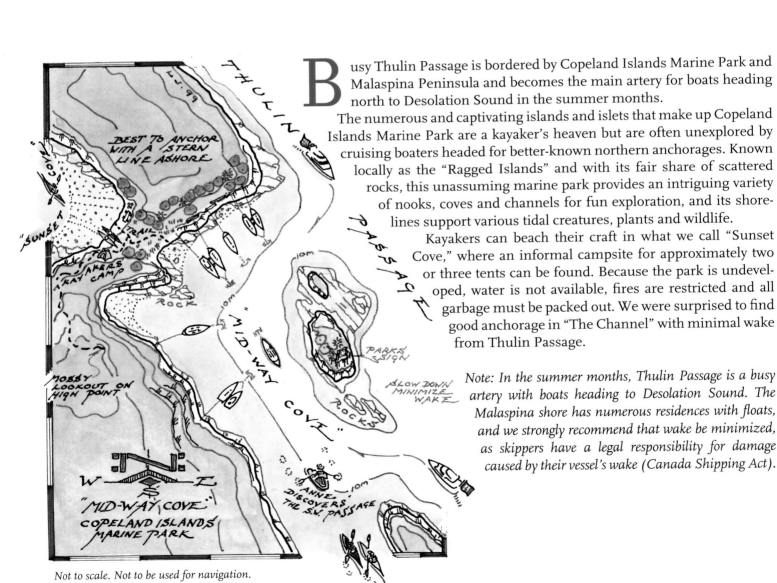

Not to scale. Not to be used for navigation.

Busy Thulin Passage is bordered by Copeland Islands Marine Park and Malaspina Peninsula and becomes the main artery for boats heading north to Desolation Sound in the summer months.

The numerous and captivating islands and islets that make up Copeland Islands Marine Park are a kayaker's heaven but are often unexplored by cruising boaters headed for better-known northern anchorages. Known locally as the "Ragged Islands" and with its fair share of scattered rocks, this unassuming marine park provides an intriguing variety of nooks, coves and channels for fun exploration, and its shorelines support various tidal creatures, plants and wildlife.

Kayakers can beach their craft in what we call "Sunset Cove," where an informal campsite for approximately two or three tents can be found. Because the park is undeveloped, water is not available, fires are restricted and all garbage must be packed out. We were surprised to find good anchorage in "The Channel" with minimal wake from Thulin Passage.

Note: In the summer months, Thulin Passage is a busy artery with boats heading to Desolation Sound. The Malaspina shore has numerous residences with floats, and we strongly recommend that wake be minimized, as skippers have a legal responsibility for damage caused by their vessel's wake (Canada Shipping Act).

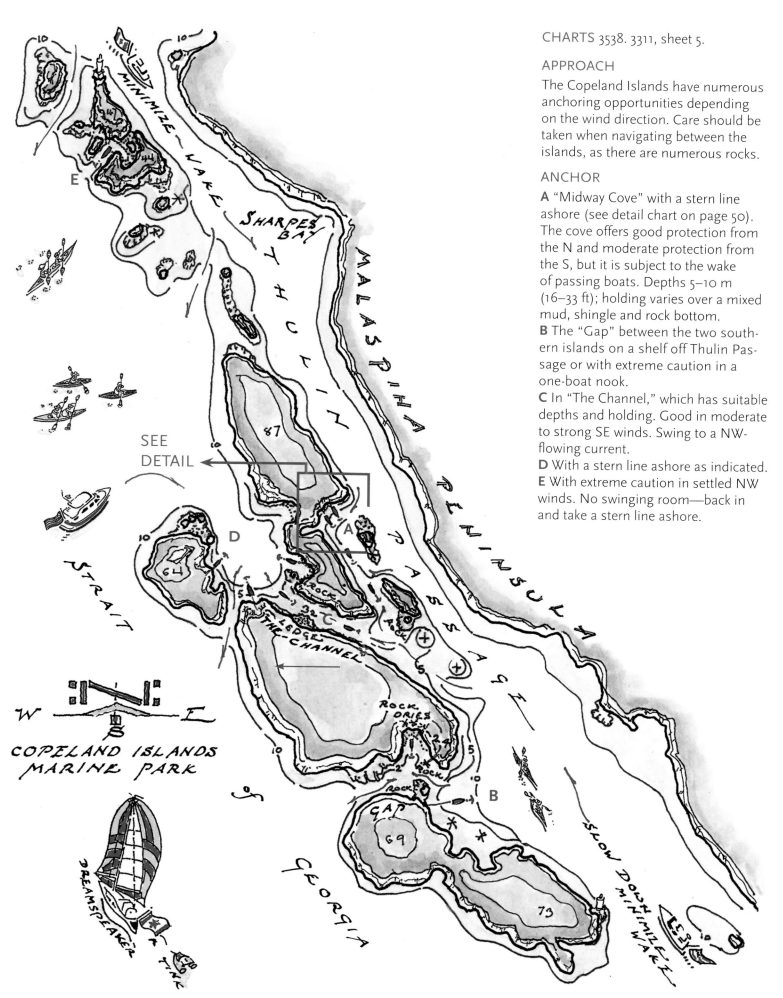

CHARTS 3538. 3311, sheet 5.

APPROACH

The Copeland Islands have numerous anchoring opportunities depending on the wind direction. Care should be taken when navigating between the islands, as there are numerous rocks.

ANCHOR

A "Midway Cove" with a stern line ashore (see detail chart on page 50). The cove offers good protection from the N and moderate protection from the S, but it is subject to the wake of passing boats. Depths 5–10 m (16–33 ft); holding varies over a mixed mud, shingle and rock bottom.
B The "Gap" between the two southern islands on a shelf off Thulin Passage or with extreme caution in a one-boat nook.
C In "The Channel," which has suitable depths and holding. Good in moderate to strong SE winds. Swing to a NW-flowing current.
D With a stern line ashore as indicated.
E With extreme caution in settled NW winds. No swinging room—back in and take a stern line ashore.

COPELAND ISLANDS MARINE PARK

SEE DETAIL

Not to scale. Not to be used for navigation.

5.3 Desolation Sound Marine Park

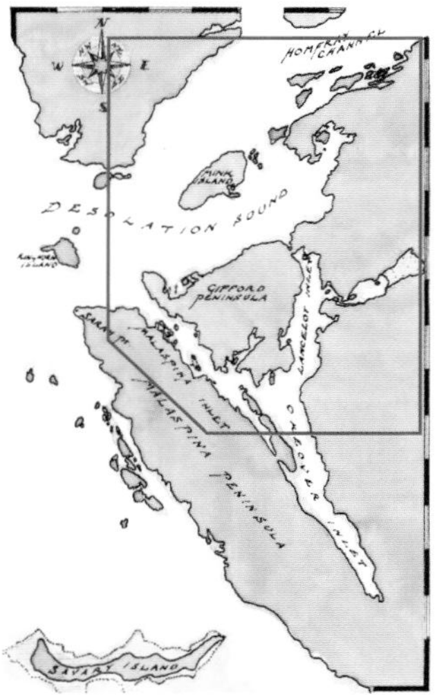

50° 5.0' N 124° 48.7' W

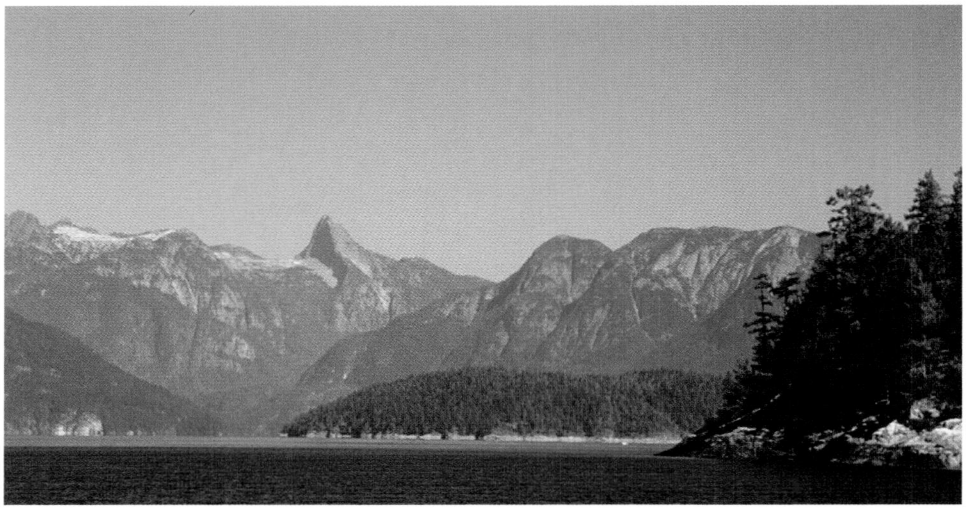

On rounding Sarah Point, the full majesty of Desolation Sound comes into view.

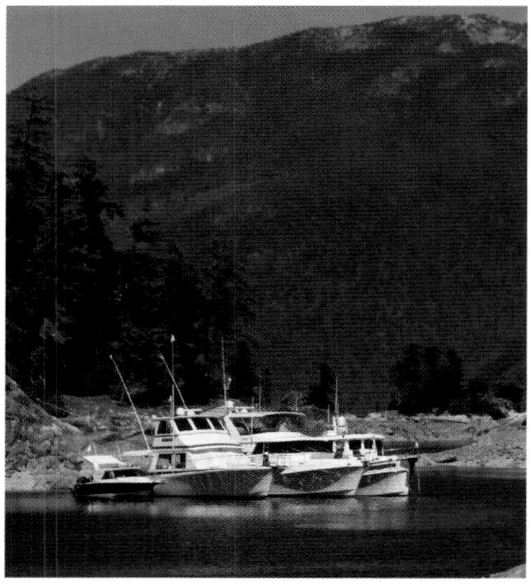

Prideaux Haven.

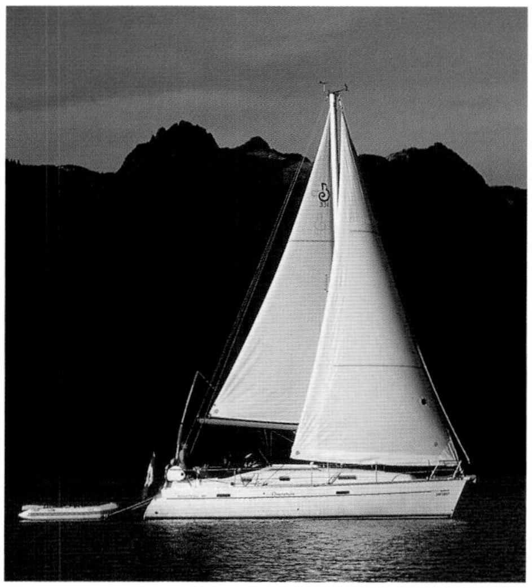

Sailing on the evening breeze in Desolation Sound.

British Columbia's largest marine park encompasses one of the most beautiful cruising areas in the world. Desolation Sound Marine Park is blessed with remarkably warm waters, a variety of safe anchorages and spectacular scenery, and it is only accessible by watercraft. The park is also protected by a "minimal development policy" to ensure that its 60 km (37.3 mi) of wilderness are preserved for future generations.

Desolation Sound Marine Park's popularity as the "ultimate destination" for local and visiting boaters and kayakers leads to overcrowding in the major anchorages during the busy summer months of July and August. However, boaters willing to venture into the lesser-known coves will often be rewarded with solitude.

In this chapter we cover the five all-time favourite anchorages in the park: Grace Harbour (see page 54), Tenedos Bay (see page 64) and Prideaux Haven and Melanie and Laura Coves (see page 68). We also include eleven lovely alternative anchorages.

It should be noted that four parcels of private land still remain within the park and due respect should be paid to their boundaries.

Note: The local road goes from Lund (see page 48) to the tip of Malaspina Peninsula, where small craft can be launched. Alternatively, use the launch at Okeover Arm (see page 60).

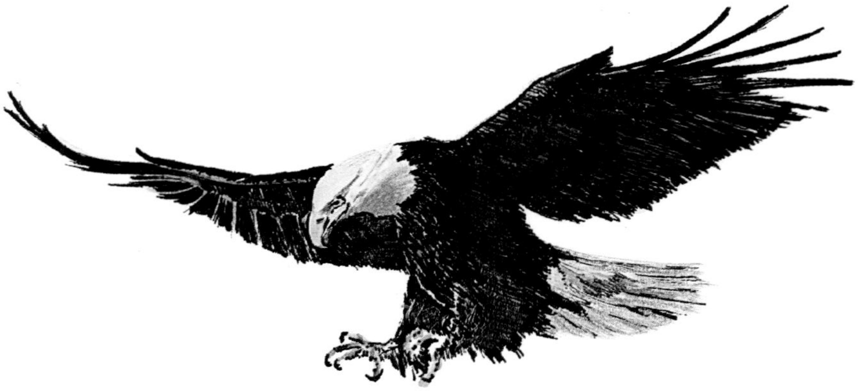

Bald eagles inhabit the park.

FEATURED ANCHORAGES

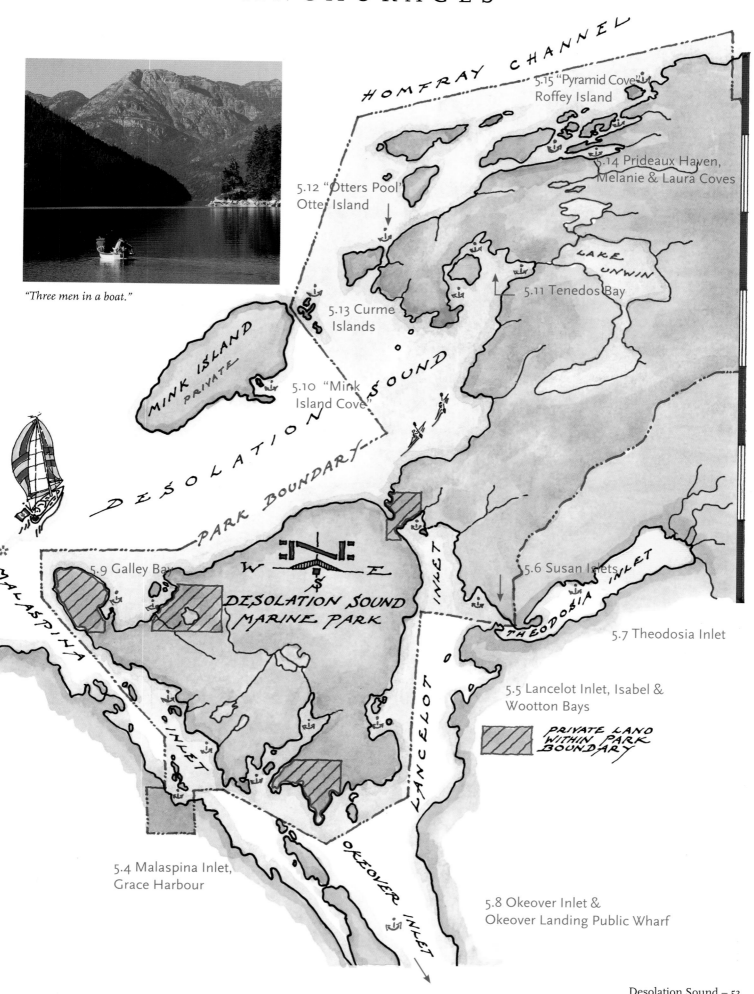

"Three men in a boat."

HOMFRAY CHANNEL

5.15 "Pyramid Cove"
Roffey Island

5.14 Prideaux Haven,
Melanie & Laura Coves

5.12 "Otters Pool"
Otter Island

LAKE
UNWIN

5.11 Tenedos Bay

5.13 Curme
Islands

DESOLATION SOUND

MINK ISLAND
PRIVATE

5.10 "Mink
Island Cove"

PARK BOUNDARY

5.9 Galley Bay

5.6 Susan Islets

DESOLATION SOUND
MARINE PARK

THEODOSIA INLET

5.7 Theodosia Inlet

LANCELOT INLET

MALASPINA

5.5 Lancelot Inlet, Isabel &
Wootton Bays

PRIVATE LAND
WITHIN PARK
BOUNDARY

INLET

5.4 Malaspina Inlet,
Grace Harbour

OKEOVER INLET

5.8 Okeover Inlet &
Okeover Landing Public Wharf

✿ 50° 3.1' N   124° 46.9' W

CHARTS 3559. 3312, pages 12 & 13.

APPROACH: MALASPINA INLET
When approaching the inlet be sure to leave Rosetta Rock to the N.

ANCHOR
Temporary anchorage can be found along the inlet's NE shore and to the SW of the Cochrane Islands. Depths 4–10 m (13–33 ft). Holding varies in a mix of rock, sand and mud.

Evening row in Grace Harbour.

The hidden charms of Malaspina Inlet, well known to kayakers, are often missed by boaters en route to Grace Harbour or Lancelot, Theodosia and Okeover Inlets. Protected from most prevailing summer winds, these hideaway anchorages can often accommodate only one or two boats, but they provide the perfect opportunity to pick fresh oysters and explore tidal pools teeming with life.

Although careful navigation is required to avoid the numerous unmarked rocks in the inlet, there are four cozy spots to choose from.

1. After giving Rosetta Rock off Cross Islet a wide berth, tuck into the nook we've named "Eagles Island," take a stern line ashore and watch the world pass by from the comfort of your cockpit.

2. The snug bight behind Neville Islet is backed by a small rocky beach and fed by a freshwater stream—a truly beautiful spot to watch the sun go down.

3. The peaceful one-boat cove between Kakaekae and Scott Points requires a bit of tricky manoeuvring and a stern line ashore, but it is well worth the effort for the solitude that it provides.

4. Protected anchorage can be found southwest of the Cochrane Islands. The oyster-covered reefs and tidal pools are wonderful to explore at low water as the warm waters and tidal currents of Malaspina Inlet encourage the development of a large variety of intertidal life.

Evening light over the Gifford Peninsula.

HARBOUR, DESOLATION SOUND MARINE PARK

Grace Harbour, one of Desolation Sound Marine Park's most protected and popular all-weather anchorages, also wins hands down for attracting the largest quantity of non-stinging jellyfish to its warm, sheltered waters (generators beware!). At the head of the basin, the spot we dubbed "Sunset Boulevard" retains light the longest, providing the most idyllic spot to relax and sip a long, cool sundowner. "Cabin Cove"—also our own name—behind Jean Island, offers alternative anchorage for boaters in a less sociable mood. Kayakers can set up camp in the northern arm of the harbour, where wooden camping platforms and pit toilets are provided. A half-mile trail leads from there to a small lake overgrown with vegetation.

Note: Stock up on your favourite brand of mosquito repellent to ensure a peaceful night's sleep at anchor or while camping.

APPROACH: GRACE HARBOUR
Enter between Scott and Moss Points, leaving Jean Island to the N.

ANCHOR
With a stern line ashore. Good all-weather protection can be found throughout the harbour. Depths 2–8 m (6.5–26 ft). Holding good in dense mud.

Note: The anchorage is well used in the summer. Stern lines are recommended.

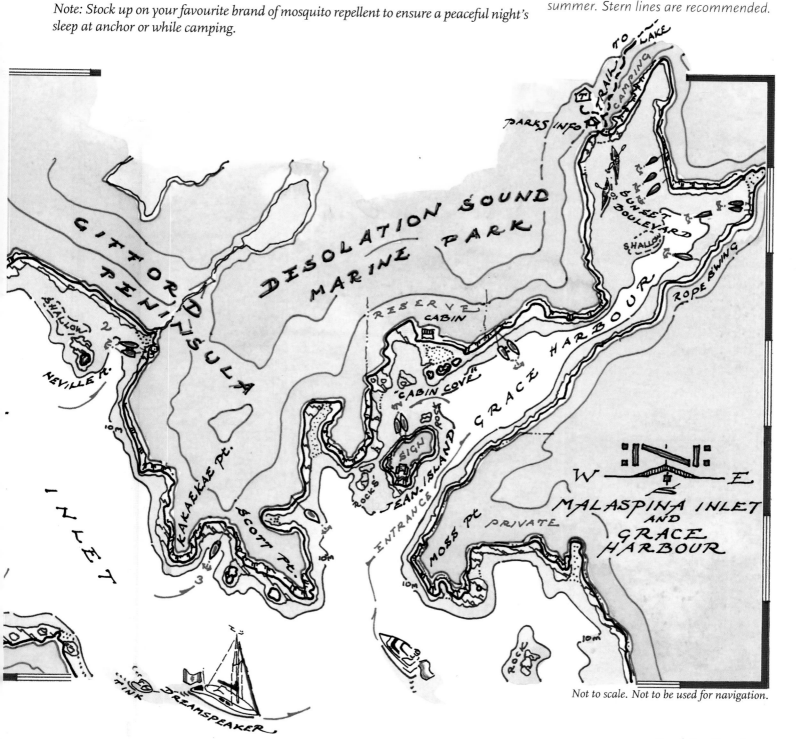

Not to scale. Not to be used for navigation.

✳ 50° 2.3' N   124° 43.5' W

CHARTS 3559. 3312, pages 13–15.

APPROACH: LANCELOT INLET

Lancelot Inlet branches N from the junction of Malaspina and Okeover Inlets.

Steep-sided Lancelot Inlet, sandwiched between Gifford Peninsula and the main-land, penetrates deep into Desolation Sound Marine Park and affords numerous anchorages waiting to be discovered. Two parcels of private land still exist within the park—one at the northwestern end of Wootton Bay, the other south of the entrance to Theodosia Inlet.

Ancient navigational symbol!

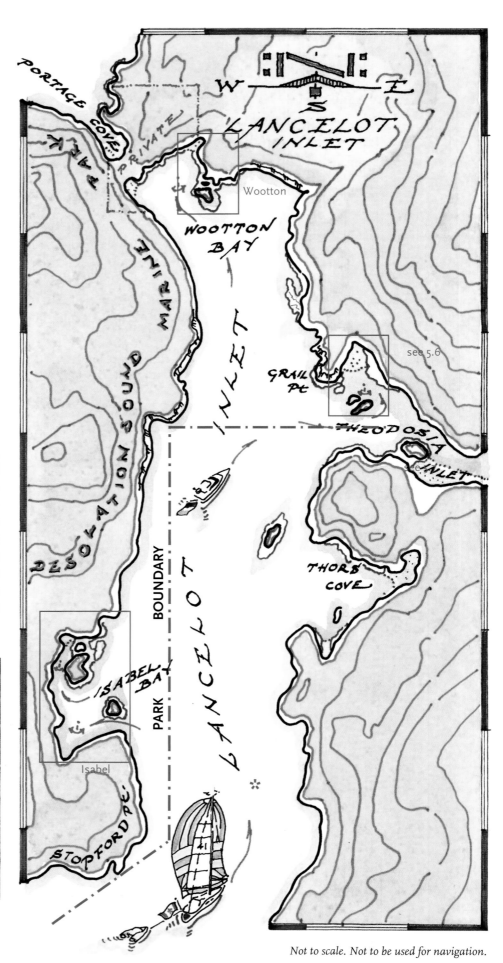

Not to scale. Not to be used for navigation.

WOOTTON BAYS, DESOLATION SOUND MARINE PARK

ANCHOR: ISABEL BAY

Good all-weather protection can be found NW of Madge Island. Take a stern line ashore as there is little room to swing. Alternative anchorage in the SW corner, giving good protection from the SE. Depths, holding and bottom conditions vary.

Note: Passage is possible S of Polly Island, but favour the Polly Island shore. If entering or exiting between Polly and Madge Islands, watch out for a rock that lies N of Polly Island.

Lovely Isabel Bay offers protected, though limited, anchorage tucked behind Polly and Madge Islands, but be prepared to find an alternative spot in the busy summer months. If you're one of the lucky ones, be sure to take a stern line ashore; then hop into your dinghy or kayak and set out to discover the "sights," including a suspended outhouse and a skinny-dipping hideaway.

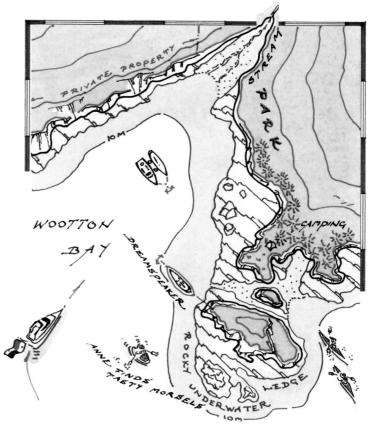

Not to scale. Not to be used for navigation.

ANCHOR: WOOTTON BAY

Although it seems rather open, the NE corner provides reasonable protection from outflow and southeasterly winds. Depths 8–12 m (26–39 ft), holding fair over a sand and rock bottom.

Note: Give a wide berth to the rocky underwater ledges that extend a deceptively long way S of the islet.

Wootton Bay is a pleasant alternative to Isabel Bay and is reasonably protected from prevailing summer winds. Flat, mossy camping ledges and a bountiful supply of fresh shellfish have made the bay a kayaker's haven.

Note: There is no public access to Portage Cove from Wootton Bay because the land is privately owned.

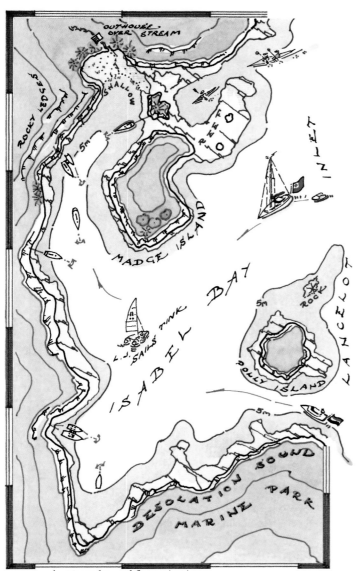

Not to scale. Not to be used for navigation.

Dreamspeaker *seeks shelter in Isabel Bay.*

5.6 SUSAN ISLETS, DESOLATION SOUND MARINE PARK

⁂ 50° 4.1' N 124° 42.1' W

CHARTS 3559. 3312, page 15.

APPROACH
From the W out of Lancelot Inlet, turning N to enter the anchorage between Susan Islets and the mainland.

ANCHOR
N of the islets and E of the rocks. Depths 4–8 m (13–26 ft). Holding good in mud.

Note: It is possible to pass between the smaller northern islet and the rocks to the S of Grail Point.

A quiet little anchorage can be found just north of the narrow entrance to Theodosia Inlet, tucked behind wooded Susan Islets. This is a wonderful spot to observe wildlife from the comfort of your cockpit, although the conical rock on the smaller islet has become a favourite with local birds, which often stop to view the antics of cruising boaters at anchor! This intimate bay also provides lovely views down Lancelot Inlet and great sunsets.

An intimate bay, a place to commune with nature.

Not to scale. Not to be used for navigation.

CHARTS 3559. 3312, page 15.

APPROACH

From the W, to the S of Susan Islets. The channel to Theodosia Inlet has a minimum charted depth of 2.4 m (nearly 8 ft). Stay in the centre of the channel and watch for rocks just visible at HW off the northern shore.

ANCHOR

Generally a good anchorage with fair protection, although the winds do whistle down off the surrounding mountains. Depths 4–6 m (13–19.5 ft). Holding good in mud.

❉ 50° 4.1' N   124° 42.1' W

Navigating Theodosia Inlet's entrance and narrow, snake-like channel is straightforward if you anticipate the currents, stay in the centre and keep a careful lookout for wayward boulders just visible at high water off the northern shore. The narrows suddenly open up to reveal a beautiful lake-like anchorage with the coastal mountain range creating a stunning backdrop. The inlet itself is fairly well protected, but boats can also tuck in behind the northern islet or between the rock bluff and the grassy isthmus farther east. When logging operations are in progress, a water taxi transports loggers out of the inlet by evening, leaving you alone to enjoy the tranquil surroundings. The logging road can also be used for hiking after hours, and the expansive mud flats are fun to explore by dinghy or kayak at high water.

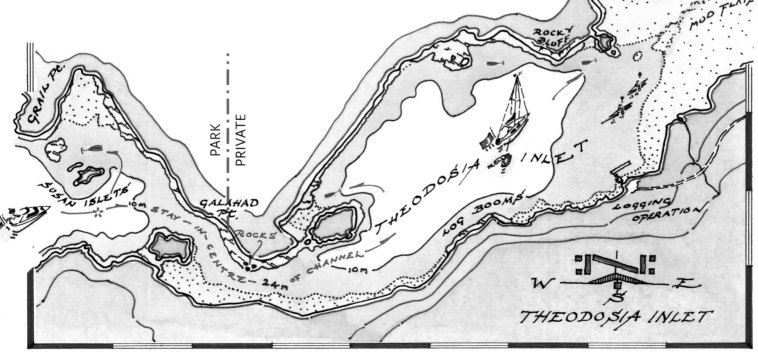

Not to scale. Not to be used for navigation.

5.8 OKEOVER INLET & "OKEOVER LANDING" PUBLIC WHARF

✳ 50° 1.5' N   124° 43.5' W

CHARTS 3559. 3312, page 14.

APPROACH
Okeover Inlet is deep with few navigational obstructions. Approach "Okeover Landing" from the NE. The building housing the restaurant on the hillside above the wharf is the most noticeable landmark.

Note: Leave Boundary Rock, off the southern tip of Coode Peninsula, to the N.

ANCHOR
Due to the steep-to shoreline, there are limited anchoring possibilities.

PENROSE BAY
Well protected from the NW but open to southeasterlies. Depths 4–10 m (13–33 ft), holding good in sand.

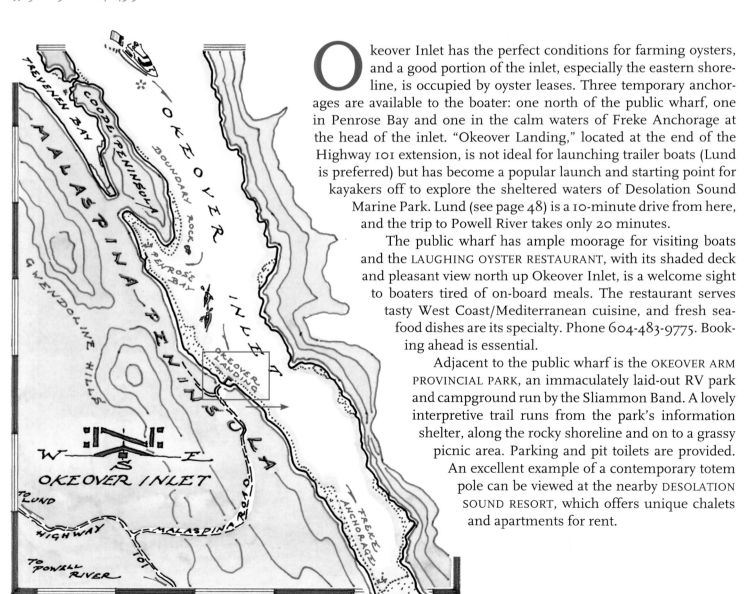

Not to scale. Not to be used for navigation.

Okeover Inlet has the perfect conditions for farming oysters, and a good portion of the inlet, especially the eastern shoreline, is occupied by oyster leases. Three temporary anchorages are available to the boater: one north of the public wharf, one in Penrose Bay and one in the calm waters of Freke Anchorage at the head of the inlet. "Okeover Landing," located at the end of the Highway 101 extension, is not ideal for launching trailer boats (Lund is preferred) but has become a popular launch and starting point for kayakers off to explore the sheltered waters of Desolation Sound Marine Park. Lund (see page 48) is a 10-minute drive from here, and the trip to Powell River takes only 20 minutes.

The public wharf has ample moorage for visiting boats and the LAUGHING OYSTER RESTAURANT, with its shaded deck and pleasant view north up Okeover Inlet, is a welcome sight to boaters tired of on-board meals. The restaurant serves tasty West Coast/Mediterranean cuisine, and fresh seafood dishes are its specialty. Phone 604-483-9775. Booking ahead is essential.

Adjacent to the public wharf is the OKEOVER ARM PROVINCIAL PARK, an immaculately laid-out RV park and campground run by the Sliammon Band. A lovely interpretive trail runs from the park's information shelter, along the rocky shoreline and on to a grassy picnic area. Parking and pit toilets are provided. An excellent example of a contemporary totem pole can be viewed at the nearby DESOLATION SOUND RESORT, which offers unique chalets and apartments for rent.

"OKEOVER LANDING"

N of public wharf and submarine cable. Very temporary. Depths 4–10 m (13–33 ft). Holding dependent on getting the anchor to set in hard-packed shingle.

FREKE ANCHORAGE

N of the mud flats. Good shelter from the SE, exposed to the N. Depths, holding and bottom condition unrecorded.

PUBLIC WHARF

Managed by the Okeover Harbour Authority, 604-483-3258, VHF 66A. Moorage for visiting boats on the inside of the floating breakwater. No power or water. Half-day rate (four hours) for visitors to the park and restaurant. Dock below the rock breakwater used by local aquaculture boats.

BOAT LAUNCH

Public.

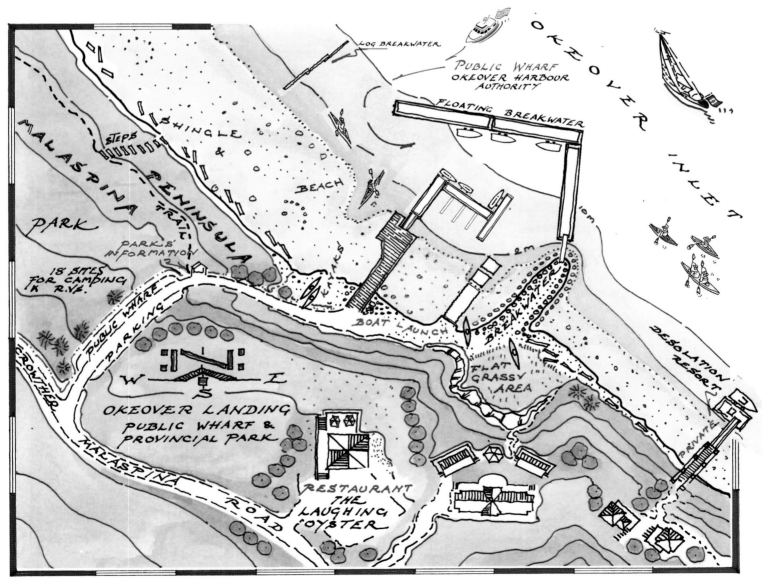

Not to scale. Not to be used for navigation.

5.9   GALLEY BAY, DESOLATION SOUND MARINE PARK

✻ 50° 4.4' N 124° 47.2' W

CHARTS 3559. 3312, page 12.

APPROACH

From the N.

Note: There are rocks in the centre of the bay and to the N of the little peninsula that forms what we call "Buff Cove."

ANCHOR

SE of what we have dubbed "Maiden Island," with good protection from prevailing winds. Depths 4–10 m (13–33 ft), moderate holding over a sand and gravel bottom. Alternatively in "Buff Cove," which is often subject to overnight outflow winds and chop from Desolation Sound. Depths, holding and bottom condition unrecorded.

Note: Galley Bay is well protected from southerly winds.

Galley Bay, tucked behind Zephine Head, is the first major anchorage available to the cruising boater after rounding Sarah Point and entering Desolation Sound.

Two parcels of land within the park are privately owned, and their boundaries should be respected. "Buff Cove," the westernmost anchorage, housed an alternative, back-to-basics community in the '60s and '70s, and, although its reputation lives on, the rustic cabins have been replaced with well-appointed private homes. The cove provides fairly sheltered protection and easy access to the park on its eastern shoreline. A second, more protected anchorage behind "Maiden Island" is also backed by private homes and is a lovely spot to explore at low water.

Not to scale. Not to be used for navigation.

CHARTS 3538. 3312, page 9.

APPROACH
From the E. Beware of the rocky ledges that fringe the anchorage.

ANCHOR
In the NW corner for the best protection or to the S of "Goat Islet" with stern anchor or line ashore.

✳ 50° 6.3' N   124° 45.1' W

Mink Island is privately owned, with large signs displayed along the shoreline requesting "No Fires at Any Time TIME PLEASE."

Good protection, warm water and an unobstructed view up Homfray Channel to the snow-capped mountains beyond make locally named "Mink Island Cove" a good temporary anchorage in the summer months, and boaters should be aware that float planes frequent the private dock. The rocky ledges surrounding "Goat Islet" are fun to explore by dinghy at low water, and the small lagoon behind provides delightful warm-water swimming.

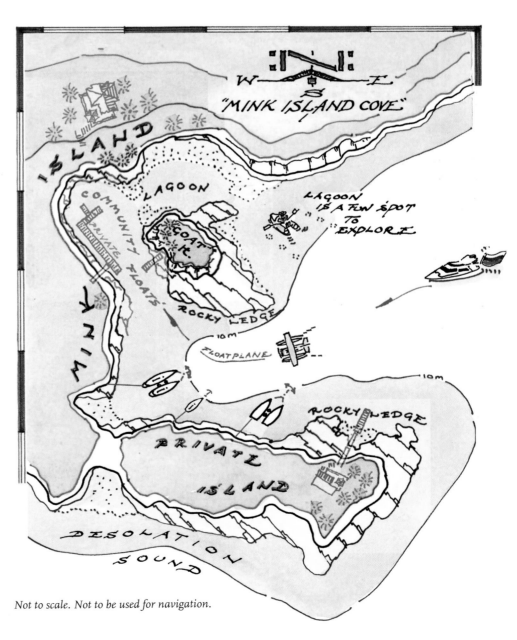

Not to scale. Not to be used for navigation.

Boys with their toys.

5.11 TENEDOS BAY, DESOLATION SOUND MARINE PARK

❋ 50° 6.8' N 124° 42.3' W

Approaching the entrance to Tenedos Bay.

Dreamspeaker *with a line ashore.*

Nestled between Bold Head and Mount Spooner, the clear but extremely deep waters of Tenedos Bay are still able to provide the visiting boater with four lovely spots suitable for anchoring. Keep a careful lookout for prominent rocks hidden just below the surface and lying in wait for the distracted skipper. The bay is extremely popular in the summer months, as news of blissful, warm-water swimming in Unwin Lake has spread.

1. The pocket anchorage in the southwest corner of the bay is quiet, secluded and subject to overnight outflow winds. It should only be entered via the northwest passage.

2. A cozy, three-boat spot west of what we call "Woodchuck Island" has become known locally as "Three Fathom Cove" over the years. Backed by high cliffs and grassy ledges, it is also a favourite with kayakers setting up camp for the night. A drying tombolo connects the island to the mainland at low water.

3. Good protection can be found in the spacious northwest cove. It provides the most secure overnight anchorage, with easy access by dinghy to the trails linking Unwin Lake with the east cove (4).

4. The convenient and popular cove below the bluff in the northeast corner is exposed to the west, but it has the best sunset views and is closest to the warm-water swimming at Unwin Lake. Kayakers can beach their craft at the head of the cove and pitch their tents in the old orchard campsite beside a freshwater stream. Pit toilets are provided, but all garbage must be packed out. The lake trail begins at the park's information shelter and divides about halfway along.

The less demanding southern route leads to the head of Unwin Lake, jammed with a wonderful variety of sun-bleached logs. It is best to continue on a little way from here if you plan to swim. Hiking along the northern trail is a little more rigorous but quite lovely as you wind your way through the forest ,passing small waterfalls and deep freshwater pools en route to bathing rocks on the lake's edge. From here you can take a blissful warm-water swim, but make your presence known well in advance as skinny-dipping is often the norm.

CHARTS 3538. 3312, page 9.

APPROACH

From the S. Enter the bay by leaving the rock off Bold Head to port. Watch for isolated rocks.

ANCHOR

1. Reasonable protection can be found behind the small islets in the SW corner.
2. For all-weather protection, locally named "Three Fathom Cove" is hard to beat. Note the shallow entrance bar, approximately 1.5 m (5 ft) at chart datum.
3. Alternative anchorage is possible in the roomy NW corner.
4. The popular anchorage below the bluff in the NE corner is exposed to the W. Depths, holding and bottom condition vary. Stern lines are recommended.

Morning tranquility in the NE corner.

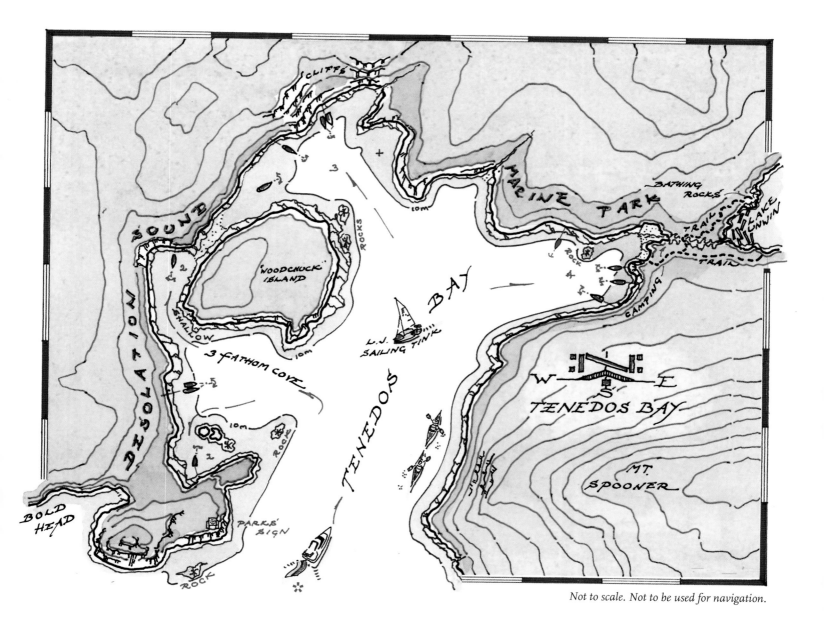

Not to scale. Not to be used for navigation.

"OTTERS POOL," OTTER ISLAND, DESOLATION SOUND MARINE PARK

✳ 50° 7.4' N 124° 43.7' W

CHARTS 3538. 3312, page 9.

APPROACH

Slowly from the SW, out of Desolation Sound, or from the N, out of Homfray Channel.

ANCHOR

Temporary anchorage can be found within the passage between Otter Island and the mainland. Depths 4–8 m (13–26 ft), holding varies over a rocky bottom.

Note: Sky Pilot Rock lies N of Otter Island.

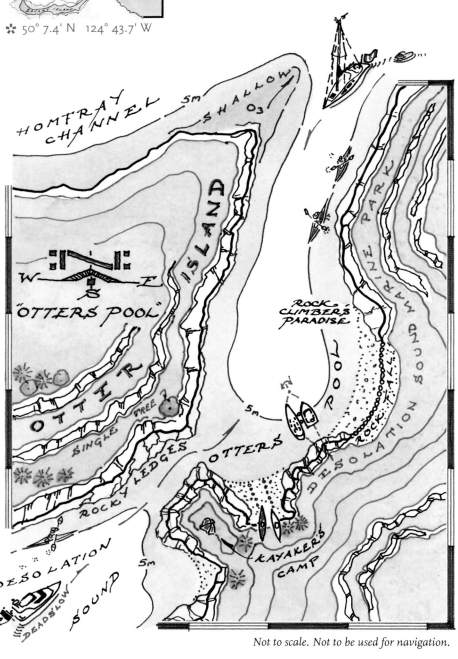

Not to scale. Not to be used for navigation.

The lovely anchorage we have dubbed "Otters Pool" is tucked between Otter Island and the mainland. Unfortunately it is also a convenient passage for runabouts and other speedy craft en route to or from nearby anchorages. Boaters should slow down, reduce their wake and allow the peace and solitude to be enjoyed by all.

Sheltered stern-to anchorage can be found south of the steep, rocky ledges—a rock climber's paradise. Stones have also been cleared in the little nook south of the anchorage, making it possible for kayakers to beach their craft and camp on the grassy spot overlooking the pass.

"Otters Pool" provides an unlikely anchorage.

CURME ISLANDS, DESOLATION SOUND MARINE PARK 5.13

CHARTS 3538. 3312, page 9.

APPROACH
This is not a recommended spot for deep-draft boats and should only be navigated on a rising tide. Beware of rocks that lie to the N in the entrance. The head of the channel is shallow and dries on a zero tide.

ANCHOR
Temporary anchorage is possible for a small boat. Swinging or turning room is limited. Stern lines ashore are a must.

✵ 50° 7.1' N 124° 44.6' W

Kayakers camping above rocky beach.

The tranquil Curme Islands are a kayaker's heaven. Temporary anchorage for one small, shallow-draft boat is also possible. Clustered off the northeast shore of Mink Island and now included in the marine park's boundaries, the islands provide flat, grassy spots for camping, rocky ledges and beaches for exploring and an abundance of trees for shade and protection. It would be easy to spend a few restful days here enjoying the simplicity of nature—until your food and water supplies run low.

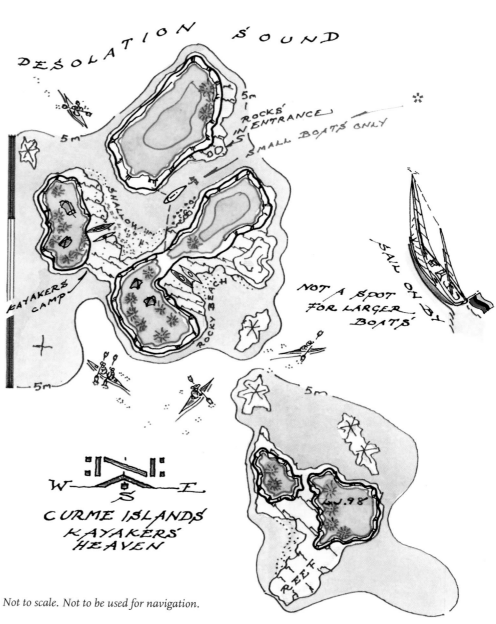

Not to scale. Not to be used for navigation.

5.14 PRIDEAUX HAVEN, MELANIE & LAURA COVES,

Majestic, snow-capped mountains, awe-inspiring vistas and remarkably warm waters lie in wait for the cruising boater voyaging north to the three most popular anchorages in Desolation Sound Marine Park. Prideaux Haven and Melanie and Laura Coves lie snuggled between the mainland and a small string of islands that form a protective barrier from wind and seas in exposed Homfray Channel. The narrow pass between Lucy Point and Oriel Rocks off William Islands provides the only safe entrance into Prideaux Haven.

Spectacular Prideaux Haven has become legendary for two diverse reasons: its roomy and protected harbour, warm and sheltered waters, open vistas, and choice of cozy nooks and crannies come first and foremost, while its reputation as the "power haven" for a large assortment of luxury yachts in the busy months of July and August takes a close second.

CHARTS 3555. 3312, page 11.

APPROACH: PRIDEAUX HAVEN
From the NW between Scobell and Eveleigh Islands. Head for the parks sign prior to turning to starboard and entering between Lucy Point and the Oriel Rocks.

ANCHOR
All-weather protection may be found throughout the haven. Depths 2–12 m (6.5–39 ft), holding good over a mud bottom.

Desolation Sound Marine Park

APPROACH: MELANIE COVE

Melanie Cove branches E from Melanie Point within Prideaux Haven. Note the drying reef at the entrance.

ANCHOR

Good all-weather protection can be found in depths of 4–8 m (13–26 ft), holding good in mud. Note the drying rocks and mud flats at the head of the cove.

APPROACH: LAURA COVE

From the N; enter between the rocky ledge off Copplestone Point and the isolated rock off Copplestone Island. Best approached at LW when the rocks are clearly visible and the isolated rock is just visible.

ANCHOR

Good all-weather protection in depths of 3–9 m (10–29.5 ft), holding good in mud.

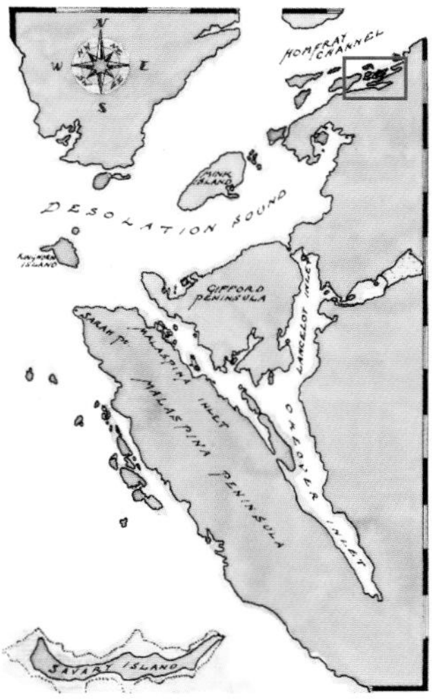

50° 8.8' N 124° 41.1' W

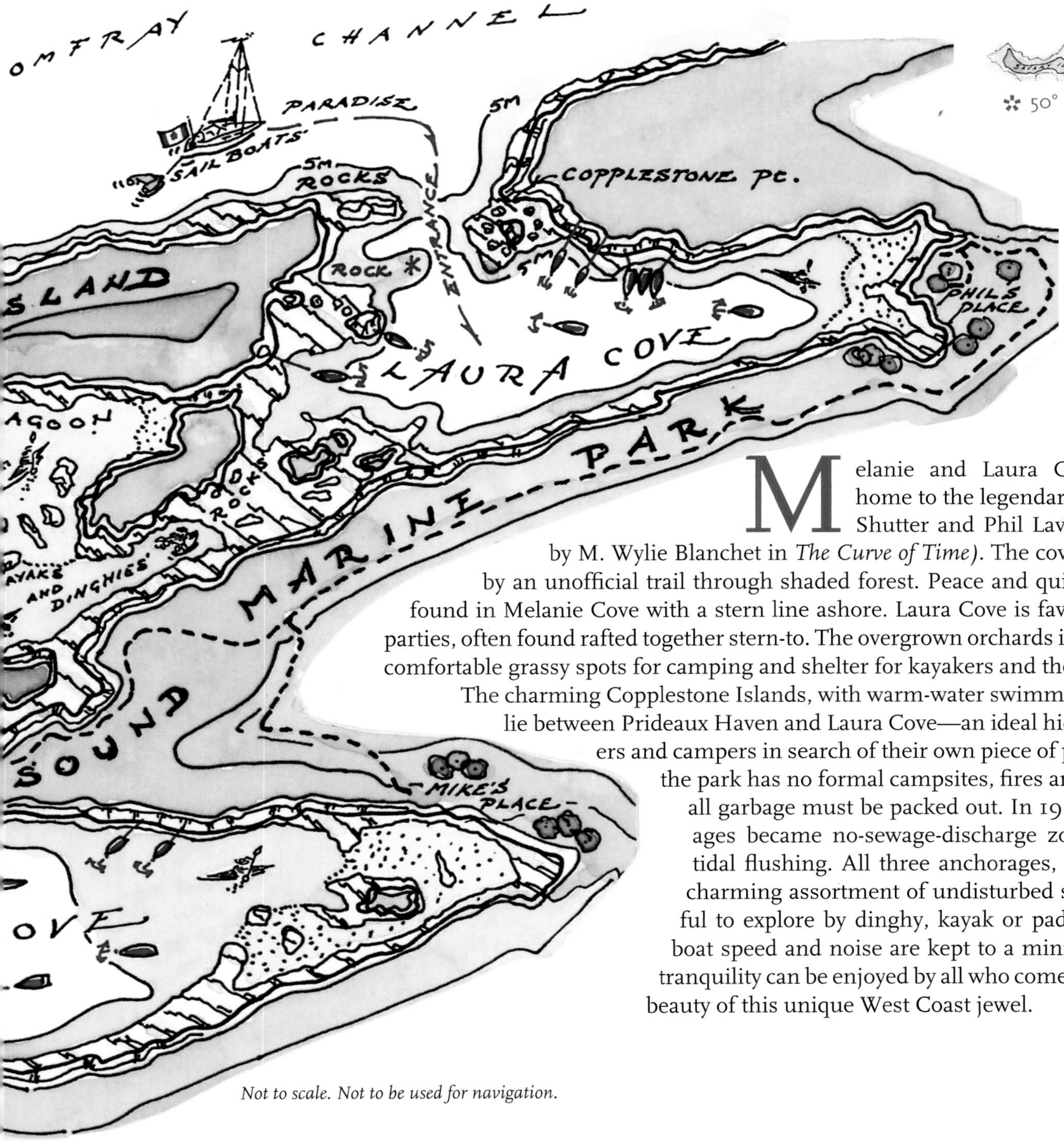

Not to scale. Not to be used for navigation.

Melanie and Laura Coves were once home to the legendary Andrew "Mike" Shutter and Phil Lavine (as described by M. Wylie Blanchet in *The Curve of Time*). The coves are still linked by an unofficial trail through shaded forest. Peace and quiet can usually be found in Melanie Cove with a stern line ashore. Laura Cove is favoured by sailboat parties, often found rafted together stern-to. The overgrown orchards in both coves offer comfortable grassy spots for camping and shelter for kayakers and their craft.

The charming Copplestone Islands, with warm-water swimming in the lagoon, lie between Prideaux Haven and Laura Cove—an ideal hideaway for kayakers and campers in search of their own piece of paradise. Because the park has no formal campsites, fires are prohibited, and all garbage must be packed out. In 1998, these anchorages became no-sewage-discharge zones due to poor tidal flushing. All three anchorages, the lagoon and a charming assortment of undisturbed spots are wonderful to explore by dinghy, kayak or paddle board and, if boat speed and noise are kept to a minimum, the park's tranquility can be enjoyed by all who come to experience the beauty of this unique West Coast jewel.

✳ 50° 9.2' N   124° 39.8' W

CHARTS 3555. 3312, page 11.

APPROACH

From the NW at LW because the shoreline is fringed by rocky ledges that extend into deep water. An alternative approach is from the S via a "tricky pass" between two prominent rocks.

ANCHOR

Temporary anchorage for three or four boats, in depths of 2–5 m (6.5–16 ft). Holding varies over a sand and rock bottom.

Note: The passage to the S is tricky because of a reef extending S from the western rock.

A rocky but undisturbed hideaway for three or four boats can be found in what we call "Pyramid Cove," between the rocky outcrops of Roffey Island and the mainland. Those willing to venture beyond popular Prideaux Haven and navigate a somewhat tricky pass into the cove will be rewarded with quiet and solitude beneath towering mountains. The less restricted entrance into the cove is north of Roffey Island. This anchorage provides reasonable protection from prevailing summer and overnight outflow winds, with limited room to swing. A stern anchor or line ashore is advised.

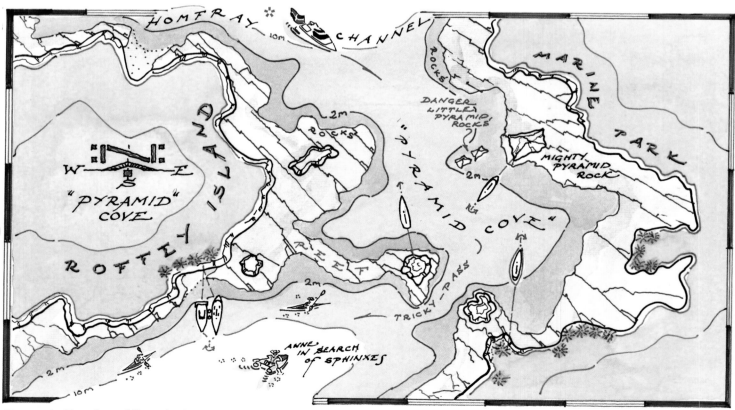

Not to scale. Not to be used for navigation.

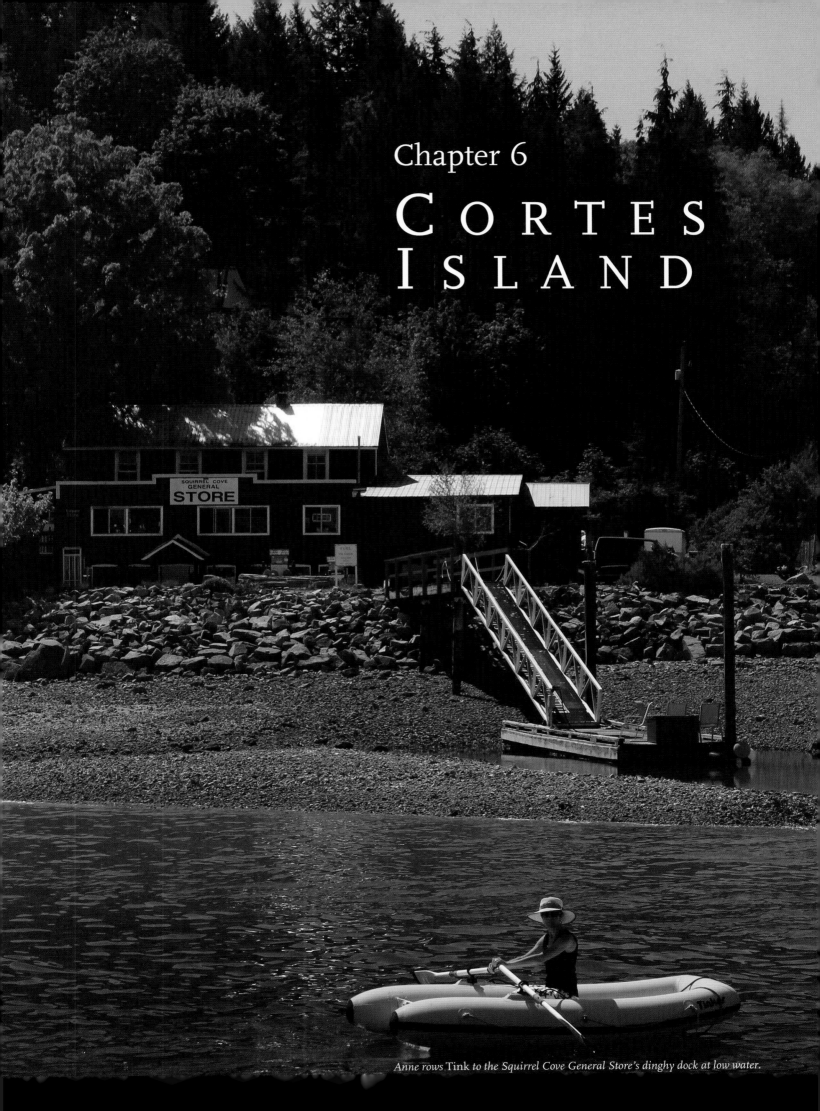

Chapter 6
CORTES ISLAND

Anne rows Tink to the Squirrel Cove General Store's dinghy dock at low water.

Chapter 6
CORTES ISLAND

A real sandy beach at Mansons Landing.

TIDES

Canadian Tide and Current Tables, Volume 5
Reference Port: Point Atkinson
Secondary Ports: Twin Islands, Gorge Harbour, Whaletown

CURRENTS

Note: Although there are no reference or secondary current stations, tidal currents may be encountered at the entrance to Cortes Bay, Gorge Harbour, Von Donop Inlet and Squirrel Cove and at the entrances of tidal lagoons.

WEATHER

Note: No specific reporting station covers this chapter. Summer winds are usually moderate, but they tend to funnel and accelerate through the anchorages. A forecast for a strong northwesterly in Johnstone Strait or the Strait of Georgia (northern half) will equate to strong northwesterly winds over Cortes Island.

CAUTIONARY NOTES

Three dangers to keep a keen lookout for while circumnavigating the island:

(1) Rocks to the N of Three Islets as one approaches Cortes Bay;

(2) The reef off Sutil Point, the southernmost tip of Cortes Island;

(3) The rock off the southern boundary of Mansons Landing Marine Park, especially when covered at HW.

I f a quick circumnavigation of the globe just will not fit into this year's busy boating schedule, consider treating yourself to a comfortable one or two-week cruise around Cortes Island—the heart of the magnificent cruising grounds encompassed in this chapter.

Although Cortes is only 16 km (10 mi) across at its widest point and 32 km (20 mi) in length from north to south, its varied coastline offers easy picnic nooks, tranquil coves and safe all-weather anchorages. Provisioning stops, cafés and restaurants are scattered around the island and offer fresh and organic produce in season. White sandy beaches, warm-water swimming, crystal-clear lakes and the gentle pace of island life complete this wonderful package.

Seaplanes operate daily flights into Cortes Bay and Mansons Landing, making these stops convenient pick-up and drop-off points; they also provide protected bays in which to anchor. Mansons Landing Marine Park invites you to enticing sandy beaches, a saltwater lagoon and freshwater swimming in Hague Lake. Welcoming Gorge Harbour Marina Resort offers moorage, an excellent restaurant, squeaky-clean showers, a swimming pool and hot tub and a fully stocked store. Good anchorage can be found throughout the bay. Shark Spit, just a short hop north, offers an idyllic picnic anchorage and the opportunity to dig for clams, swim or simply lounge on the beach.

Whaletown's gruesome history as a whaling station in the late 1800s has been eclipsed by its importance as a ferry terminal connecting Cortes Island with Quadra and Vancouver Islands. Farther north, three lovely fair-weather anchorages surrounded by a lush recreational reserve can be found in Carrington Bay, and Quartz Bay provides protected overnight anchorage. A quick side trip across Sutil Channel takes you to Read Island, where peaceful Evans Bay provides spectacular mountain views.

Protected Von Donop Inlet, with its beautiful marine park, offers a rich variety of anchorages and is still a firm favourite with cruising boaters who enjoy relaxing in the park's calm, sheltered waters. A trail leads from here to Squirrel Cove, the most popular anchorage on Cortes Island due to its reputation for abundant, safe anchorage. The community of Squirrel Cove, just a short dinghy ride from the anchorage has a public wharf, a fully stocked general store, shower and laundry facilities and a charming waterfront restaurant.

FEATURED DESTINATIONS

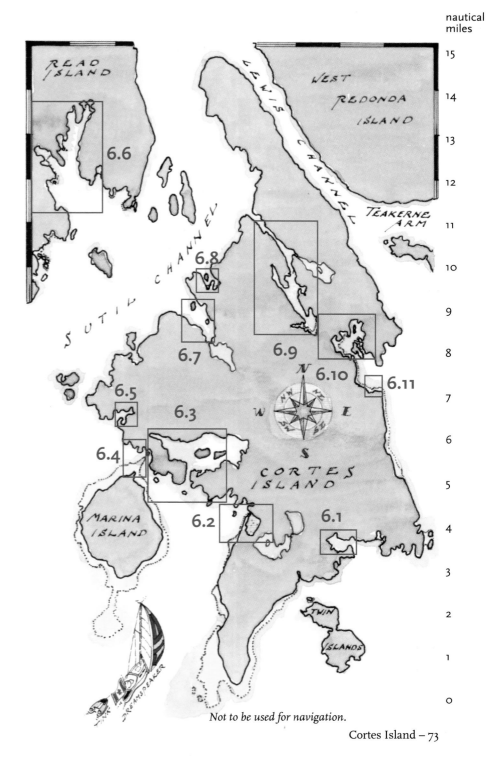

Not to be used for navigation.

6.1 CORTES BAY, CORTES ISLAND

✻ 50° 3.8' N   124° 55.3' W

Active float plane traffic in Cortes Bay.

Misty Isles *at anchor.*

Distracted skippers beware: the rocks that lie between the northern shoreline and the starboard light at the entrance to Cortes Bay are well covered at high water. Be sure to enter the bay south of the distinctive red-and-white tower.

This large bay provides a convenient stopping point for boaters journeying north from Comox as well as a gentle introduction to island life for those prepared to venture farther than the public wharf. At the time of writing, Karl Triller was still the official King of Cortes. Unfortunately, WOLF BLUFF CASTLE, which he built by hand, is under repairs and not open to the public.

The Royal Vancouver Yacht Club has an extensive outstation at the head of the bay, and the Seattle Yacht Club sits comfortably on the southern shore. Seaplanes operate scheduled and chartered flights into and out of Cortes Bay, making it a convenient pick-up and drop-off point for friends, family and crew.

For panoramic views and a little exercise, take the Squirrel Cove road to Easter Bluff. Pop into LINNAEA FARM for organic vegetables, an informal tour or a quiet wander through its beautiful gardens. For idyllic, warm-water swimming, visit Hague Lake, a 30-minute walk along Bartholomew Road. A walk to Gunflint Lake, northwest of Cortes Bay, takes about 20 minutes.

ANCHORING NOTE: *Cortes Bay is known locally as Windy Bay. A forecast for moderate to strong north westerly will funnel wind through the bay at 15–30 knots. Many visiting boaters have difficulty setting their anchors and find themselves dragging. The trick is to carefully reverse laying out the chain and rode. Wait ten minutes to allow the anchor to penetrate the loose upper layer of mud prior to the final pullback, which should see the anchor set in the dense lower layer and allow you a good night's rest.*

CHARTS

3538. 3312, page 8. 3311, sheet 5.

APPROACH

From the E; enter between the starboard light (red) and the cliffs on the southern shore.

ANCHOR

The bay is well protected, and anchorage is possible throughout. However, the bottom condition of loose mud over a dense lower level, creates anchoring challenges. Make sure that your anchor is well set. Depths vary.

PUBLIC WHARF

Managed by Cortes Harbour Authority—call the harbour manager at 250-935-0007. Primarily used by local boats. Power up to 30 amps, but no water on the float. Garbage drop-off for a fee. Cortes Bay is a float plane operations zone with a designated float at the public wharf.

MARINA

Both marinas are private.

BOAT LAUNCH

The public Blind Creek boat launch is alongside a private float.

CAUTIONARY NOTE

Ensure that your anchor is well set. Anchors tend to drag when the winds shift in direction.

Delightful yellow house at the head of Cortes Bay.

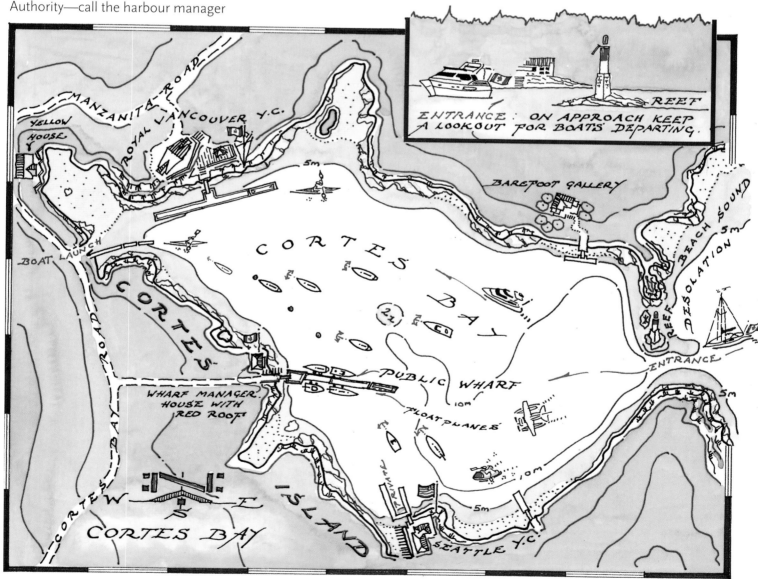

Not to scale. Not to be used for navigation.

MANSONS LANDING MARINE PARK, CORTES ISLAND

Approach to Mansons Landing from the SW.

At anchor in Manson Bay.

In settled weather, Mansons Landing Marine Park is an idyllic spot to drop anchor, dig out your bucket and spade and just have fun for a few days. With two inviting bathing spots—saltwater and freshwater—clean, white sandy beaches and magnificent views out to snow-capped mountains, who could wish for more?

Most boaters anchor in Manson Bay, to the north of "Cat and Sheep Islets" and off the shallows at the lagoon entrance. The saltwater lagoon is wonderful to explore by dinghy, kayak or paddle board at high water. At low water dig for clams and collect oysters, but be sure to respect legal limits.

The public wharf is a colourful place, with visiting boats and local runabouts all happily rafted up together. Shops for provisioning are a 15–20-minute walk up Sutil Point Road. The CORTES MARKET has a good selection of provisioning items, fresh and frozen produce, a deli and coffee bar, ice and hardware. They also offer free Wi-Fi and the use of their computer for 50 minutes. The market is open 7 days a week and free delivery to your boat can be arranged; call 250-935-6626. The popular MARKET TAKE-OUT stand in the parking lot specializes in freshly made fish and chips and burgers, and also serves ice cream.

CORTES NATURAL FOOD CO-OP is open seven days a week and specializes in organic and local produce. They have an excellent in-house bakery and café that serves freshly made sandwiches, hot and cold wraps and baked goods. The CAFÉ and ESPRESSO BAR are open Mondays, Wednesdays and Fridays from 9 a.m. to 3 p.m. Wi-Fi and the use of a computer are available.

MARNIE'S BOOKSTORE has a great selection of new and used titles and carries art supplies. For local crafts, freshly baked goods and local produce visit the farmers' market, which takes place every Friday at Mansons Hall from 12 p.m. to 3 p.m. year-round.

The white sandy beach and clean, warm water of Hague Lake can be reached by taking the Seaford Road route (off Sutil Point Road) or by hiking along the lovely lagoon-side trail to what we call the "Skinny-Dipping Rocks," where sunbathing *au naturel* is favoured. Alternatively, relax on the family beach or take an exhilarating swim to the big smooth rocks on the lake's eastern shore. Because Hague Lake provides drinking water for lakeside residents, motorboats are forbidden, the use of soap or shampoo is prohibited and dogs are not allowed on the beach or in the water.

CHARTS 3538. 3313, sheet 5.

APPROACH

From the SW, maintaining a safe distance from the Cortes shore to clear the rocks off the park's SW boundary.

ANCHOR

In Manson Bay. Good protection from NW and SE winds. Open to the W/SW summer winds. However, these winds are generally light and diminish in the early evening. Depths 4–12 m (13–39 ft). Holding good in sand.

PUBLIC WHARF

Managed by Cortes Harbour Authority—call the harbour manager at 250-935-0007. Generally occupied by a mixture of local and visiting boats. Power up to 30 amps but no water on the float. Garbage drop-off for a fee. Pay phone at the top of the ramp.

BOAT LAUNCH

Public and tidal into the lagoon for kayaks and shoal-draft boats.

Note: Manson Bay is a float plane operations zone with a designated float at the public wharf.

The lagoon is a magical place.

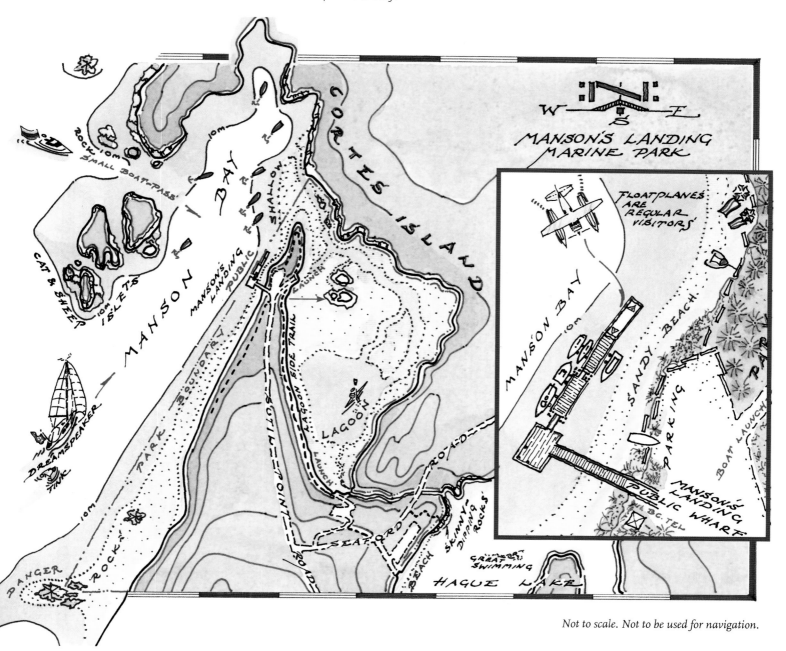

Not to scale. Not to be used for navigation.

6.3 Gorge Harbour, Cortes Island

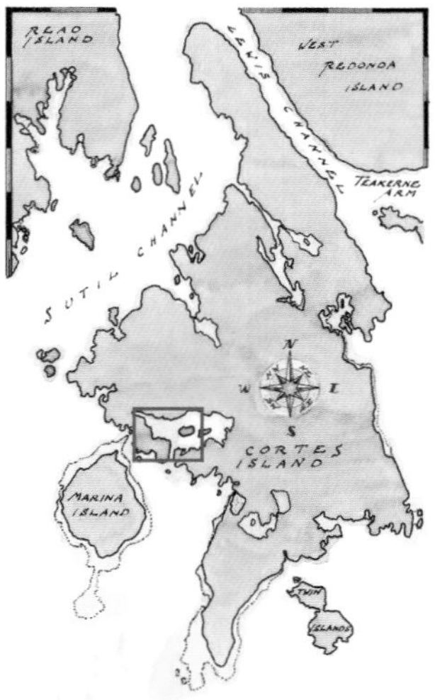

50° 4.6' N 125° 0.8' W

Entrance to Gorge Harbour.

Boat-watching from the fireside patio, Gorge Harbour Marina.

The appropriately named Guide Islets mark the bottleneck entrance to The Gorge, with its high, steep cliffs depicting First Nations petroglyphs at low water. Be sure to leave Tide Islet to starboard on entering Gorge Harbour, which offers protected anchorage with some secluded coves and a variety of islets to explore.

GORGE HARBOUR MARINA RESORT has a warm and inviting ambience and is artistically landscaped with island stonework, native plants, cedar boardwalks and green lawns sweeping down to the water. Visiting boaters (including those at anchor) are welcome to enjoy the resort's family amenities, which include a pool and hot tub, a volleyball court and kids' play area, morning yoga, a covered gazebo for boating rendezvous, and clean showers and laundry facilities. The fireside patio overlooking the marina and harbour has sturdy picnic tables and nightly entertainment during July and August.

The fully stocked store (open 7 days a week) includes a BC Liquor Store outlet and carries a good selection of provisioning items, local and organic produce, bread, meat and seafood; mail service, tide tables, CHS charts and propane are also available. Garbage disposal is for a fee but recycling is complimentary and well organized. Don't miss the Saturday farmers' market from 10 a.m. to 2 p.m. for locally made crafts, preserves, fruit pies, pastries, bread and garden produce (summer only). The resort is an ideal base for kayakers to set up camp with tent sites and RV camping in the old apple orchard. Guest rooms and a cottage are also available.

The charming FLOATHOUSE RESTAURANT with its shaded deck and waterfront view started its life as a float home near Kingcome Inlet and was moved to its present location in 1979. Today it is noted for its excellent selection of unique dishes, seafood specials and cordial service. This is the perfect spot to while away a few hours before retiring to the cockpit for an après-lunch nap. The restaurant is licensed and open for lunch and dinner. Reservations are a must in the busy summer months, call 250-935-6433.

Hikes from Gorge Harbour include a 2.4 km (1.5 mi) energetic walk to historic Whaletown (see page 81) and a pleasant ramble along the community trails of Whaletown Commons, just off Whaletown Road. The CORTES CONNECTION operates a minibus service to Campbell River five times a week and reservations are necessary.

CHARTS

3538. 3312, page 19. 3311, sheet 5.

APPROACH

From the S. The narrow entrance pass is easy to see below the towering cliffs on the western side located to the N of the Guide Islets. Leave Tide Islet to the E.

Note: Tidal currents up to 4 knots may be encountered in the entrance pass.

ANCHOR (EAST)

There are many opportunities for anchoring throughout the eastern harbour with excellent protection in strong SE winds. Depths vary. Good holding in a mix of sand and mud.

ANCHOR (WEST)

There are a variety of nooks and bights throughout the harbour. Convenient anchorage between private buoys off the marina in the NW corner. Depths vary, good holding in a mix of mud and sand.

PUBLIC WHARF

Managed by Cortes Harbour Authority—call the harbour manager at 250-935-0007. A single float lies along the northern shore and is primarily used by local boats. No power or water. Garbage drop-off for a fee.

MARINA

The Gorge Harbour Marina Resort has a full-service marina with extensive visitor moorage, call 250-935-6433, VHF channel 66A. Water, power up to 50 amps and free Wi-Fi. Kayak and paddle board rentals available.

BOAT LAUNCH

At the public wharf.

FUEL

Fuel dock at the marina. Gasoline, diesel, (propane at the store), ice, snacks, ice cream, fishing tackle, local books and boating guides.

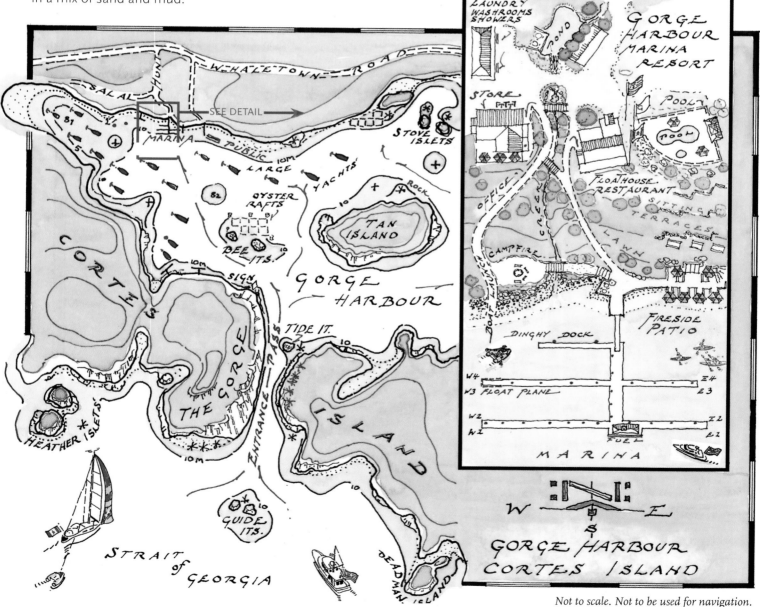

Not to scale. Not to be used for navigation.

UGANDA PASSAGE, SHARK SPIT, MARINA ISLAND

✳ 50° 5.0' N   125° 2.0' W

CHARTS

3538. 3312, page 19. 3311, sheet 5.

APPROACH

Either from the S off Heather Islets or from the W out of Sutil Channel. Uganda Passage is best transited prior to HW, when the spit is still visible.

ANCHOR

On a shallow shingle ledge to the E of Shark Spit. The spit offers good protection from NW seas while exposed at LW. Depths of 2–6 m (6.5–19.5 ft), holding good in mud and shingle.

Shark Spit looking out to Uganda Passage.

Whaletown's charming little post office.

The rather narrow and sinuous Uganda Passage is well marked as it twists around the shallows off Shark Spit and the scattered rocks and shoals off western Cortes Island. The long, fin-shaped gravel-and-shell beach that forms Shark Spit extends out from the northern tip of Marina Island, creating an idyllic picnic anchorage with crystal-clear waters and mountain views. Many relaxing hours can be spent swimming, digging clams, beach-combing or collecting driftwood for the design of beach encampments and sculptures. Excellent dinghy sailing can be found in the lee of the spit, and walks to the tip of the spit at low water can prove exhilarating when boats navigating Uganda Passage pass close by.

Not to scale. Not to be used for navigation.

WHALETOWN BAY, CORTES ISLAND

CHARTS

3538. 3312, page 19. 3311, sheet 5.

APPROACH

Either from the S midway between the starboard (red) buoy and the Cortes shore or from the W between the same buoy and the port-hand light.

ANCHOR

NE of the port-hand day beacon off the public wharf or E of the ferry terminal between boats on buoys. Depths 2–6 m (6.5–19.5 ft). Holding good in thick, sticky mud.

PUBLIC WHARF

Managed by Cortes Harbour Authority—call the harbour manager at 250-935-0007. Power up to 30 amps but no water. Primarily used by local boats.

Note: Whaletown Bay is the terminus for the ferry from Heriot Bay, Quadra Island. Stay well clear of its channel and terminal.

✿ 50° 6.2' N   125° 3.3' W

A regular ferry service to and from Heriot Bay on Quadra Island operates from sleepy Whaletown Bay. Temporary anchorage is available at the head of the bay, and moorage at the public wharf is possible if you can find a spot between the local runabouts or are prepared to raft up.

A short walk up Whaletown Road will take you to the charming little post office (open Monday, Wednesday and Friday) and mailbox, the small local library and the picturesque white mission church, St. John the Baptist. A public notice board listing local events can be found at the post office.

In season, and if you are in luck, juicy blackberries can be found nearby, so take a container just in case.

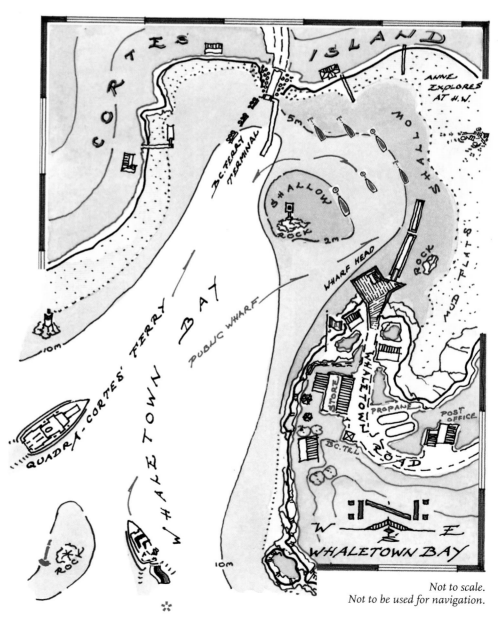

Not to scale.
Not to be used for navigation.

6.6 EVANS BAY, READ ISLAND

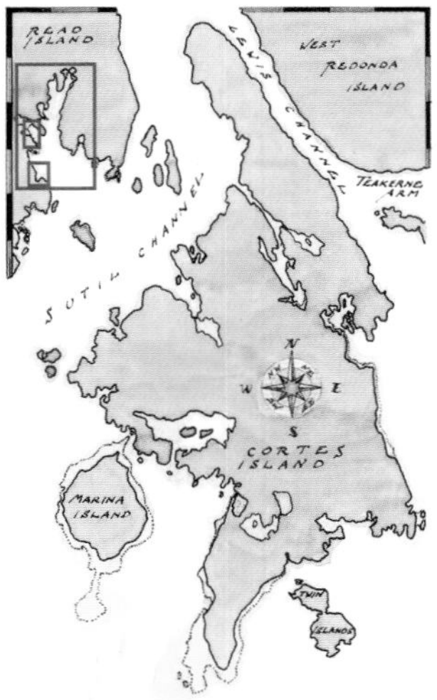

✲ 50° 11.0' N 125° 4.3' W

CHARTS 3538. 3312, page 19.

APPROACH

From the SE.

EVANS BAY: Has numerous small coves to anchor in, all temporary because they are exposed to the south. However, in prevailing northwesterly winds, they form snug overnight anchorages. Shelter from the SE can be found in the cove S of the public wharf between local boats on buoys.

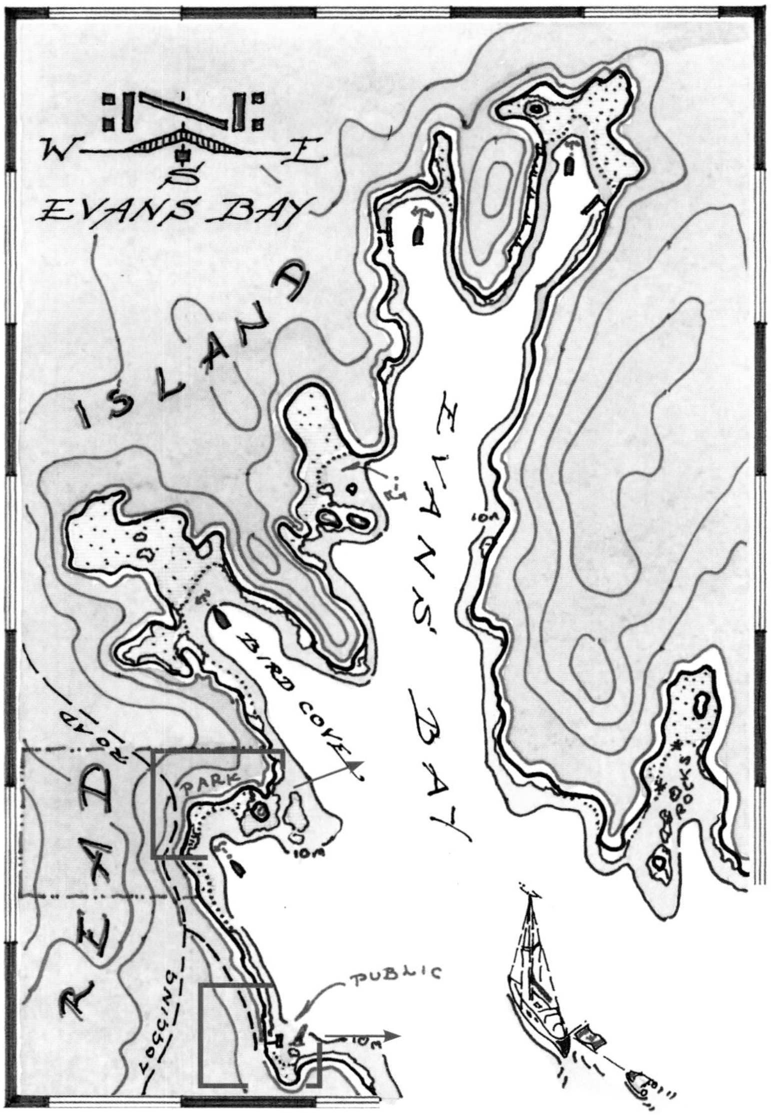

Not to scale. Not to be used for navigation.

The small public wharf is filled with local boats but offers moorage if you are prepared to raft up. It also provides access to the island's main road, which connects the bay with Surge Narrows public wharf, if you're up for an energetic hike (see page 145).

A charming two-boat anchorage north of the public wharf provides spectacular mountain views, a lovely pink gravel beach, easy access to the main road and delightful Lambert's Beach Park. There are islets and rocky ledges to explore and, although the bay loses its light early, the sunset's afterglow creates a wonderful backdrop to this tranquil spot.

The property surrounding Bird Cove is privately owned, but the drying mud flats at the head of the cove are wonderfully peaceful and fun to explore by dinghy or kayak at high water. A more sheltered anchorage can be found north of Bird Cove, tucked behind three charming islets, and two other temporary spots are available at the head of the bay in either the western or the eastern arm.

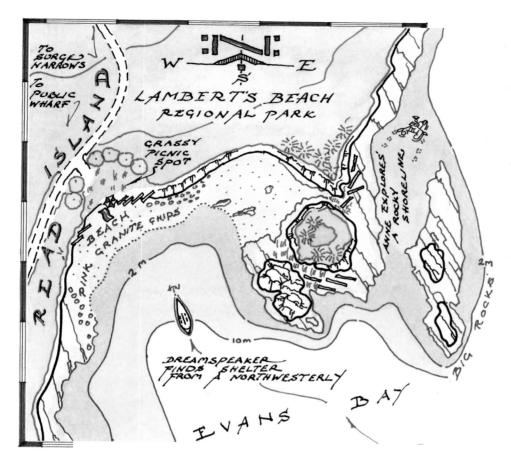

Not to scale. Not to be used for navigation.

Delightful Lambert's Beach Park.

LAMBERT'S BEACH PARK: A small park and picnic spot fringed by a rocky islet. There is a reasonable anchorage with good protection from the northwest. Depths 4–6 m (13–19.5 ft), holding good over a gravel and mud bottom.

READ ISLAND PUBLIC WHARF: A small public wharf used by local boats lies in the southwest corner of Evans Bay.

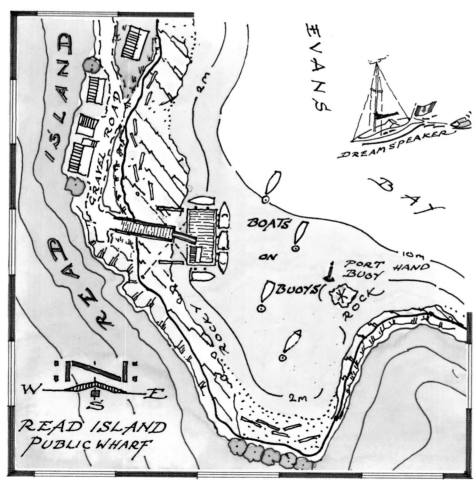

Not to scale. Not to be used for navigation.

Approach to Evans Bay public wharf.

6.7 CARRINGTON BAY, CORTES ISLAND

✹ 50° 8.8' N   125° 1.0' W

CHARTS 3538. 3312, page 19.

APPROACH
From the NW. Jane Islet may be passed via the northern channel or by the southern passage, but watch for the unmarked rocks that lie due S of the islet.

ANCHOR
Carrington Bay offers good protection from the SE but is relatively open to prevailing northwesterly winds. Protection from the NW can be found behind Jane Islet or between what we call "Lucy and Ronnie Islets" and the Cortes shore. Depths 8–12 m (26–39 ft), holding fair over a rock and mud bottom.

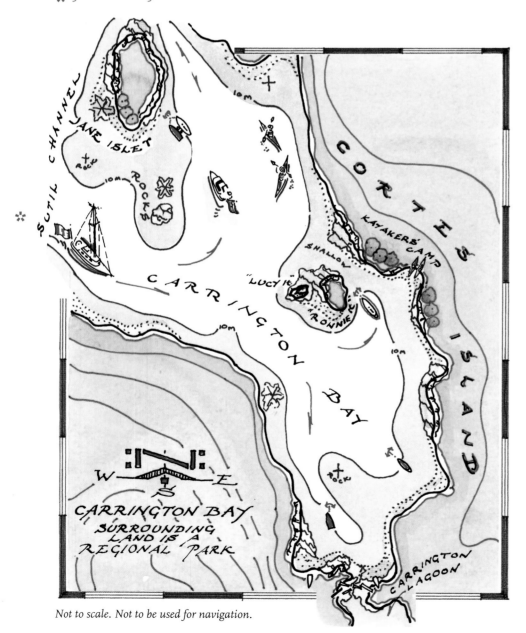

Not to scale. Not to be used for navigation.

Surrounded by a provincial recreational reserve, three pleasant fair-weather anchorages await the intrepid explorer willing to take a detour into Carrington Bay on Cortes Island's western shoreline.

The two ideal spots to drop your anchor are behind "Lucy and Ronnie Islets" or Jane Islet, as they afford some protection from the northwesterly winds known to spring up in the late afternoon or early evening. The third anchorage, at the head of the bay, is the most exposed, although in settled weather it provides easy access to Carrington Lagoon, which is fun to explore by kayak or paddle board if you don't mind a tricky portage over piled-up driftwood. Carrington Bay is also known for its glorious sunsets.

Carrington Bay is fun to explore.

CHARTS 3538. 3312, page 19.

APPROACH

From the NW out of Sutil Channel. The passage into the inner anchorage between the peninsula and the islets is deep.

ANCHOR

Good all-weather protection can be found in this snug anchorage. Depths 8–14 m (26–46 ft), holding good in mud.

❀ 50° 9.7' N   125° 0.3' W

I f you need a little more protection than Carrington Bay offers in a strong northwesterly, take a short hop north to Quartz Bay. Sheltered anchorage is possible behind the islet and drying isthmus in the bay's westernmost arm. Private homes look down from the eastern shoreline, making the anchorage more suitable for a quick overnight stop than an extended stay.

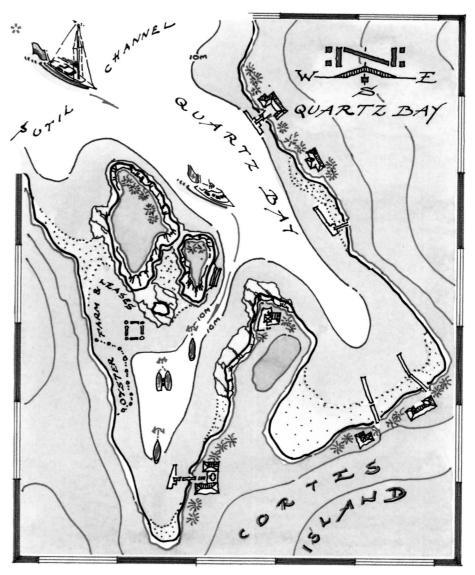

Not to scale. Not to be used for navigation.

HÁTHAYIM MARINE PARK, VON DONOP INLET, CORTES ISLAND

✵ 50° 11.0' N   124° 58.8' W

V on Donop Inlet is almost 5 km (3 mi) in length and rather narrow in spots as it twists and turns, almost dividing Cortes Island. BC Parks, in partnership with the Klahoose First Nation, declared the inlet and surrounding lands a marine park in 1994 and preserved this magical spot for all to enjoy.

Although sheltered Háthayim Marine Park can become crowded in the summer months, it still offers a rich variety of nooks and crannies to anchor in as well as peaceful lagoons to explore and forested trails to hike.

The most popular anchorage is at the head of the inlet, where a trail leads to Squirrel Cove (see pages 88–89) and "Buccaneer Cove." The small lagoon is enchanting to explore at high water.

Just east of the inlet's narrow entrance is what we like to call "Lagoon Falls," a favourite rendezvous at high water as dinghies and kayaks get ready to enter Von Donop Lagoon. Passage into the lagoon at any other time is hindered by swift currents and a profusion of boulders.

One of the most serene anchorages in the inlet, which we've dubbed "Buccaneer Cove," has a shallow bar at its entrance, dries at the southern end at low water and can only fit two or three boats comfortably. Once settled, you could spend a few blissful days walking the trails, lounging in the cockpit or dining *al fresco*. The grassy point at the entrance to the cove comes with an excellent view of the inlet.

CHARTS 3538. 3312 page 19.

APPROACH

From the NW. The most obvious landmark is the park's sign on the NE shore. Although the entrance appears narrow and shallow, there is more than adequate width (50 m/164 ft) and depth (4.3 m/14 ft) in its narrowest part. However, danger lurks in the form of a rock with less than 2 m (6.5 ft) of water above it, a rock only visible at LW. Favour the western shoreline to clear.

ANCHOR

Good all-weather anchorage exists throughout the length of the inlet in depths of 4–12 m (13–39 ft), holding good in sticky mud. There are also two excellent anchoring options in "Buccaneer Cove" and "Lagoon Falls," next page.

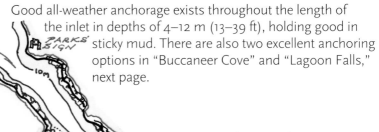

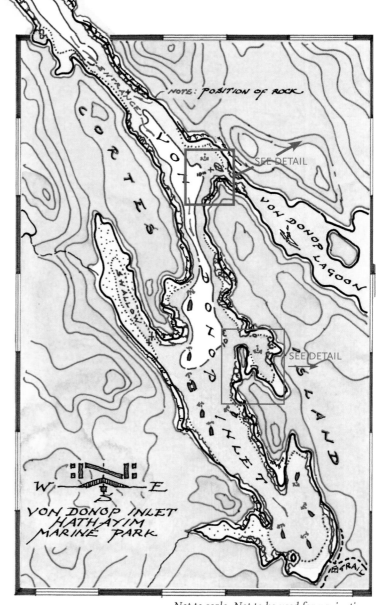

Not to scale. Not to be used for navigation.

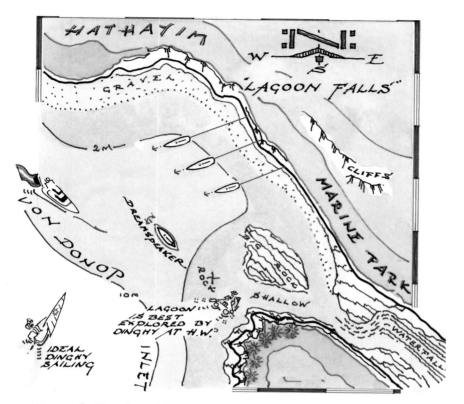

Not to scale. Not to be used for navigation.

ANCHOR

"LAGOON FALLS" Just inside the entrance. Anchor in depths of 3–9 m (10–29.5 ft).

Note: Passage into the lagoon is only possible at HW by dinghy or kayak.

"Lagoon Falls" sparkles on a sunny day.

ANCHOR

"BUCCANEER COVE" On the eastern shore midway down the inlet. A bar guards the entrance, charted at 1.8 m (6 ft). Depths of 2–3 m (6.5–10 ft).

Note: The wind funnels and accelerates throughout the inlet.

Two "buccaneers' ships" in "Buccaneer Cove."

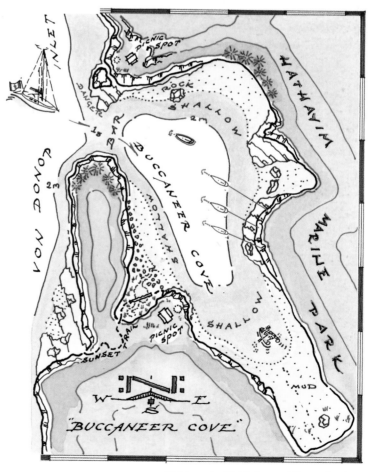

Not to scale. Not to be used for navigation.

6.10 SQUIRREL COVE, CORTES ISLAND

✤ 50° 7.7' N   124° 55.1' W

Entrance to Squirrel Cove anchorage.

A good place to raft and rendezvous with friends.

Knowing your position in Squirrel Cove comes in handy.

B e sure to enter the anchorage of Squirrel Cove west of Protection Island, as the eastern passage is strewn with rocks and boulders. This large and protected cove (more of a bay) can accommodate many boats in the busy summer months, with its northern portion being the most popular. Safe alternative anchorage for larger boats can be found west of Protection Island. The mouth of "Squirrel Cove Lagoon" provides fun and entertainment on both flood and ebbing tides—kids and adults alike shoot the rapids in dinghies, kayaks and tubes. The swing rope on the upper northeast shore is a must-try. Visitors should be aware that property surrounding the cove is either private or part of the Klahoose First Nation Reserve.

For many years, boaters visiting Squirrel Cove were able to enjoy a special treat thanks to Bill Rendall and his famous cinnamon buns. Although Bill and his small, rustic bakery are no longer found in the cove, his legend will certainly live on.

TRAILS

Squirrel Cove to Von Donop Inlet and Háthayim Marine Park (see page 86).

Squirrel Cove is a surprisingly good base for all levels of hikers. As we found no official map, Laurence has located the trailheads as follows (see inset map):

A After an initial climb the trail splits N to Von Donop Lagoon and W to Von Donop Inlet—both hikes are a good 2.5 km (1.6 mi).

B HW tidal access to the trailhead (check the tide tables). This is a light NW hike of 0.5 km to Von Donop Inlet.

C Beach your dinghy near the cabin on shore. The initial trail of 0.75 km snakes S along a stream bed then intersects a meticulously groomed trail S to Whaletown Road (0.5 km) and N to Von Donop Inlet (2 km). From here extend your hike (a good hour) to "Buccaneer Cove." A large number of these trails pass through Klahoose First Nation land—please be respectful.

CHARTS 3555. 3312, page 10.

APPROACH

From the SE, having given the starboard day marker off Boulder Point a wide berth. A sign indicating the Klahoose First Nation is a prominent landmark that overlooks the entrance.

ANCHOR

Good all-weather protection can be found throughout the cove. However, chop from SE seas does penetrate the anchorage. Both northwesterly and southeasterly winds whistle through. Depths of 4–14 m (13–46 ft), holding good in sticky mud.

Note: Signs at the entrance to the cove inform all boaters that harvesting of shellfish is prohibited and that it is illegal to discharge sewage into the bay.

Anne rows Tink *through the reversing rapids into Squirrel Cove.*

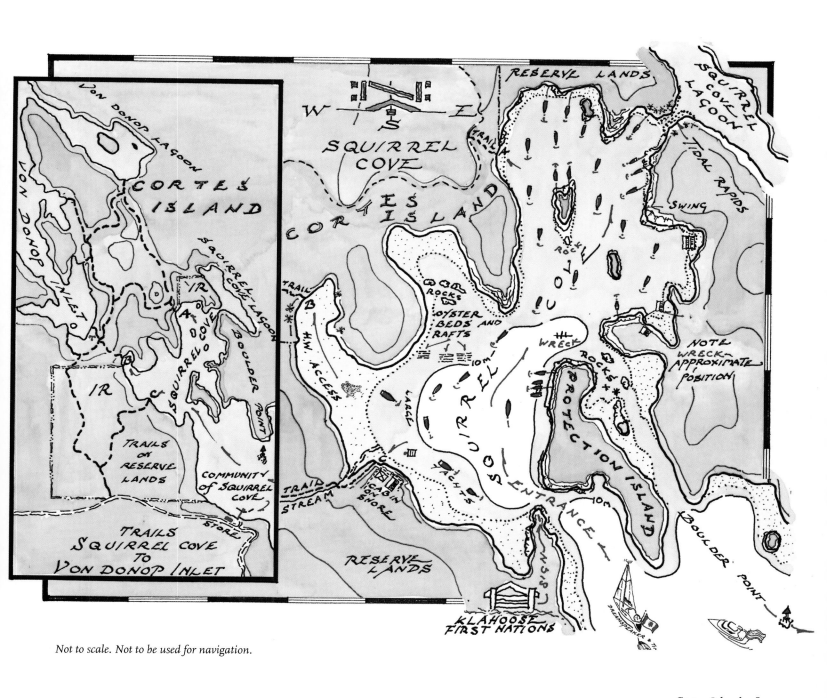

Not to scale. Not to be used for navigation.

6.11 Community of Squirrel Cove, Cortes Island

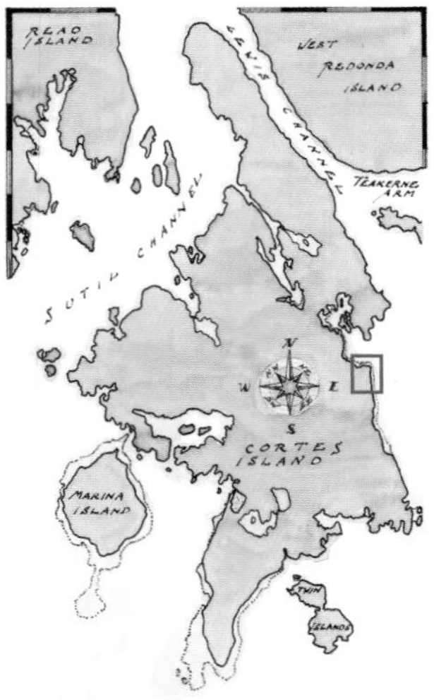

✲ 50° 7.2' N 124° 54.6' W

CHARTS 3555. 3312, page 10.

APPROACH

From the NE, the Squirrel Cove General Store and community buildings being the most visible landmarks.

ANCHOR

If the public wharf has no available moorage, temporary anchorage can be found to the NW of the wharf. Depths of 4–6 m (13–19.5 ft), holding good in mud. For all-weather anchorage, see 6.10 (page 88).

PUBLIC WHARF

Managed by Cortes Harbour Authority—call the harbour manager at 250-935-0007. Power up to 30 amps but no water on the float. Garbage drop-off for a fee. Extensive moorage is available at two floats, but they are very busy and used as temporary moorage by islanders and visitors going ashore for provisions.

FUEL

At the dock W of the public wharf. Dries at LW. Owned by the store and open year-round, 250-935-6327. Portable water, marked diesel, gasoline and propane available. This is also a convenient dinghy dock for quick access to the store.

The public wharf and SQUIRREL COVE TRADING COMPANY are located near the entrance to Squirrel Cove. The well-stocked store carries everything you might need, including fresh and organic produce, propane, ice, specialty gifts, charts, boating guides and an excellent selection of marine supplies and hardware. It also has a post office, BC Liquor Store outlet, Wi-fi, and an ATM. Laundry and shower facilities are close by. THE FLYING SQUIRREL take-out stand serves up tasty hamburgers, freshly make fish tacos and wraps, and ice cream.

The CORTES CRAFT SHOP, a co-op of island artists and artisans, carries unique handmade gifts and treasures. The COVE RESTAURANT is open May to mid-September and features a variety of fresh, homemade seafood dishes with octopus cocktail being a specialty. They serve lunch and dinner, and brunch on Sundays, and you can watch the boat traffic from the shaded deck. Call 250-935-6350 for reservations. Don't miss the Sunday farmers' market (12 p.m.–3 p.m. summer only), where you can stock up on baked goods, preserves and local handmade crafts.

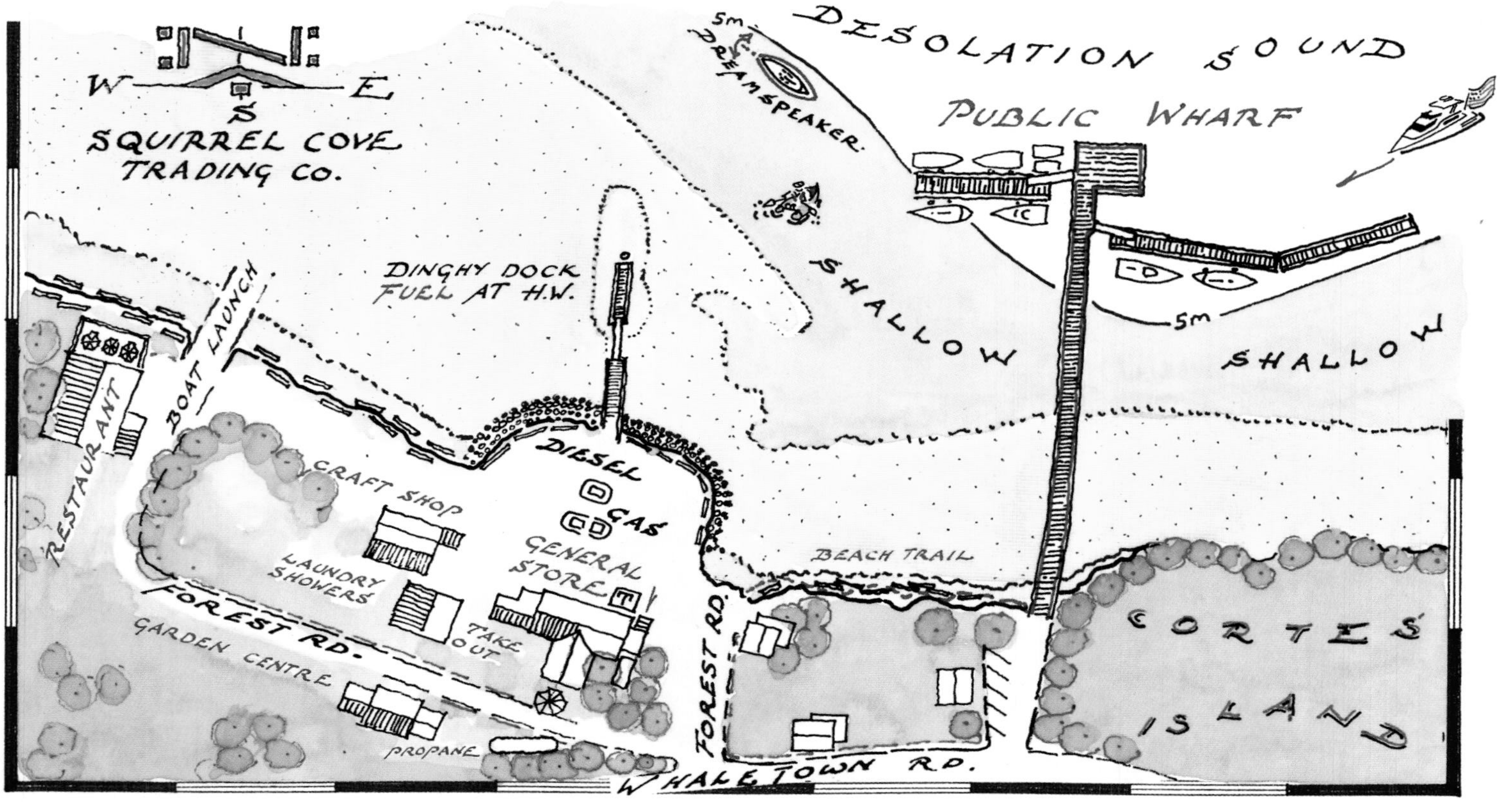

Not to scale. Not to be used for navigation.

Chapter 7
THE
REDONDA
ISLANDS

Roscoe Bay, a landlocked paradise at low water.

Chapter 7
THE REDONDA ISLANDS

The schooner Adventuress *in spectacular Toba Inlet.*

TIDES

Canadian Tide and Current Tables, Volume 5
Reference Port: Point Atkinson
Secondary Ports: Prideaux Haven, Channel Islands

CURRENTS

Although there are no reference or secondary current stations covering the waters in this chapter, tidal currents stream through the inlets and channels at rates of 1–2 knots. Currents of 3 knots may occur at the northern entrance to Waddington Channel.

WEATHER

No specific reporting station covers this chapter. Summer winds tend to be moderate and take their directions from the inlets or channels through which they funnel. Nightly outflow winds can wake one in the early hours but are usually absent by daybreak.

CAUTIONARY NOTES

Anchoring is in predominantly deep water with a stern line ashore. Be well experienced in this technique. If you need direction, ask some of the old salts for advice.

The steep-sided inlets and channels create barriers for VHF coverage, which is poor in Waddington Channel, Pendrell Sound and Toba Inlet and nonexistent in Roscoe Bay.

If you are in search of cascading waterfalls, freshwater lakes, warm-water swimming, energetic hikes and the serene beauty of coastal wilderness, this chapter is for you. From spectacular Cassel Falls in Teakerne Arm Provincial Park to the warm waters of Pendrell Sound and the wild beauty of Toba Inlet, these often-bypassed spots have so much to offer the more enterprising boater or kayaker.

Teakerne Arm Provincial Park offers the perfect picnic stop and a chance to stretch your legs and indulge in a warm-water wash and brush-up in Cassel Lake. Refuge Cove, a major provisioning stop, welcomes boaters with reasonably priced moorage, excellent provisioning and warm island hospitality. Regular seaplane service is also available from here.

The cozy anchorage in Roscoe Bay Provincial Park turns into a tranquil, landlocked paradise at low water, and the warm waters of Black Lake offer excellent bathing and diving rocks and a fun day of paddling for those willing to portage their kayaks or paddle boards along the much frequented trail.

The warmest water can be found in Pendrell Sound, designated a shellfish reserve, as it provides the perfect location for producing Pacific oyster spat. Visiting boaters are requested to maintain a wake-free speed within the sound. Serene "Oyster Cove" (our name for it) provides protected anchorage, a delightful picnic spot with a view atop a rocky bluff and an enticing saltwater lagoon just waiting to be explored.

Breathtaking Toba Inlet lures you to its head with the promise of icefields, roaring waterfalls and open vistas—and you won't be disappointed. The easiest way to explore the inlet is by setting up base at the Toba Wilderness Marina.

Finally, charming Walsh Cove Provincial Park, the last protected anchorage in Waddington Channel, offers you the opportunity to hunt for hidden petroglyphs, fine warm-water swimming and great views of the East Redonda mountains.

FEATURED DESTINATIONS

nautical miles

Not to be used for navigation.

7.1 TEAKERNE ARM PROVINCIAL PARK
WEST REDONDA ISLAND

✻ 50° 11.7' N 124° 50.9' W

Anchoring is possible below the falls.

Anchored below the park sign with stern lines ashore.

The main attractions of Teakerne Arm Provincial Park on West Redonda Island include the invitingly warm waters of Cassel Lake and its spectacular cascading falls.

Cassel Lake is the perfect place to picnic and treat yourself to a freshwater wash and brush-up. It's an energetic hike that takes the well-worn trail leading from the dinghy dock to a ledge of smooth, clean bathing rocks on the lake's southern shore. A helpful haul-out rope has been placed here for your convenience. Taking a detour off the path, you will discover an abandoned, rusty logging donkey, slowly being hidden by grass and leafy salal bushes. For those of us who have always wondered why these machines were called "donkeys" but have never bothered to ask, June Cameron supplies the answer in her memoirs of the island's early logging practices, *Destination Cortez Island*: "the early engines had less than one horsepower, so were called 'donkeys' and the name stuck." Simple as that.

It's difficult to anchor close to Cassel Falls as water is very deep right up to the rocky shoreline. The first lucky boats can tie up to the rope lines provided. We enjoyed the most exhilarating full-pressure shower under the falls then towelled dry on the warm boulders just up from the small beach; good footwear is advised as the rocks under the falls are very slippery.

Stern-to anchorage is possible in the popular nook west of the falls or along part of the northwest shoreline as indicated, although both are subject to afternoon chop. Kayakers can beach their craft and set up camp atop the rocky spine or the dry grassy spots.

Note: At the time of writing we observed logging operations in the southeast portion of Teakerne Arm.

CHARTS 3538. 3312, page 8.

APPROACH

From the SW. The park's sign on the rocky promontory W of the waterfall is the most clearly visible landmark.

ANCHOR

Temporary anchorage can be found near Cassel Falls and along the NW shoreline with a stern line to the lines or rings provided. The deep water shelves rapidly to shallow water. Depth, holding and bottom condition vary.

Note: Not recommended as an all-weather anchorage because Teakerne Arm tends to funnel northwesterly and southeasterly winds and chop into its upper reaches. In settled summer weather, though, afternoon winds tend to die off in the early evening, leaving glassy water for a peaceful night.

Anne takes a swim in Cassel Lake.

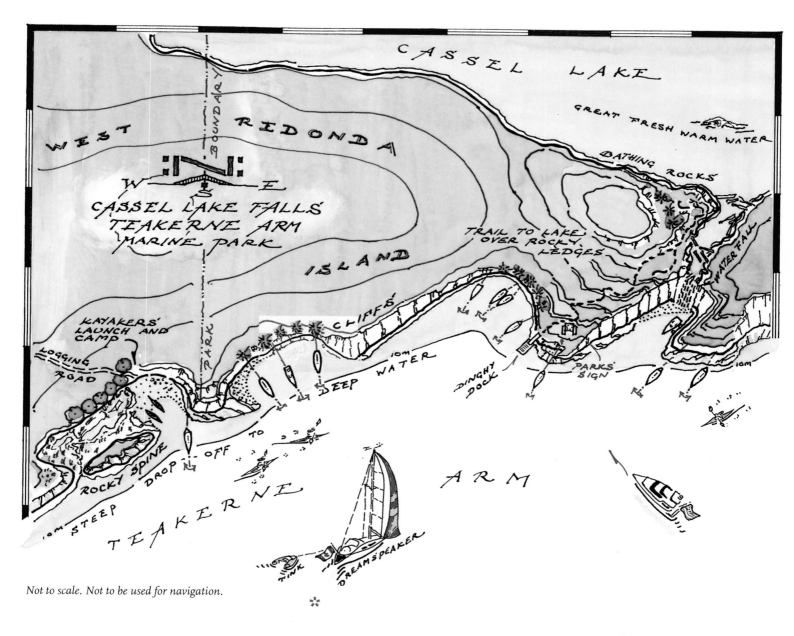

Not to scale. Not to be used for navigation.

7.2   REFUGE COVE,
WEST REDONDA ISLAND

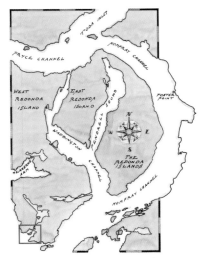

⚜ 50° 6.9' N   124° 51.2' W

The community of Refuge Cove, complete with moorage and store.

Refuge Cove has a friendly pioneering charm.

Welcoming Refuge Cove is cooperatively owned and operated and certainly lives up to its name. This sociable, enterprising community happily accommodates many visiting boats in the summer months and then leads a quiet, secluded life the rest of the year.

Moorage is available at the public wharf and marina. Clean showers (no time limit) and laundry facilities are located at the top of the ramp, opposite the second-hand bookstore. The GENERAL STORE, which also collects moorage fees, carries an excellent selection of fresh and frozen produce, baked goods, ice, propane, charts, boating guides, books, gifts, specialty items, hand-scooped ice cream and fishing supplies. It also houses a BC Liquor Store outlet and post office (mail drop and pick-up on Monday, Wednesday and Friday).

Don't pass up the opportunity to sample a delicious, freshly made hamburger or cinnamon bun at UPCOAST SUMMERS. The sociable café has an on-site bakery and serves breakfast, lunch, pastries and coffee on the shaded deck overlooking the cove; as of 2017 it will also be offering dinner, with beer and wine. Open 8 a.m. until late, mid-June to mid-September (weather dependent). The REFUGE COVE GALLERY, with its lofty ceilings and windows, is fronted by a shaded water-view patio. Here you will find a selection of one-of-a-kind gifts ranging from local First Nations art to ceramics and jewellery. It also carries a colourful range of boat shoes, recycled sail bags, quality wool sweaters, cards and books.

Deep anchorage is possible in the cove opposite the wharf and marina or in a more protected little cove to the north, but watch for two rocks at its narrow entrance. DAVE'S GARBAGE BARGE alongside Centre Island will take your garbage and dispose of it, for a fee.

Refuge Cove is a popular rendezvous for cruising boaters and a convenient location to pick up or drop off family, friends and crew because seaplanes operate regular chartered and scheduled flights to and from Vancouver and Campbell River.

CHARTS 3538. 3555. 3312, page 10.

APPROACH

From the SW. Deep-water channels exist to both the N and the S of the unnamed island in the centre of the cove.

ANCHOR

To the W of the public wharf and marina. Depth is approximately 15 m (49 ft), holding good in mud. Alternative anchorage may be found at the head of the cove, but many local boats occupy this spot during the summer.

PUBLIC WHARF & MARINA

The wharf and marina offer visitor moorage with a 4-hour courtesy tie-up. Power (15 amps), water and Wi-Fi are available. Moorage fees administered by the General Store, 250-935-6659. Store and fuel dock open June 1–September 15, 9 a.m.–5 p.m. (9–6 July and August). Fuel dock is also open the rest of the year on Monday, Wednesday and Friday, 1–3 p.m.

FUEL

Gasoline, diesel oil and propane are available from the fuel float operated by the General Store.

Note: In summer the public wharf and marina are a hive of activity. Anchoring off is fine. Rumours of "old logging equipment fouling the bottom" are, locals say, untrue.

Approaching the marina.

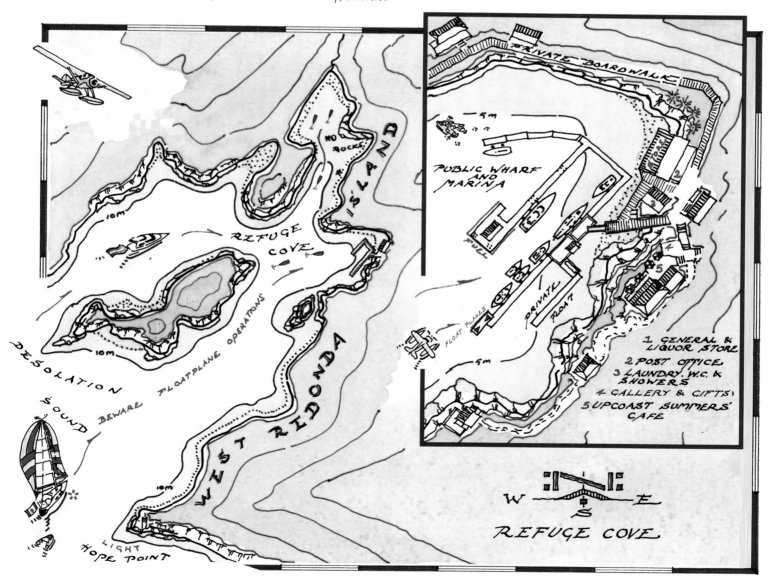

Not to scale. Not to be used for navigation.

7.3 Roscoe Bay Provincial Park, West Redonda Island

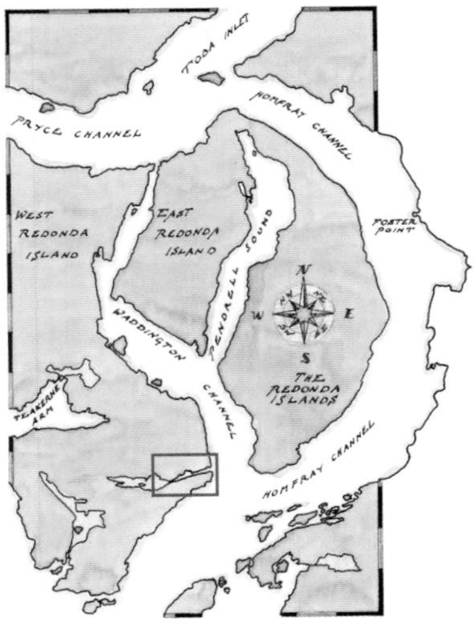

50° 9.7' N 124° 44.7' W

An evening gathering aboard Dreamspeaker.

With a stern line ashore, it's time to relax in Roscoe Bay.

The safest time to enter or exit Roscoe Bay is at high water and preferably on a rising tide as the shallow bar at the entrance turns this surprise anchorage into a landlocked paradise at low water. To ensure ultimate tranquility, Roscoe Bay Marine Park is also surrounded by steep, forested slopes and fed by a freshwater lake.

Once inside the bay, visitors are presented with a large, all-weather anchorage that affords reasonable depths; a flat, grassy spot to beach kayaks or set up camp; and warm-water swimming at its best. These factors have contributed to the popularity of the park, making it a favoured rendezvous in the busy summer months. Boaters appreciate and respect the peace and quiet of the bay and any form of noise is considered an intrusion.

The trail to Black Lake is reasonably easy to hike, so you can portage a kayak or paddle board for a fun day of paddling. Excellent bathing, swimming and a smooth expanse of rocks for diving can be found just beyond the mouth of the lake, strewn with logs and water lilies. Farther along the trail, more private beaches lie in wait for the adventurous and an energetic hike along the grassy ledges on the bay's northwest shore will take you to a mossy picnic spot with a bird's-eye view of the activities below.

A few blissful days could be spent exploring this lovely marine park or just relaxing in the cockpit, a book in one hand and a cool drink in the other.

The unofficial 6 km (3.6 mi) trail to Mount Llanover begins from the park's northern shore with an elevation gain of 650 metres (2,132 feet). We chatted with a hiker who had enjoyed his magnificent climb to Llanover's peak. Views from the peak were spectacular as he looked across to Homfray and Lewis Channels and Teakerne Arm and southwest to Refuge Cove and Savary Island. To the east, 1,600-metre (5,249-foot) Mount Addenbroke towered over East Redonda Island; go well prepared with water, a picnic lunch and good binoculars.

A note for those who miss the high-water deadline: safe anchorage is possible just outside the shallow bar, with good views of Waddington Channel and an extra half-hour of light at sunset.

CHARTS 3538. 3312, page 9.

APPROACH

The outer entrance lies N of Marylebone Point. The park's sign on the northern shore is the most obvious landmark. A bar that dries on a zero tide creates a tidal gate to the inner bay and anchorage.

ANCHOR

Good all-weather anchorage, room for numerous boats. Depths of 3–9 m (10–29.5 ft), holding good in sticky mud.

Note: Time arrival and departure according to your draft. As a general rule, enter and exit on a rising tide as close to HW as possible. Post a bow lookout, and initially favour the southern shore and then the centre channel prior to entering the inner bay.

The outer entrance from Waddington Channel.

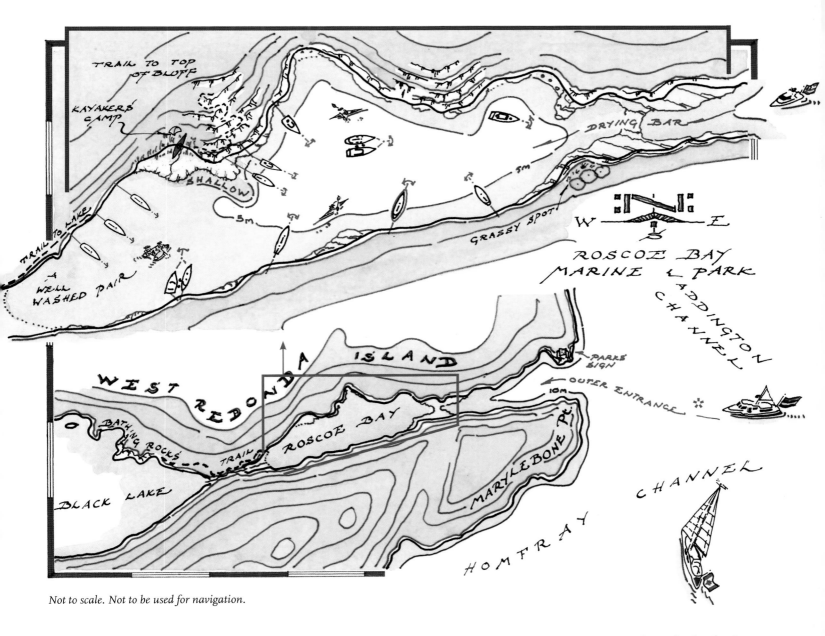

Not to scale. Not to be used for navigation.

The Redonda Islands – 99

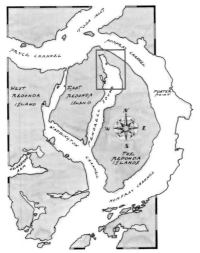

✳ 50° 16.0' N 124° 42.8' W

CHARTS 3541. 3312, page 16.

APPROACH

At a wake-free speed. The water is deep and free of obstructions.

ANCHOR

In settled weather, deep-water anchorage with a stern line ashore is possible in numerous nooks at the head of the sound, as indicated. Depth, holding and bottom conditions vary.

Note: The rock at the head of the sound has less than 2 m (6.5 ft) of water over it at LW.

An exhilarating spinnaker run.

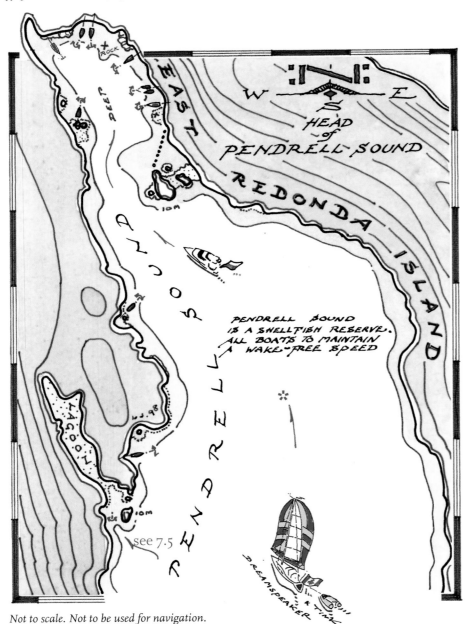

Not to scale. Not to be used for navigation.

Pendrell Sound intersects with Waddington Channel and almost divides East Redonda Island in half. The island's eastern side has a unique ecosystem and is protected as an ecological reserve, enabling scientists to preserve and study its stunning variety of natural vegetation.

The waters of Pendrell Sound are extremely deep, with little tidal exchange and practically no currents, helping water temperatures to reach 25°C (80°F) in the summer months. The sound is also protected from prevailing winds by high mountains and is worth exploring, as oysters and mussels abound. Any activity causing pollution is prohibited.

A trip to the head of the sound will reveal a peaceful anchorage with spectacular views of snow-capped mountains. Because of the deep water, stern lines ashore are essential. This is the perfect spot, in settled weather, for boaters wishing to get away from the crowds. Days can be spent swimming, kayaking and paddle boarding or just relaxing in the cockpit enjoying oysters steaming on the barbecue.

Spectacular vistas in "Oyster Cove."

CHARTS 3541. 3312, page 16.

APPROACH

"Oyster Cove" (our name for it) lies on the western shore of Pendrell Sound.

ANCHOR

Temporary anchorage with the best protection in Pendrell Sound. A stern line ashore is recommended because the water is deep and swinging room is limited. Depths of 6–8 m (19.5–26 ft), holding fair over a shingle and mud bottom.

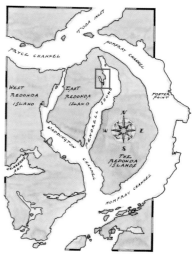

✱ 50° 16.2' N   124° 43.5' W

Protected anchorage in relatively shallow water can be found behind what we call "Shell Island" in lovely "Oyster Cove." From here you can simply lounge in your cockpit, taking in the serene mountain views, or jump into your kayak or dinghy to explore the saltwater lagoon at high water.

The cove is definitely stern-line territory, enabling a good number of boats to tuck in for the night and enjoy the natural pleasures of Pendrell Sound. Mount Bunsen towers over the anchorage's western shore, where views out to mighty Mount Addenbroke are wonderfully uninterrupted. A hike along the northern shore's rocky bluff leads up to a charming picnic spot with a backdrop of the glacier and twin peaks of Mount Whieldon and Mount Grazebrooke. On your return, stop to pick fresh sea asparagus growing haphazardly alongside the spot we dubbed "Spatt Islet."

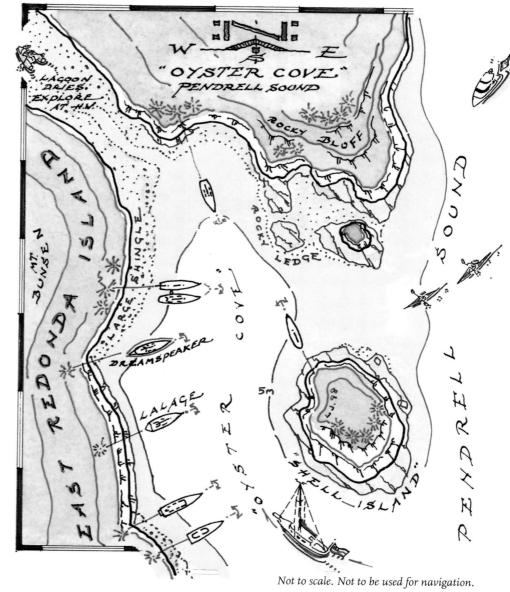

Not to scale. Not to be used for navigation.

7.6 Toba Inlet and Homfray Channel

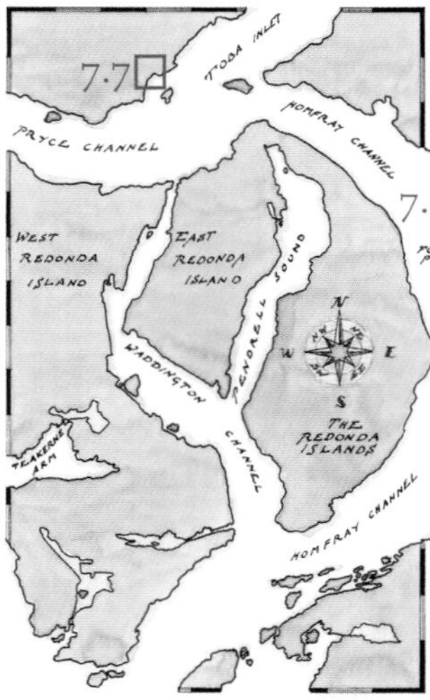
7.7
TOBA INLET
HOMFRAY CHANNEL
PRYCE CHANNEL
7.8
WEST REDONDA ISLAND
EAST REDONDA ISLAND
FOSTER POINT
PENDRELL SOUND
N
W
E
S
WADDINGTON CHANNEL
THE REDONDA ISLANDS
TEAKERNE ARM
HOMFRAY CHANNEL

50° 19.2' N 124° 46.2' W

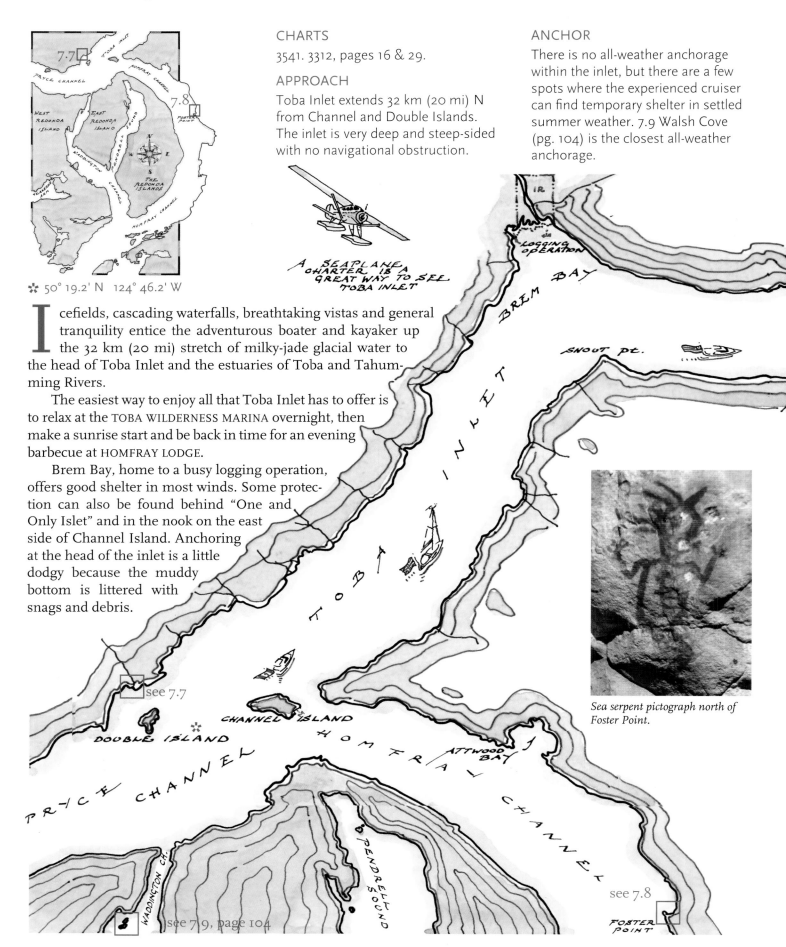

CHARTS

3541. 3312, pages 16 & 29.

APPROACH

Toba Inlet extends 32 km (20 mi) N from Channel and Double Islands. The inlet is very deep and steep-sided with no navigational obstruction.

ANCHOR

There is no all-weather anchorage within the inlet, but there are a few spots where the experienced cruiser can find temporary shelter in settled summer weather. 7.9 Walsh Cove (pg. 104) is the closest all-weather anchorage.

Icefields, cascading waterfalls, breathtaking vistas and general tranquility entice the adventurous boater and kayaker up the 32 km (20 mi) stretch of milky-jade glacial water to the head of Toba Inlet and the estuaries of Toba and Tahumming Rivers.

The easiest way to enjoy all that Toba Inlet has to offer is to relax at the TOBA WILDERNESS MARINA overnight, then make a sunrise start and be back in time for an evening barbecue at HOMFRAY LODGE.

Brem Bay, home to a busy logging operation, offers good shelter in most winds. Some protection can also be found behind "One and Only Islet" and in the nook on the east side of Channel Island. Anchoring at the head of the inlet is a little dodgy because the muddy bottom is littered with snags and debris.

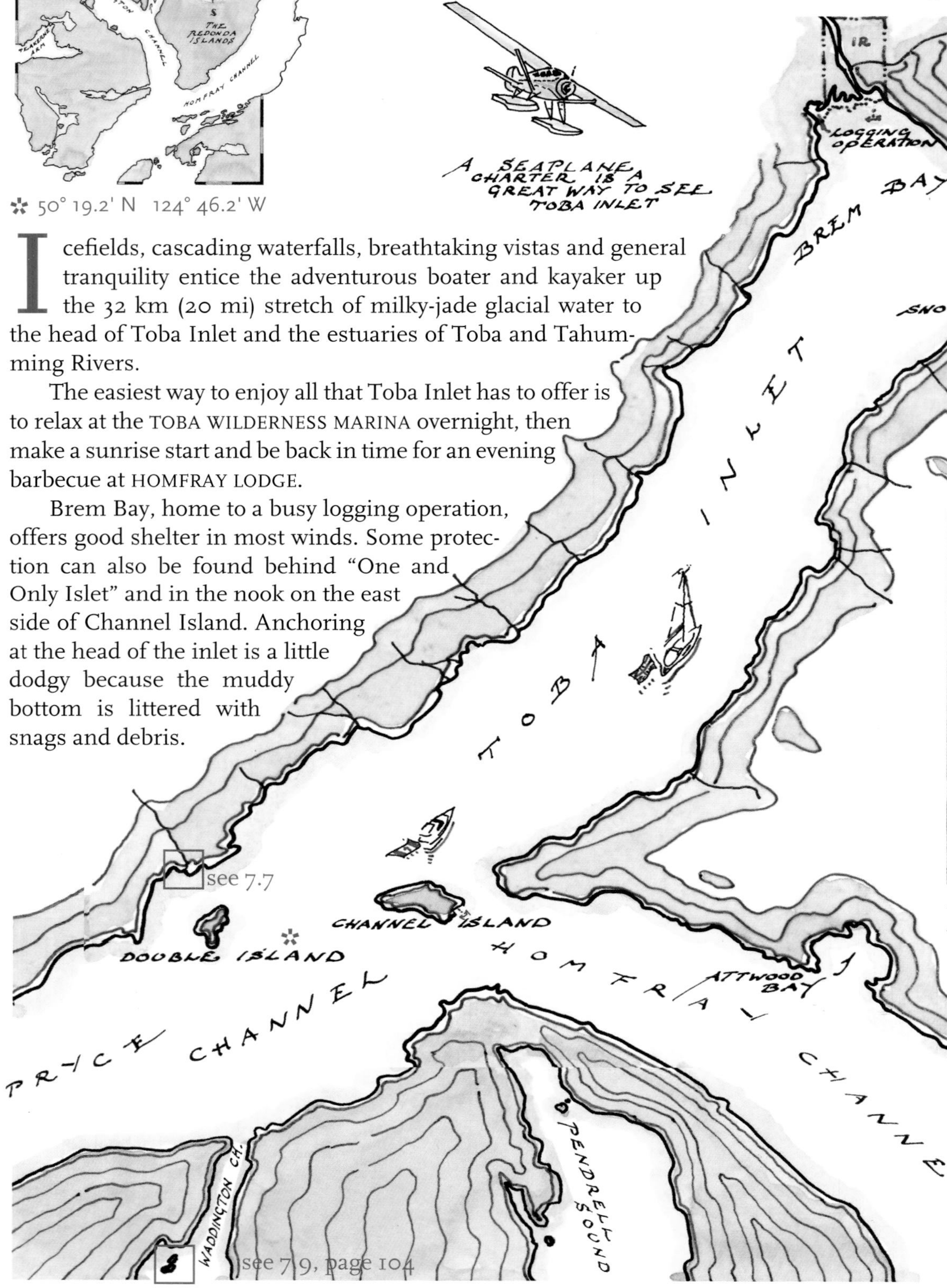
A SEAPLANE CHARTER IS A GREAT WAY TO SEE TOBA INLET
IR
LOGGING OPERATION
BREM BAY
SNOUT pt.
TOBA INLET
see 7.7
CHANNEL ISLAND
DOUBLE ISLAND
HOMFRAY CHANNEL
ATTWOOD BAY
PRYCE CHANNEL
WADDINGTON CH.
PENDRELL SOUND
see 7.9, page 104
see 7.8
FOSTER POINT

Sea serpent pictograph north of Foster Point.

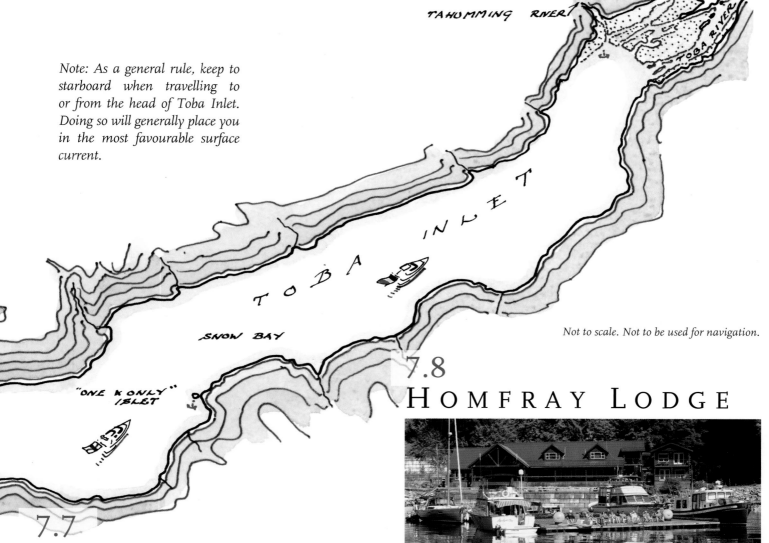

Note: As a general rule, keep to starboard when travelling to or from the head of Toba Inlet. Doing so will generally place you in the most favourable surface current.

Not to scale. Not to be used for navigation.

7.7
TOBA WILDERNESS

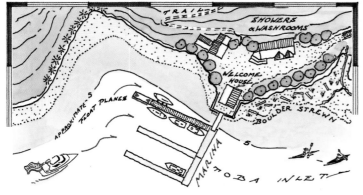

APPROACH
The marina lies due N of Double Island and can be approached from the S or SE in deep water with no obstructions.
MARINA
Extensive visitor moorage with power up to 50 amps, water and Wi-Fi on the docks—250-830-2269. Call VHF 66A for tie-up instructions.

Tucked inside Double Island at the mouth of Toba Inlet lies Toba Wilderness Marina. Complete with sturdy concrete docks and deep-water moorage, their all-inclusive visitor package includes showers, Wi-Fi, a bag of ice and one garbage drop-off per day. Extensive maintained trails lead to dramatic viewpoints and a spectacular waterfall.

7.8
HOMFRAY LODGE

Enjoying the floating deck.

APPROACH
The marina and lodge from the NW or by rounding Foster Point from the S.
MARINA
Limited visitor moorage alongside the floating deck and two mooring buoys. Call 604-740-6032, VHF 66A. Water, ice and free Wi-Fi, no power. Shower and laundry facilities. Reservations in July and August. Club rendezvous can raft.

Relaxed and friendly, the resort offers visitor moorage and a communal BBQ and firepit. Enjoy the glorious view up Homfray Channel from the shaded lodge porch or colourful Adirondack chairs neatly set out on the deck. The grounds also include pleasant hiking trails.

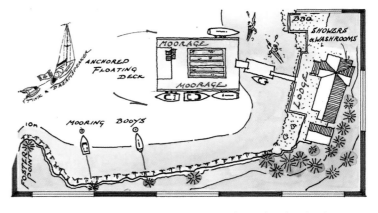

7.9 Walsh Cove Provincial Park, West Redonda Island

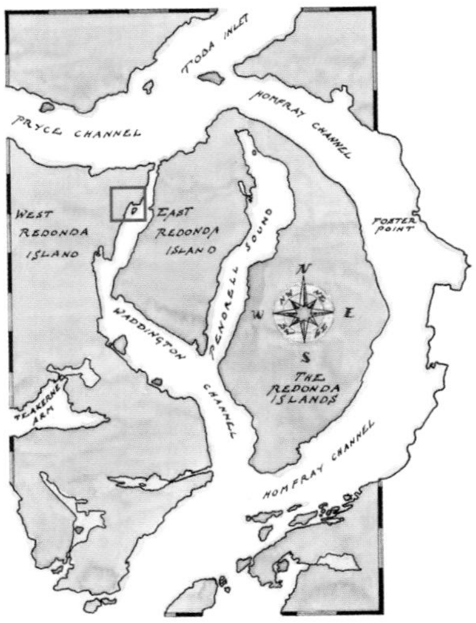

50° 15.9' N 124° 48.1' W

CHARTS 3541. 3312, page 16.

APPROACH

From the S, the park's sign on the Gorges Islands, atop Bluff Point, is the most clearly visible landmark.

ANCHOR

The cove offers reasonable protection, but the winds do whistle through it. Depths of 5–15 m (16–49 ft) over a mixed bottom of shingle, mud and rock.

Note: False Pass is navigable by recreational craft, but this is best done at LW when the rocks on either side of the passage are visible.

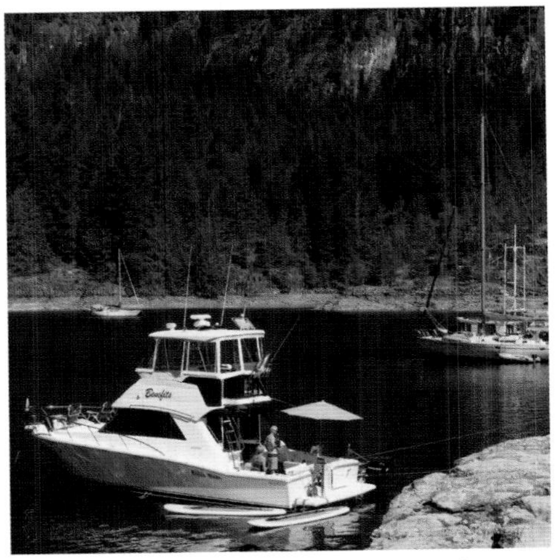

A popular summer spot. Boaters tie stern lines to Gorges Islands.

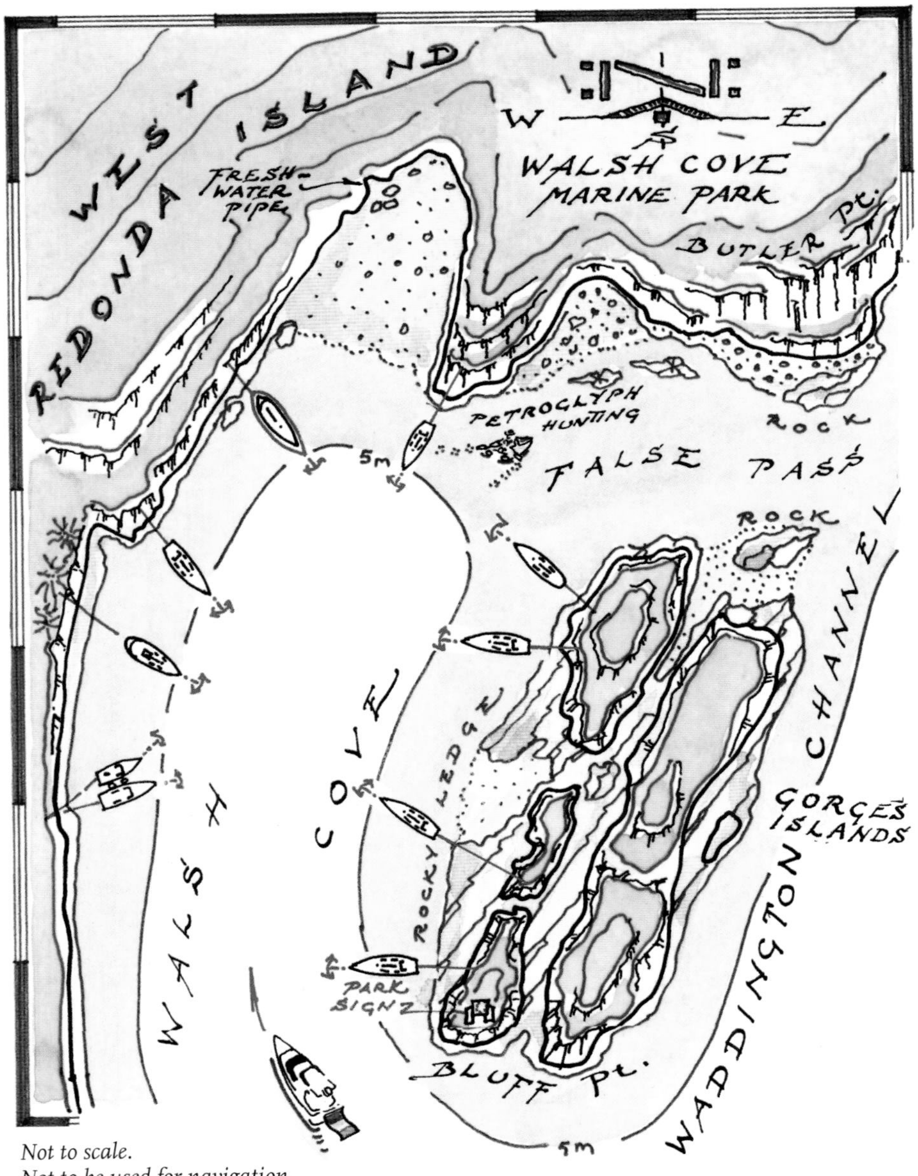

Not to scale.
Not to be used for navigation.

Boaters planning an expedition up breathtaking Toba Inlet should note that the last protected anchorage available in Waddington Channel is tucked in behind Gorges Islands, in lovely Walsh Cove Provincial Park. The alternative is moorage at TOBA WILDERNESS MARINA (see page 103). Safe entrance to steep-sided Walsh Cove can be found west of Bluff Point. False Pass should only be attempted at low water and with careful navigation. Once you are inside, this charming marine park offers adequate stern-to anchorage, an opportunity to hunt for petroglyphs at Butler Point, excellent swimming and great views over to the East Redonda mountains. Take some time to explore the enchanting wooded islets, where wild onion and thyme still grow and sun-heated rock ledges provide warm-water swimming as the tide rises.

Clean and piped fresh water can be found at the head of the small, drying nook on the western side of the cove, which comes as a nice surprise if you are beginning to run a little low and don't plan to leave Walsh Cove for another day or two.

Chapter 8
Calm Channel to Bute Inlet

Avocet moored at Waddington Harbour, Bute Inlet.
PHOTO LYNN OVE MORTENSEN

Sailing in Calm Channel.

Chapter 8
CALM CHANNEL TO BUTE INLET

TIDES

Canadian Tide and Current Tables, Volume 5
Reference Port: Point Atkinson
Secondary Ports: Redonda Bay, Orford Bay & Waddington Harbour (Bute Inlet)

CURRENTS

Although there are no specific reference or secondary current stations, weak tidal currents (usually less than 2 knots) can be encountered in Whiterock Passage. A perpetual southerly surface current, which can attain 2 knots, exists in Bute Inlet.

WEATHER

In the summer months, Calm Channel tends to be in a wind shadow, from the prevailing northwesterlies. However, Bute Inlet funnels the daytime inflow wind and nighttime outflow wind along its length. Strong outflow winds are more common in winter, early spring and late fall than in summer. These winds can often reach gale force.

CAUTIONARY NOTE

If venturing up Bute Inlet, check your stock of provisions and top up with fuel and water. To date, there is no mall in Waddington Harbour to replenish supplies.

I n the busy summer months, Calm Channel turns into a bustling water highway filled with pleasure boats and commercial craft because it provides a safe and convenient link between the two most popular cruising areas: Desolation Sound and the Discovery Islands. This chapter invites boaters to slow down and discover a few enchanting but lesser-known treasures before continuing with their voyages.

At first glance, the low-lying Rendezvous Islands seem to hold little excitement; on closer inspection, they offer two charming picnic anchorages, a community nature park and hiking trails. Undeveloped South Rendezvous Island has been preserved as a provincial park.

A detour up the small, steep-sided inlet of Ramsay Arm is worth the effort, and protected overnight anchorage can be found nearby in peaceful Frances Bay. Bute Inlet offers few protected anchorages and has no marina, but the adventurous boater will find the beauty of this tranquil 65 km (40 mi) fjord irresistible. In settled weather, a few days spent exploring the inlet's spectacular shoreline will prove both worthwhile and memorable.

Included in this chapter is Whiterock Passage, which provides a convenient shortcut to Surge Narrows public wharf on Read Island and the enticing anchorages along Quadra's eastern shoreline. The deeply dredged but narrow boat passage can be successfully navigated on a rising tide with the aid of a lookout and the large leading marks provided, although both skipper and crew need their wits about them as there is little margin for error in this boulder-lined pass.

Featured Destinations

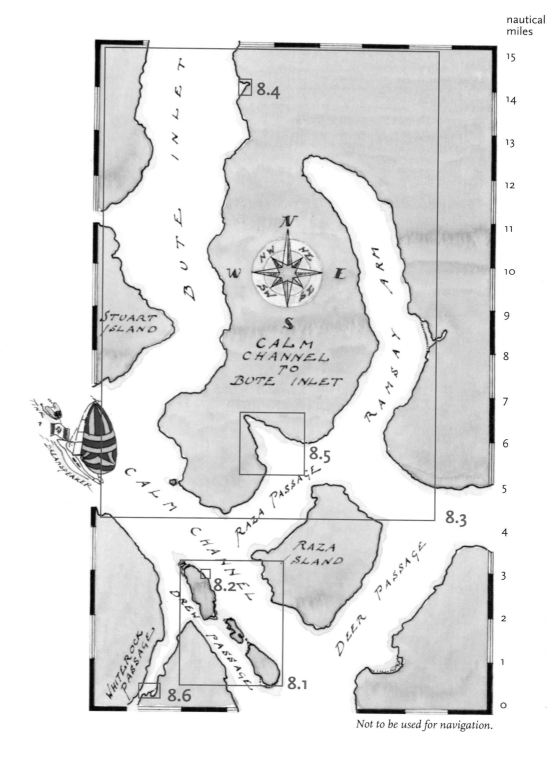

Not to be used for navigation.

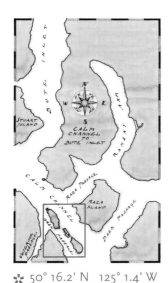

✳ 50° 16.2' N   125° 1.4' W

CHARTS 3541. 3312, page 17.

APPROACH

The waters of both Calm Channel and Drew Passage are deep right up to the shoreline. Navigation between the middle island and S Rendezvous Island is possible with local knowledge.

ANCHOR

Temporary anchorage is possible in the spots as indicated on the shore-line plan below; stern lines ashore are required. Depths, holding and bottom condition unrecorded.

Note: Boaters are requested to slow down and minimize wake when transiting Calm Channel, especially when passing the community docks of the Rendezvous Islands.

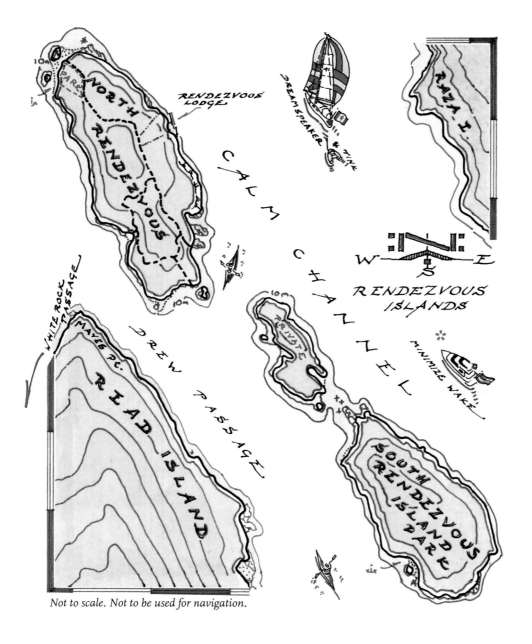

Not to scale. Not to be used for navigation.

At first glance, the Rendezvous Islands seem to offer little excitement for the cruising boater heading north. Yet a few tempting surprises await for those willing to slow down and take a little time to explore the hideaway picnic anchorages.

Undeveloped South Rendezvous Island has been set aside as a provincial park with 112 hectares (268 acres) of upland and 51 hectares (122 acres) of foreshore to explore. Temporary anchorage is possible on the southwest shore, tucked in behind an islet. The middle island is private, and space in the small cove is taken up by a private mooring buoy.

In the early 1900s, the population of North Rendezvous Island was large enough to support a school and post office. Today the island is home to a small, enterprising community of people who wish to preserve the enchantment of island life. Temporary anchorage is possible in a nook below the Community Nature Park at the northern end of the island, and a fairly good road and trail system circles the island and provides excellent hiking opportunities. Kayakers can set up camp on the islet, joined to the park at low water.

RENDEZVOUS LODGE,
NORTH RENDEZVOUS ISLAND

An unexpected treat in Calm Channel.

CHARTS 3541. 3312, page 17.

APPROACH
From the E out of Calm Channel. The lodge and flags comprise the most obvious landmark.

MARINA
The lodge has limited moorage for visiting boaters.

✳ 50° 17.5' N   125° 3.7' W

Unfortunately, at the time of writing, Rendezvous Lodge was not open for business and was up for sale. We hope that it will reopen in the future. This inviting lodge, with its licensed restaurant and fine dining, provided the perfect spot for lunch or dinner while exploring Calm Channel and Bute Inlet.

Primarily a "wilderness vacation lodge," it offered small boat moorage, and visiting boaters could tie up at the private dock. Glorious views across Calm Channel and up Bute Inlet certainly made this side trip worthwhile. Overnight guests could stretch their legs on the local hiking trails or relax in the outdoor hot tub. Showers were also available.

Note: The dock float is exposed to the wash from passing boats.

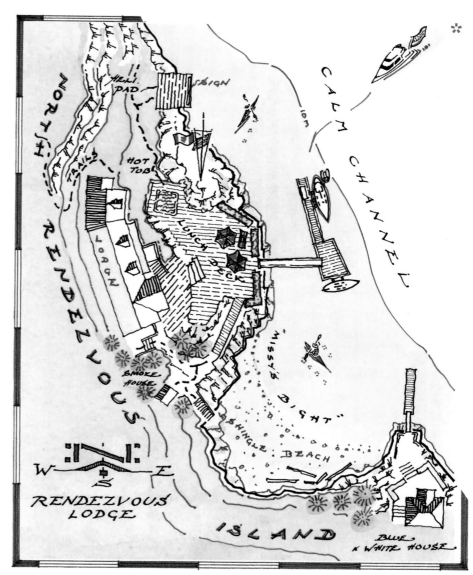

Not to scale. Not to be used for navigation.

8.3 BUTE INLET & RAMSAY ARM

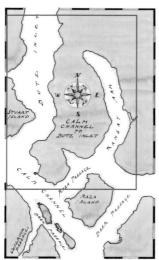

Looking up Bute Inlet from Rendezvous Islands.

❋ 1) 50° 21.2' N   125° 6.6' W, Bute Inlet
❋ 2) 50° 20.5' N   124° 58.8' W,
    Ramsay Arm

Entrance to the Southgate River, head of Bute Inlet. PHOTO LYNN OVE MORTENSEN

The 65 km (40 mi) stretch of glacial water from the mouth to the head of Bute Inlet and the Homathko River estuary is often considered out of bounds by the cruising boater in search of convenient marinas, safe anchorages and predictable weather. Bute Inlet's reputation for being somewhat daunting and forever shrouded in mist is not unfounded, but if the forecast calls for settled weather and you're within close proximity, treat yourself to a few memorable days exploring the inlet's spectacular shoreline and experiencing its isolated tranquility. The great beauty of Bute Inlet is difficult to appreciate fully unless you are prepared to take the plunge and venture to its upper reaches, where you'll be surrounded by breathtaking vistas of snow-capped mountains and the dazzling expanse of Homathko Icefield.

Temporary deep-water anchorages are available en route, and an overnight stop in Waddington Harbour is possible if you are able to tie up at one of the logging floats or alongside an anchored log boom. Although depths are suitable for anchorage, the open exposures, murky waters, shifting silt and hidden debris make anchoring hazardous. It's possible to explore the two glacial rivers by dinghy or kayak, but be aware that hazards are often obscured by the opaque waters. Study the tide tables carefully, beginning and ending your journey on a rising tide.

"Leask Cove," below Fawn Bluff (now with private uplands), provides good anchorage in settled weather and is a convenient overnight stop for boaters planning a dawn start up Bute Inlet.

The small inlet of Ramsay Arm, with its towering cliffs and eerie solitude, is interesting to explore by boat if you have the time, although the only protected anchorage available is off Raza Passage in secluded Frances Bay (see page 113). In settled weather, drop your anchor in nearby Quatam Bay. Picnic or dig for clams at low water.

CHARTS 3541. 3542. 3312, pages 17, 27, 28.

APPROACH

From Calm Channel, both Bute Inlet and Ramsay Arm are deep-water channels.

ANCHOR

The spots as indicated on the adjacent shoreline plan are temporary and require careful sounding close to shore. These locations are remote and demand cautious preplanning. Depth, holding and bottom condition vary.

Note: Strong outflow winds can be experienced in the inlet during the summer months, when the weather pattern is about to change.

Afternoon inflow winds occur during settled, sunny weather. They are generally light but can be accelerated by the inlet's length and steep-sided shoreline. Surface currents of up to 2 knots flow S and are only marginally affected by the flood and ebb tides.

Temporary moorage at commercial docks and floats is possible with permission from local logging operations.

Shaded forest undergrowth at Frances Bay.

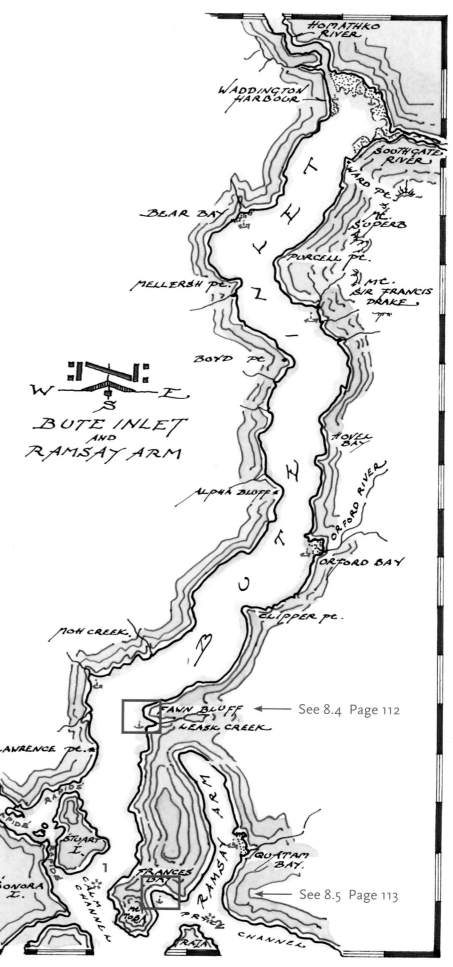

See 8.4 Page 112

See 8.5 Page 113

Not to scale. Not to be used for navigation.

8.4 "Leask Cove," Fawn Bluff, Bute Inlet

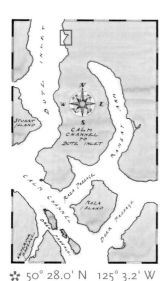

✻ 50° 28.0' N   125° 3.2' W

CHARTS 3542. 3312, page 27.

APPROACH

From the SW. "Leask Cove" and Leask Creek lie about 1 km (2/3 mi) S of Fawn Bluff.

ANCHOR

The cove is one of the better-protected anchorages off Bute Inlet: Fawn Bluff shields it from the brunt of outflow winds. Depths of 4–6 m (13–19.5 ft), with stern line to the rocky shoreline, as the bluff has a steep drop-off to deep water. Holding over a mixture of rock and mud.

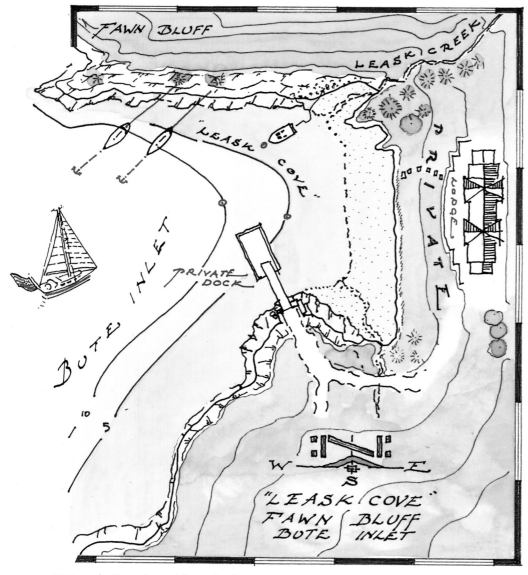

Not to scale. Not to be used for navigation.

Tucked below Fawn Bluff on the eastern shoreline of Bute Inlet, the spot we have dubbed "Leask Cove" is the only anchorage protected from outflow winds in the lower reaches of Bute Inlet.

Once the flourishing homestead of the pioneering Leask brothers, the uplands of the cove are now private with a large West Coast–style lodge looking down on the anchorage and a dock and ramp at the head of the cove.

Approaching the cove; the foreshore is now private.

FRANCES BAY/ "FANNY BAY," RAZA PASSAGE

CHARTS 3541. 3312, page 17.

APPROACH

From the SE. Frances Bay lies at the confluence of Raza Passage and the mouth of Ramsay Arm.

ANCHOR

Temporary anchorage can be found at the head of the bay. Deep-water swinging or stern lines ashore. Depth, holding and bottom condition vary.

CAUTIONARY NOTES

Exposed to the SE, although winds tend to be light from this direction in summer. Overnight outflow winds, however, do swirl down from the surrounding mountains.

Due to recent logging operations (2015) be aware of logging debris on the bottom when anchoring.

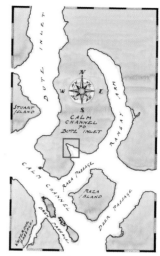

✻ 50° 20.8' N   125° 2.2' W

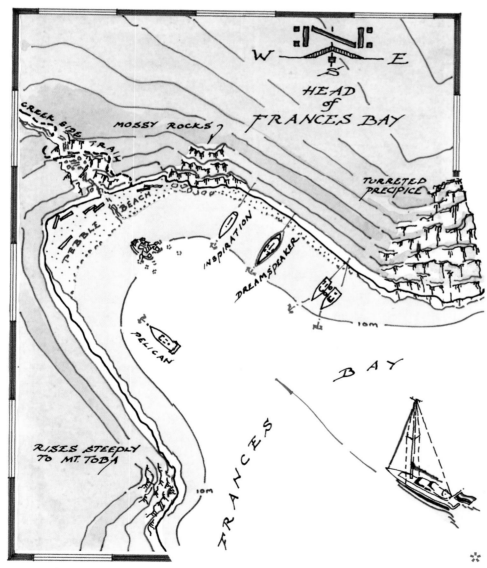

Not to scale. Not to be used for navigation.

Peaceful Frances Bay (known locally as "Fanny Bay") is a natural wonderland offering a turreted precipice, mossy picnicking rocks and a small pebble beach. The short creek trail leads into a cool forest retreat where decaying "nurse logs" form miniature gardens, and ferns and moss-covered rocks share space with huge old-growth stumps, which support new trees.

From the comfort of your cockpit, you can identify Toba Mountain to the southwest and the Downie Range rising majestically to the northwest. The stunning view down Pryce Channel is included in the package.

The head of Frances Bay.

WHITEROCK PASSAGE

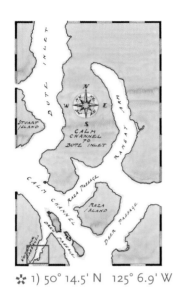

* 1) 50° 14.5' N   125° 6.9' W
* 2) 50° 15.2' N   125° 5.8' W

CHARTS 3537. 3312, page 20.

APPROACH

The approach bearings as indicated on the shoreline plan below are true bearings and refer to entering the passage from the southern and northern ends respectively. A lookout armed with binoculars is an added bonus because the dogleg turn in the centre of the passage requires a quick change of position from bow to stern.

Whiterock Passage from the south.

Boulder-strewn Whiterock Passage provides a convenient shortcut south to the Surge Narrows public wharf on Read Island (see page 145) and the inviting anchorages tucked into Quadra Island's eastern shoreline.

The dredged boat passage between the boulders can be successfully navigated on a rising tide by using the large leading ranges provided on the Read Island shore.

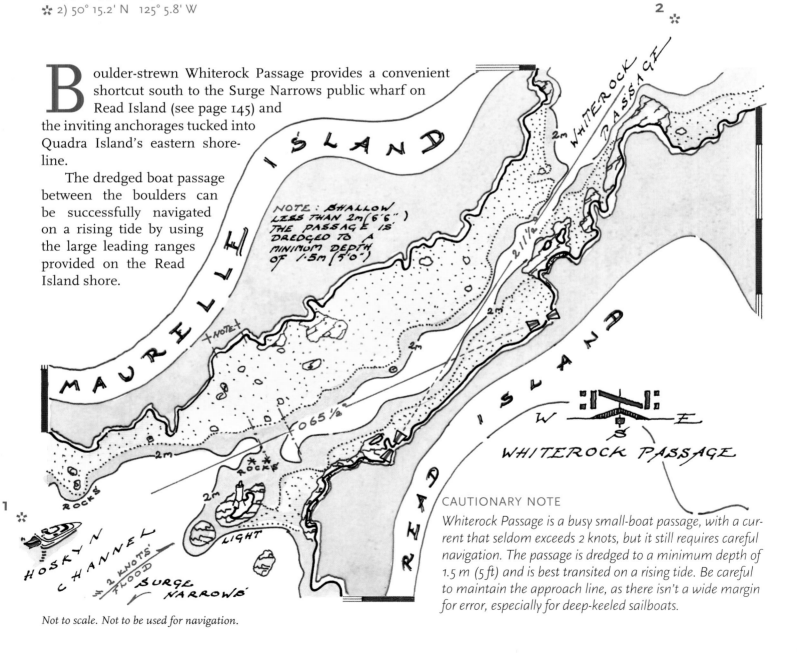

CAUTIONARY NOTE

Whiterock Passage is a busy small-boat passage, with a current that seldom exceeds 2 knots, but it still requires careful navigation. The passage is dredged to a minimum depth of 1.5 m (5 ft) and is best transited on a rising tide. Be careful to maintain the approach line, as there isn't a wide margin for error, especially for deep-keeled sailboats.

Not to scale. Not to be used for navigation.

Chapter 9
THE YUCULTAS, DENT AND ARRAN RAPIDS

A Ranger Tug transiting Dent Rapids at slack.

Chapter 9
THE YUCULTAS, DENT & ARRAN RAPIDS

TIDES

Canadian Tide and Current Tables, Volume 6
Reference Port: Campbell River
Secondary Port: Big Bay
Reference Port: Owen Bay
Secondary Port: Mermaid Bay

CURRENTS

Reference Station: Gillard Passage, Arran Rapids
Secondary Stations: Yuculta Rapids, Dent Rapids

Note: See 9.1 (page 118) for details of the Yucultas, which include the Yuculta and Dent Rapids as well as Gillard and Barber Passages.

WEATHER

No specific reporting stations. The boater is entering an area where the topography has a big effect on wind and wind direction. In summer, in periods of high pressure, the mornings are usually overcast, but by midday the sun breaks through, having burned away the cloud cover.

View from the Dent Island Lodge.

CAUTIONARY NOTES

The prudent navigator should always transit the rapids at or close to slack water. Big engines below may be no match for nature. Don't be caught in the wrong place at the wrong time, because these rapids are exceedingly hazardous, especially to small craft.

This essential chapter serves as a gateway to the inviting cruising grounds that lie beyond the charms of Desolation Sound in the cooler, more challenging waters of the Discovery Islands. From here on, the all-important *Canadian Tide and Current Tables* should always be studied diligently and kept close at hand.

The legendary Yucultas, almost always pronounced "Uke-la-taws" or jokingly called "Yuks," are a string of rather daunting rapids that require careful navigation when journeying north from Calm Channel (Chapter 8) to Cordero Channel (Chapter 10). They are composed of the Yuculta Rapids proper, the Dent Rapids and Gillard and Barber Passages, and they present a fearsome obstacle at all times except on or close to slack water. The exceptionally strong tidal currents that flow through all four passes come with associated overfalls and whirlpools, and the freshwater overlays and aerated boils also reduce the buoyancy of a displacement hull. Boaters should keep in mind that these passes are still the preferred route for tugs towing log booms south, resulting in partly submerged debris often in the form of dreaded deadheads. To top it off, some thoughtless skippers are determined to storm through these rapids at top speed, causing unnecessary wakes and added turbulence, sometimes more frightening and dangerous than the mighty rapids themselves.

With careful planning, you can transit all three rapids in one go, but we recommend a more relaxed approach and encourage boaters to take the rapids one at a time, enjoying the hospitality and amenities offered in featured destinations along the way.

The community of Big Bay offers moorage, a general store, shower and laundry facilities and a hiking trail to the lake. The Dent Island Lodge, located at the eastern end of Cordero Channel, provides luxury moorage, courteous service and excellent cuisine. The hot tub overlooking "Canoe Pass" is the perfect spot to unwind and soak your weary muscles. Historic Mermaid Bay, in Cordero Channel, has a wonderful collection of tugboat names above the rocks, high in the trees, and is an interesting spot to while away a few hours waiting for slack water.

FEATURED DESTINATIONS

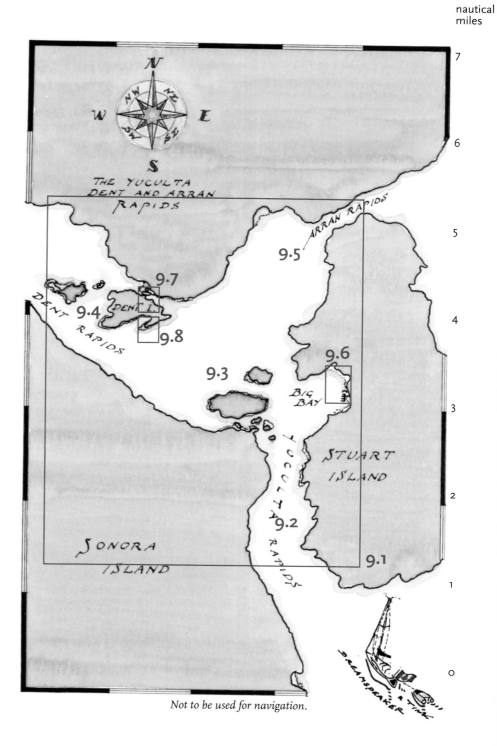

Not to be used for navigation.

9.1 THE YUCULTAS

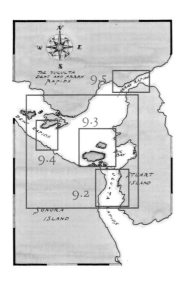

If you are heading N, approach the Yucultas off Kellsey Point on the Stuart Island shoreline an hour prior to the turn to ebb, cross over, take advantage of the northerly current that prevails along the Sonora Island shore and transit Gillard Passage. It's approximately 5 nautical miles from Kellsey Point to calmer waters in Cordero Channel N of Little Dent Island. A sailboat at 6 knots should be able to transit Dent Rapids before the ebb has had time to build to full force.

If you are heading S, the cruising plan is easier because the Dent Rapids turn to flood 15 minutes earlier than Gillard Passage. It's approximately 2 nautical miles from the Dent Rapids to Gillard Passage, so approach the Dents 15 minutes prior to the turn. At a speed of 6 knots, you should reach Gillard Passage at the turn and thus make it through the Yuculta Rapids safely.

9.2 THE YUCULTA RAPIDS

These rapids extend N from Harbott Point to Big Bay, Stuart Island, with maximum current velocities being encountered between Kellsey Point and Whirlpool Point. The secondary station lies centre channel, southwest of Whirlpool Point, attaining maximum strengths of 10 knots flood and 8 knots ebb. Dangerous whirlpools and overfalls form off Whirlpool Point.

Reference current station: Gillard Passage
Direction of flood: S
Times of slack water as follows:
  • turn to flood plus (+) 25 minutes
  • turn to ebb plus (+) 5 minutes

9.3 GILLARD & BARBER PASSAGES

These rapids extend west and north from Big Bay through Gillard and Barber Passages, respectively. Maximum current velocities encountered in the passages are recorded at the current station situated in the centre of Gillard Passage between Gillard and Jimmy Judd Islands, with a maximum flood of 13 knots and an ebb of 10 knots. Dangerous whirlpools and overfalls form between Hesler Point and the Gillard light.

Reference current station: Gillard Passage
Direction of flood: E and S

Note: Don't forget to add 1 hour in periods of daylight saving time.

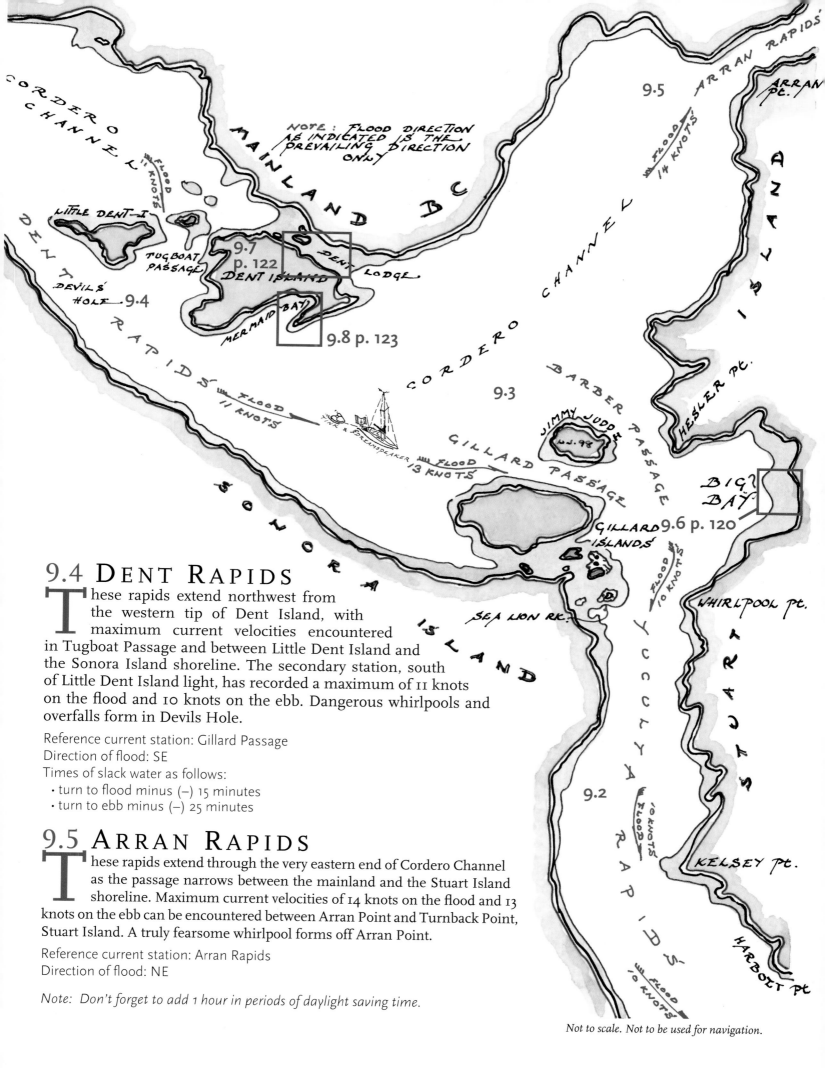

The map labels, read as they appear:

CORDERO CHANNEL

MAINLAND BC

NOTE: FLOOD DIRECTION
AS INDICATED IS THE
PREVAILING DIRECTION
ONLY

DENT RAPIDS

LITTLE DENT I.

TUGBOAT PASSAGE

DEVILS' HOLE 9.4

9.7 p. 122

DENT ISLAND

DENT LODGE

MERMAID BAY

9.8 p. 123

FLOOD 11 KNOTS

FLOOD 11 KNOTS

FLOOD 13 KNOTS

INK & DREAMSPEAKER

9.3

CORDERO CHANNEL

9.5

ARRAN RAPIDS

ARRAN PT.

FLOOD 14 KNOTS

BARBER PASSAGE

HESLER PT.

JIMMY JUDD I.
J.J. 98

GILLARD PASSAGE

SONORA ISLAND

SEA LION RK.

GILLARD ISLANDS

BIG BAY

9.6 p. 120

FLOOD 10 KNOTS

WHIRLPOOL PT.

YUCULTA RAPIDS

FLOOD 10 KNOTS

9.2

KELSEY PT.

FLOOD 10 KNOTS

STUART ISLAND

HARBOLT PT.

9.4 DENT RAPIDS

These rapids extend northwest from the western tip of Dent Island, with maximum current velocities encountered in Tugboat Passage and between Little Dent Island and the Sonora Island shoreline. The secondary station, south of Little Dent Island light, has recorded a maximum of 11 knots on the flood and 10 knots on the ebb. Dangerous whirlpools and overfalls form in Devils Hole.

Reference current station: Gillard Passage
Direction of flood: SE
Times of slack water as follows:
· turn to flood minus (−) 15 minutes
· turn to ebb minus (−) 25 minutes

9.5 ARRAN RAPIDS

These rapids extend through the very eastern end of Cordero Channel as the passage narrows between the mainland and the Stuart Island shoreline. Maximum current velocities of 14 knots on the flood and 13 knots on the ebb can be encountered between Arran Point and Turnback Point, Stuart Island. A truly fearsome whirlpool forms off Arran Point.

Reference current station: Arran Rapids
Direction of flood: NE

Note: Don't forget to add 1 hour in periods of daylight saving time.

Not to scale. Not to be used for navigation.

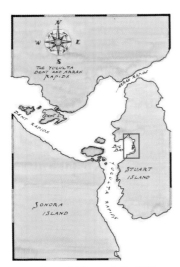

✴ 50° 23.5' N   125° 8.3' W

Stuart Island Community Dock is a popular stop in the season. PHOTO ROGER MINOR

Dreamspeaker *tucked behind the breakwater.*

The store above the community dock is a good place to meet.

Accessible by float plane, helicopter or boat, the community of Big Bay takes full advantage of its focal position and natural resources in the summer months. It offers moorage and resort facilities, professional sport-fishing guides, eco-tours and the opportunity for boaters to relax before continuing north or south through the turbulent waters of Gillard or Barber Passage and the notorious Yuculta or Dent Rapids.

After the closure of the Big Bay Marina and Resort, along with its fuel dock, the community of Stuart Island expanded the moorage and onshore facilities at the public wharf. The welcoming STUART ISLAND COMMUNITY DOCK is well maintained and offers clean shower and laundry facilities. Moorage faces out to the Yuculta Rapids giving visitors a great view of the maximum tides from their boats.

Up from the dock is the "community meeting place" and general store with a post office and BC Liquor Store outlet. The store stocks essential provisioning items, fresh and frozen produce and meat. You will also find fishing gear, cruising guides, locally produced crafts, cards, clothing, pottery, freshly roasted coffee and gift items; the book exchange is worth thumbing through. A covered area with picnic tables and BBQ facilities are available for boating groups to enjoy a rendezvous or potluck supper while taking in the stupendous scenery.

Boaters at the Community Dock are welcome to hire a professional fishing guide, visit the SONORA BAY RESORT RESTAURANT AND SPA or pop over to DENT ISLAND LODGE for lunch or dinner; reservations are essential in the busy summer months. A hiking trail through mossy forest to Eagle Lake is maintained by the Stuart Island Community Association; here you will find a communal rowing skiff, a log swimming platform and warm water.

MORGAN'S LANDING WILDERNESS RETREAT—250-287-0237, VHF 66A—is east of Dent Island Lodge. It offers visitor moorage with power and water on the docks. Shower and laundry facilities, meals by reservation and accommodation are available at the lodge. Professional guided fishing trips with the owners can also be arranged. At the time of writing the lodge was up for sale—call them for updates.

Note: Please respect private boundaries of homes on the island.

CHARTS 3543. 3312, page 26.

APPROACH

The community of Big Bay lies E of Hesler Point below the slopes of Mount Muehle. Avoid the large kelp bed over the 4 m (13 ft) patch in the centre of the bay.

ANCHOR

Anchoring off the floats isn't recommended because the waters are in a constant state of movement, either from the strong back eddies or from the sport boats zooming by.

PUBLIC WHARF

Stuart Island Community Dock has expanded moorage and lies S of the timber breakwater, 250-202-3625, VHF 66A—call ahead in the busy summer months. No power and limited water available on the docks.

CAUTIONARY NOTE

At certain stages of the tide a strong cross-current runs 90° to the community dock. We recommend that boaters come to a stop and stand off to assess the state of the current before attempting to come alongside and tie up.

Note: The bay is a zone for float plane operations.

Sonora Lodge on Big Bay's east shore.

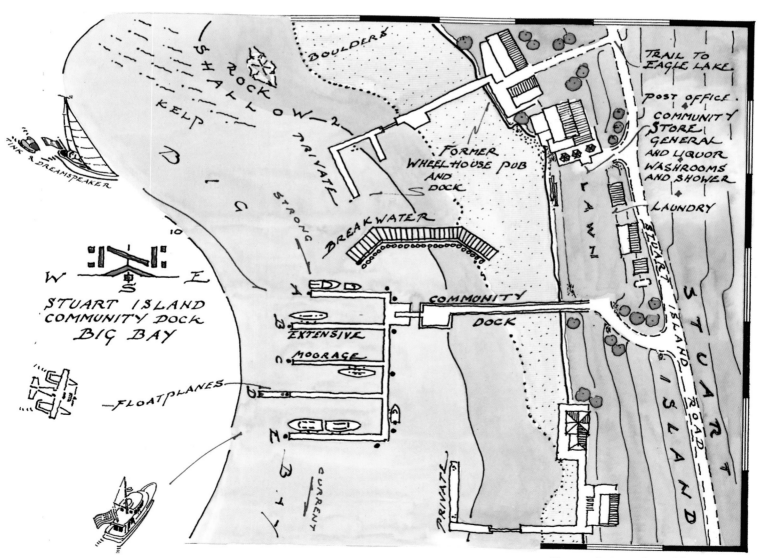

Not to scale. Not to be used for navigation.

9.7 DENT ISLAND LODGE AND MARINA, CORDERO CHANNEL

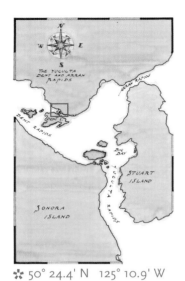

✿ 50° 24.4' N   125° 10.9' W

CHARTS 3543. 3312, page 26.

APPROACH

From the SE. The Dent Island Lodge's marina lies between Dent Island and the mainland, at the head of a small cove.

ANCHOR

Good protected anchorage for one or two boats can be found in the cove. Boats at anchor will swing to the current that flows through "Canoe Pass." Anchor in depths of 4–6 m (13–19.5 ft). Holding good in shingle and kelp.

MARINA

Dent Island Lodge requires reservations for moorage and dining in the busy summer months—250-203-2553, VHF 66A. The marina has concrete docks with moorage for boats up to 200 ft. Unlimited water and power up to 50 amps (single-phase 100 amp power upon request). Wi-Fi, ice, shower and laundry facilities. Resort amenities include a restaurant, tapas bar, library, fitness room, sauna and hot tub. Fishing trips can be arranged.

Note: "Canoe Pass" is a small-boat passage only.

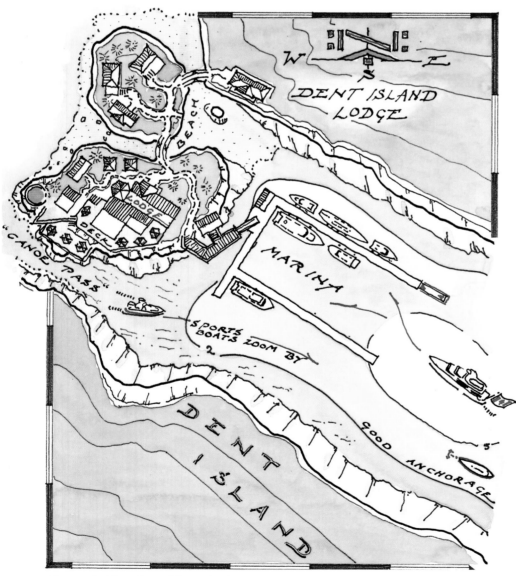

Not to scale. Not to be used for navigation.

Built in harmony with its natural surroundings, the DENT ISLAND LODGE at the southern entrance to Cordero Channel offers its guests comfortable moorage, deluxe log cabins and resort facilities with magnificent views out to "Canoe Pass" and the turbulent Dent Rapids. The lodge's laid-back luxury, pleasant service and exceptional West Coast cuisine can be enjoyed in the restaurant, which offers guests the best in fine dining, or at the more casual RAPIDS GRILL specializing in a delicious small-plate menu with a stunning view. The chef's lavish dinner menu includes a platter of fresh hors d'oeuvres served at your chosen location—try the hot tub built in the trees above the rocky shoreline of "Canoe Pass" rapids.

Approaching the lodge's west float.

CHARTS 3543. 3312, page 26.

APPROACH

From the S, by rounding the wooded peninsula.

ANCHOR

Temporary anchorage is possible off a small shingle beach. Depths of 6–12 m (19.5–39 ft), holding good in shingle and mud.

Note: If you've missed slack water, it's prudent to wait for the following slack water. If Mermaid Bay is taken up with a log boom, ask for permission to tie up alongside it or visit the Dent Island Lodge (see page 122) a short distance away.

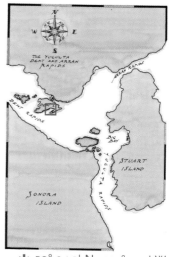

❊ 50° 24.1' N 125° 11.3' W

Tucked neatly into the southern end of Dent Island, Mermaid Bay provides a convenient temporary or emergency anchorage and is a pleasant spot to while away a few hours waiting for slack water. Historically it was used by tug skippers as a "waiting place," especially when both the Dent Rapids and Gillard Passage had to be attempted in one go. Generations of tugboat names have been painted onto driftwood or old planks and wedged into the rocks or nailed to the trees, but no mermaids have been spotted to date! Because space in the bay is limited, be prepared to tie up alongside a log boom if necessary.

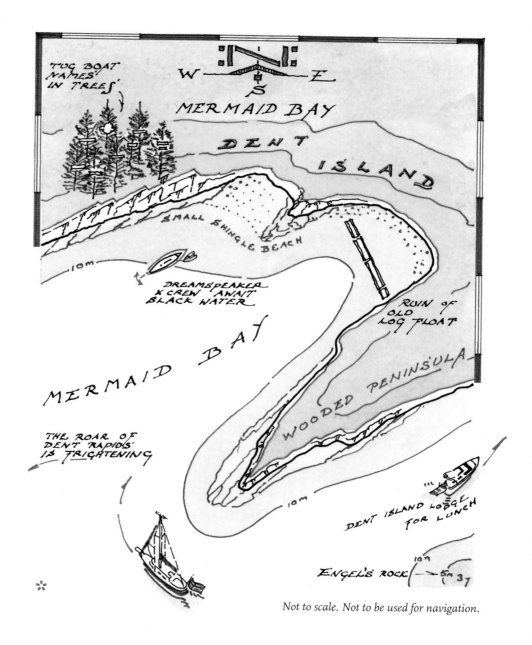

Not to scale. Not to be used for navigation.

Generations of tugboat names in Mermaid Bay.

Chapter 10
CORDERO CHANNEL

Looking across Cordero Channel from Shoal Bay.

Public wharf at Shoal Bay.

Chapter 10
CORDERO CHANNEL

TIDES

Canadian Tide and Current Tables, Volume 6

Reference Port: Owen Bay
Secondary Ports: Shoal Bay, Cordero Islands, "Blind Channel," Chatham Point

CURRENTS

Reference Station: Seymour Narrows
Secondary Station: Greene Point Rapids

WEATHER

Area: Johnstone Strait
Reporting Stations: Helmcken Island, Chatham Point

Note: The relentless currents and strong to gale-force afternoon and evening winds that plague Johnstone Strait S seldom penetrate into Cordero Channel with the same intensity.

CAUTIONARY NOTES

Once you are clear of the Dent Rapids, Cordero Channel itself is relatively free of turbulent water, but currents remain strong, especially in the western half of the channel. It's therefore advisable to travel with the prevailing tidal stream.

Don't forget, "Blind Channel" (the local name for Mayne Passage) has rapids and turbulent water in its northern reaches. Both "Blind Channel" and Greene Point Rapids shouldn't be attempted other than at or near slack water.

I n this chapter, we explore a diverse selection of destinations between the Dent and Greene Point Rapids, in Cordero Channel, in Mayne Passage (known locally as Blind Channel) and in the less travelled Nodales Channel. Should you plan to stop over or refuel at the Blind Channel Resort, keep in mind that the "Blind Channel Rapids" (the local name for the northern portion of Mayne Passage) extend as far north as Shell Point.

Historic Shoal Bay on East Thurlow Island provides a convenient base while you explore the "Gut" (as it's known locally) and Estero Basin in Frederick Arm or while you take a side trip up Phillips Arm. Anchor or tie up at the busy public wharf, take a hike to the Douglas Pine Mine and enjoy a cold beer at the pub. Bickley Bay, just around the corner, offers a pleasant alternative anchorage.

Tucked in behind Lorte Island, inviting Cordero Lodge, with its hearty German cooking, comes as a wonderful surprise as you near the end of Cordero Channel. Snuggled between the Cordero Islands and the mainland shore lies a lovely, quiet anchorage, an ideal hideaway for lounging in the cockpit and watching the world rush by.

The efficiently run BLIND CHANNEL RESORT provides the only fuelling and provisioning stop for the area covered in this chapter, and it is a welcome sight to the cruising boater running low on supplies. Family owned and operated, the resort has built an excellent reputation over the years by offering comfortable moorage, a cozy restaurant with tasty, home-cooked meals and a store that sells delicious loaves of home-baked bread. Take a walk along the well-maintained trail to the 800-year-old cedar, or picnic on the pebble beach in Charles Bay, a short hop across Mayne Passage.

Peace and solitude can be found in undeveloped Thurston Bay Marine Park, where you can dig for clams, pick blackberries and wild mint or just idle away a few blissful days surrounded by wilderness. The head of Hemming Bay on East Thurlow Island offers you sheltered anchorage, great sunsets and the opportunity to relax and explore at your leisure.

FEATURED DESTINATIONS

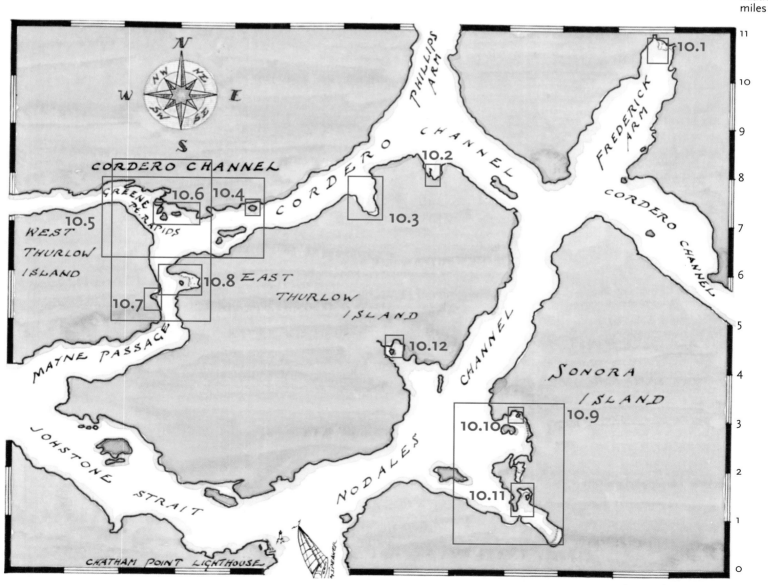

Not to be used for navigation.

10.1 THE "GUT" TO ESTERO BASIN, FREDERICK ARM

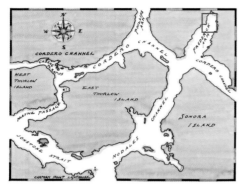

✵ 50° 29.9' N 125° 15.1' W

CHARTS 3543. 3312, page 25.

APPROACH

Use caution as you approach the head of Frederick Arm because a shallow delta extends out from the "Gut" to Estero Basin. The entrance to the "Gut" is also obscured by overhanging greenery.

ANCHOR

Temporary anchorage is possible below a cliff of bare rock. Depths of 10–15 m (33–49 ft), holding good in shingle and rock.

The "Gut" to Estero Basin.

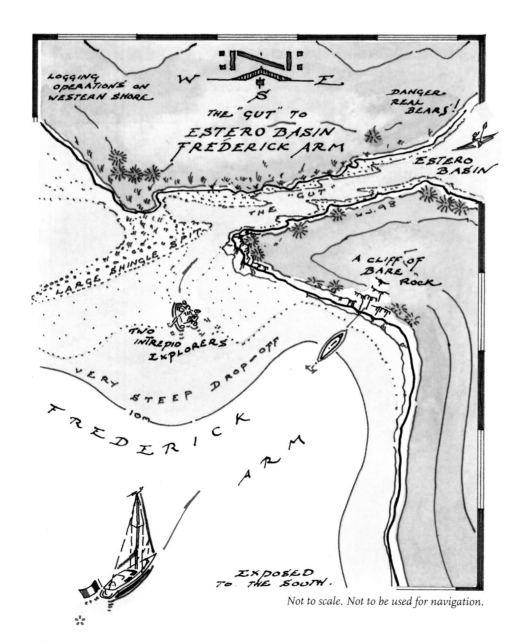

Not to scale. Not to be used for navigation.

The temporary, deep-water anchorage at the head of Frederick Arm makes an excellent day stop, as from here you can easily adventure into beautiful Estero Basin by dinghy or kayak. The tidal waters flow rapidly in and out of the basin, so timing your trip around slack water is essential unless you plan to shoot the rapids or are prepared to beach or portage your dinghy at some point. Although tugboats have been using the "Gut" (as it's known locally) for years, ascending the narrows in a deep-draft boat, even at high-water slack, isn't advisable without detailed local knowledge. Take advantage of the clear, freshwater stream that flows down into Estero Basin from the lakes on the northern shore, and pack your swimsuit. Boaters should keep in mind that this is bear country and take the usual precautions when exploring beyond the shoreline.

Note: Afternoon inflow winds can make the head of Frederick Arm choppy and sometimes untenable for safe anchorage by small craft. If you time it right, you can take the last of the flood into the basin, enjoy a 2-hour excursion, then return on an early ebb and settle into Shoal Bay (see page 129) for the night.

SHOAL BAY, EAST THURLOW ISLAND 10.2

CHARTS 3543. 3312, page 25.

APPROACH

Anchorage is possible to the NE and NW, within the vicinity of the public wharf. Good holding in sand and mud in depths of 5–15 m (16–33 ft).

PUBLIC WHARF

Popular with visitors in the summer months. There is no power or water on the floats. Be prepared to raft up. Pay moorage fees at Shoal Bay Pub where Wi-Fi, washrooms, showers and laundry facilities are available.

Note: Shoal Bay experiences overnight outflow winds emanating from Phillips Arm, making the anchorage a lee shore. Ensure that your anchor is well set prior to an overnight stay.

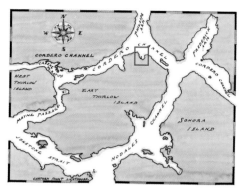

✳ 50° 27.6' N   125° 21.9' W

Shoal Bay provides a convenient base while you explore Phillips and Frederick Arms or wait for slack water at Dent and Greene Point Rapids. Although the busy public wharf in Shoal Bay has limited amenities, it's in good repair and has a great view across Cordero Channel, up Phillips Arm. It's hard to imagine that this bay was a boom town in the early 1900s, claiming a community larger than the newly established city of Vancouver.

The long jetty across the shallows leads to the waterfront SHOAL BAY PUB, where Mark and Cynthia, the owners, welcome visiting boaters to enjoy their garden, a cold beer or glass of wine and a chat. They have a well-established garden and offer "pick your own" vegetables and flowers in season (by donation); Cynthia's creative pottery is also for sale at the pub. Leashed dogs welcome. If you are in the area during the first week of August, don't miss the Shoal Bay Music Festival and BBQ.

There is a 45-minute uphill hike to the DOUGLAS PINE MINE, which once produced gold, copper and iron—a great way to get off the boat and exercise.

Note: Two rental cabins are available at the lodge—call 250-287-6818.

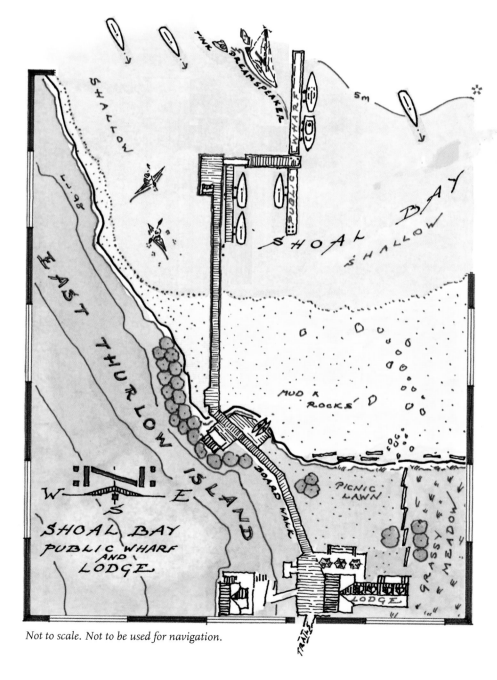

Not to scale. Not to be used for navigation.

10.3 Bickley Bay, East Thurlow Island

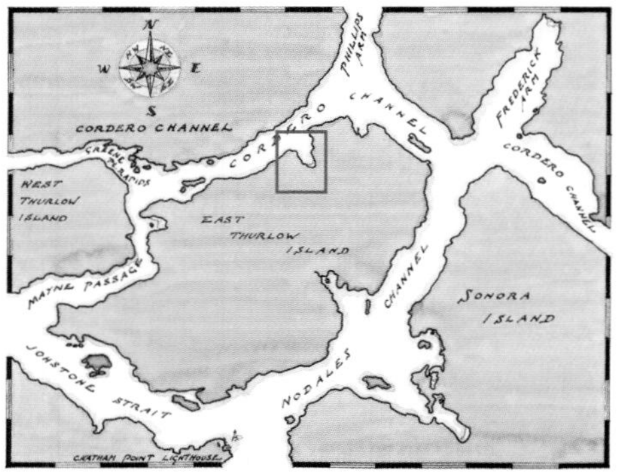

✲ 50° 27.3' N 125° 24.0' W

CHARTS 3543. 3312, pages 24 & 25.

APPROACH

From the N, between Peel Rocks and a large fish farm.

ANCHOR

Reasonably protected anchorage can be found at the head of the bay. Depths of 5–10 m (16–33 ft), holding good in mud.

Note: Overnight outflow winds from Phillips Arm make the bay a lee shore. In summer, however, the relatively light wind is offset by good holding. Ensure that your anchor is well set prior to an overnight stay.

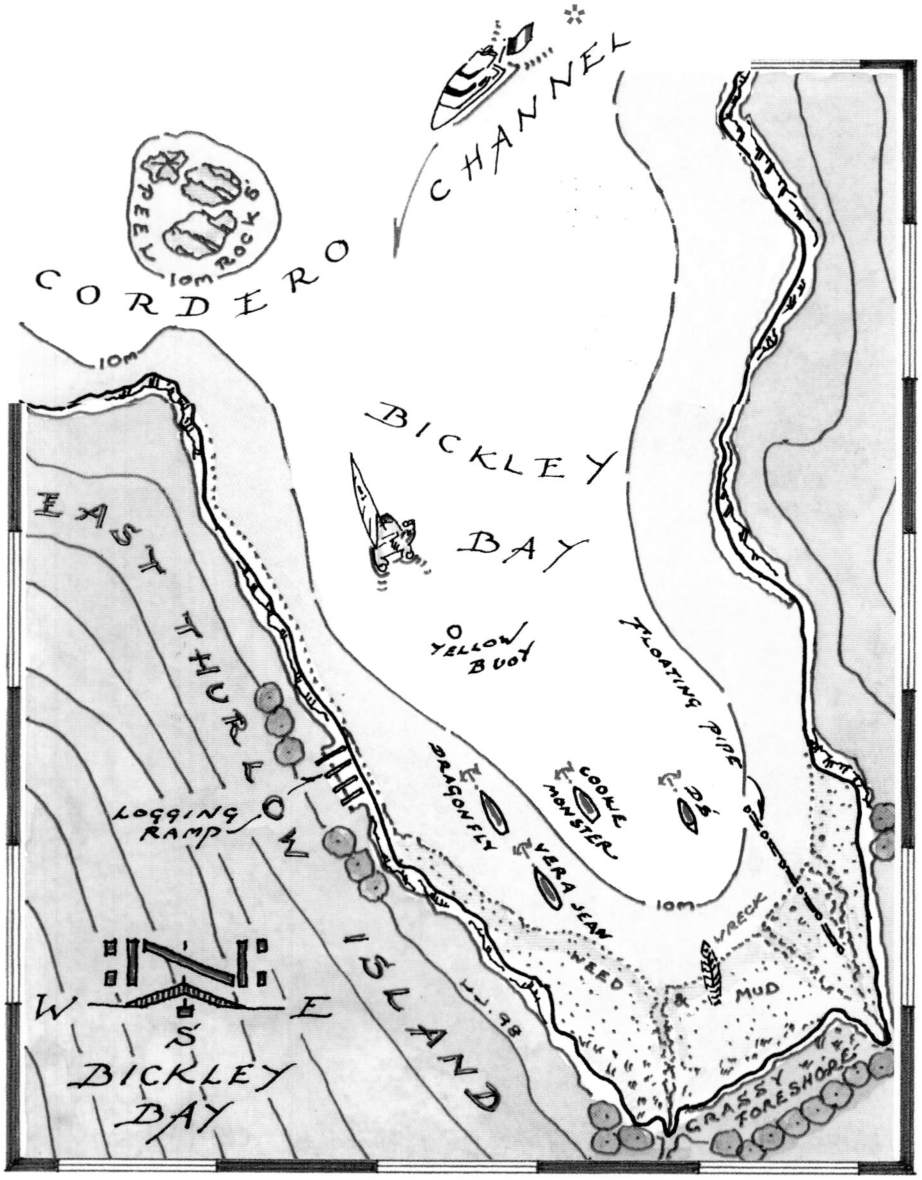

Not to scale. Not to be used for navigation.

Just around the corner from Shoal Bay lies protected Bickley Bay. It is a pleasant place to anchor overnight or use as a base while you explore Phillips Arm. It is backed by a grassy foreshore and fed by a freshwater stream. If you have a kayak on board and the tide is up, take the opportunity to paddle at leisure and observe the wildlife. When we visited one August, the stream was so low that the restless salmon were jumping around our boat but unfortunately not onto our hooks.

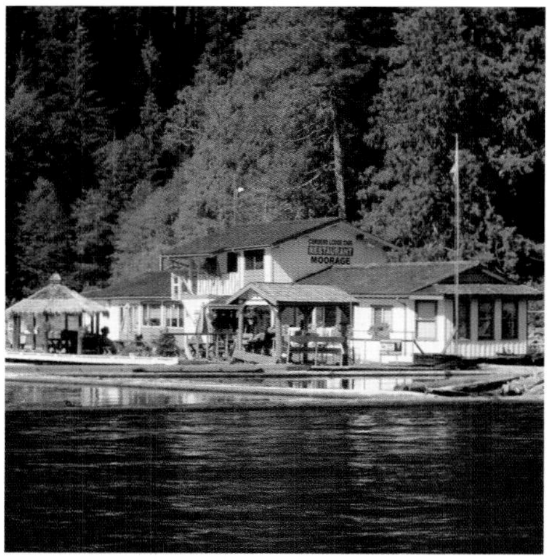

The floating Cordero Lodge.

CHARTS 3543. 3312, page 24.

APPROACH

Either from the S, out of Cordero Channel, or from the W, between the mainland and Lorte Island.

ANCHOR

W of the lodge, where reasonable protection can be found between Lorte Island and the mainland. Depths, holding and bottom condition unrecorded.

MARINA

Cordero Lodge, 250-287-0917, VHF 66. Moorage for guests and overnight visitors. Washrooms, no power and limited Wi-Fi on the docks. Summertime bookings for moorage and dinner recommended. Call ahead for updates on the lodge and restaurant.

Note: Please slow down when approaching the lodge as passing boat traffic can cause damaging wakes at the lodge floats.

CAUTIONARY NOTE

Plan your approach to the lodge's floats carefully because the strong current that swirls around Lorte Island can make docking a challenge.

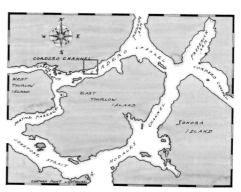

✳ 50° 26.7' N   125° 27.1' W

P lease reduce speed when you see the "SLOW" sign near the entrance to this picturesque floating lodge, bedecked with hanging baskets of flowers in the summer months.

At the time of writing, although the lodge was up for sale it was open for lunch and dinner, with excellent German dishes being the specialty. The restaurant, with a lounge, seats twenty-two but has been known to squeeze in twenty-five hungry guests and boaters.

The lodge offers overnight moorage and accommodation for up to eight guests. Relax and fish off the dock or exercise the dog with an energetic hike on the trails behind the lodge. Because the owners believe in a good night's sleep, the running of generators is restricted at night.

Note: The lodge is just a short hop from the anchorage in Bickley Bay.

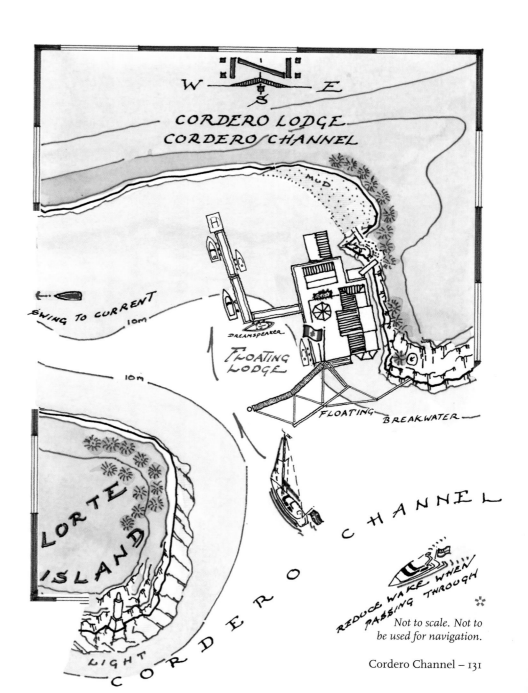

Not to scale. Not to be used for navigation.

10.5 Greene Point Rapids & West Cordero Channel

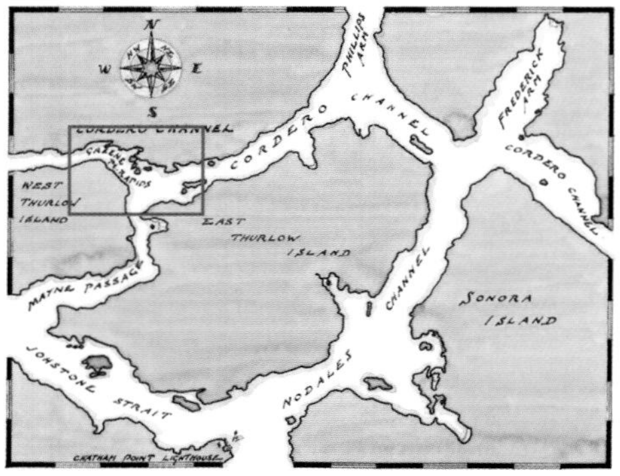

✲ 50° 26.0' N 125° 29.5' W

CHARTS 3543. 3312, page 24.

GREENE POINT RAPIDS

Approach the rapids at or near slack water and with the current turning in your favour.
Reference current station: Seymour Narrows
Direction of flood: SE
Times of slack water as follows:

- turn to flood:
  minus (–) 1 hour 25 minutes
- turn to ebb:
  minus (–) 1 hour 35 minutes

W CORDERO CHANNEL

Listed are 4 handy anchorages in Cordero Channel to overnight or await the turn of the tide.

1. **"cordero cove,"** see 10.6 (page 133)
2. **lorte island**, see 10.4 (page 131)
3. **tallac bay**, on the mainland shore, offers a comfortable temporary anchorage on its western shore. Backed by a grassy meadow, it offers good holding and is fun to explore.
4. **crawford anchorage**, in a cozy nook on the southern shore of Erasmus Island

These rapids extend both east and west from Greene Point. Strong currents of up to 5 knots are found off Erasmus Island, but they dissipate to 3 knots past Lorte Island. Maximum current velocities encountered in the rapids are recorded at the current station, situated centre channel between the Cordero Islands and West Thurlow Island, with a maximum flood of 7 knots and ebb of 5 knots. Dangerous overfalls and turbulent water form southwest off the Cordero Islands, with whirlpools and upwellings west of Greene Point and north of Edsall Islets.

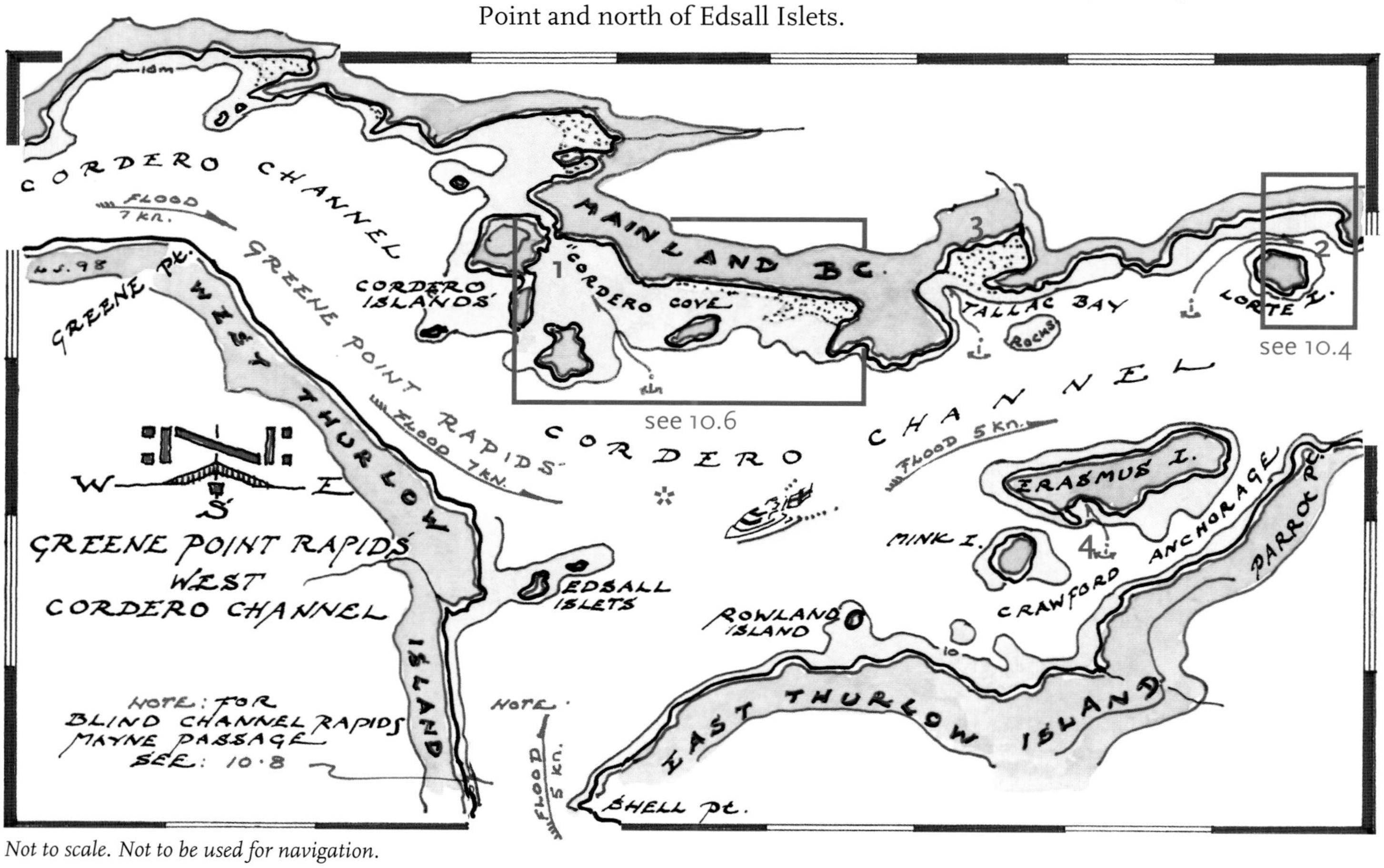

Not to scale. Not to be used for navigation.

"CORDERO COVE," CORDERO ISLANDS

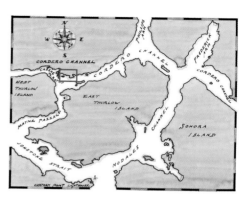

CHARTS 3543. 3312, page 24.

APPROACH
From the S; the channel between the southern islands is fringed by kelp. A rock lies off the western tip of the easternmost island.

ANCHOR
Good sheltered anchorage, away from the turbulence and eddies in Cordero Channel, can be found in the cove. Depths of 6–12 m (19.5–39 ft), holding over a mud, sand and weed bottom.

❀ 50° 26.4' N   125° 29.6' W

"Cordero Cove" is a good sheltered anchorage.

This surprise anchorage is protected from northwesterly winds and the swift current in Cordero Channel by three charming islands. The southeast basin also affords some protection in a southeasterly.

 With a pleasant view out to bustling Cordero Channel, what we call "Cordero Cove" is an ideal spot for exploring, picnicking, shell collecting and just lounging in the cockpit. Many tranquil hours can be spent basking on the smooth-rock islet in the cove's northwest corner. You'll be lulled by water music as it gushes through the narrow gap and tumbles over rocks at high water. The best spot to spread your picnic blanket is on the downy moss and grass patch on the westernmost island with a great view over to the Greene Point Rapids.

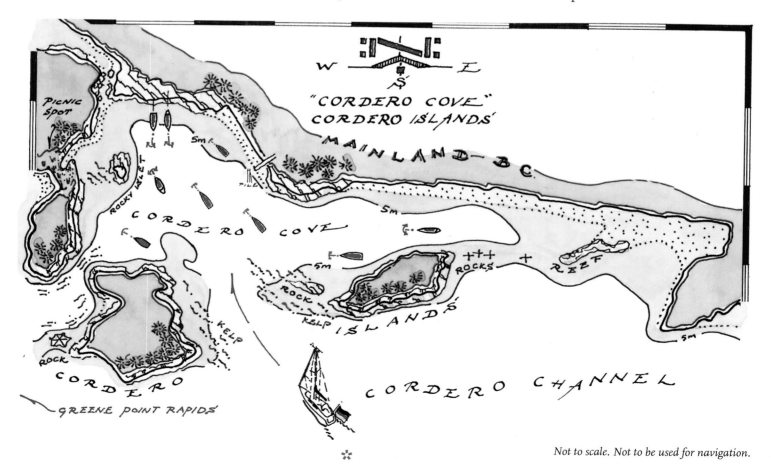

Not to scale. Not to be used for navigation.

BLIND CHANNEL RESORT, WEST THURLOW ISLAND

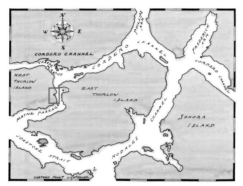

✣ 50° 24.9' N   125° 29.9' W

CHARTS 3543. 3312, page 24.

APPROACH

With caution, because a back eddy, running counter to the current in Mayne Passage, creates a strong current setting into the marina facility.

MARINA

The Blind Channel Resort marina, toll-free 1-888-329-0475, VHF 66A, has extensive visitor moorage with water, power up to 50 amps and Wi-Fi.

FUEL

Open year-round and operated by the resort. Gasoline, diesel and propane available.

The deck at Blind Channel Resort.

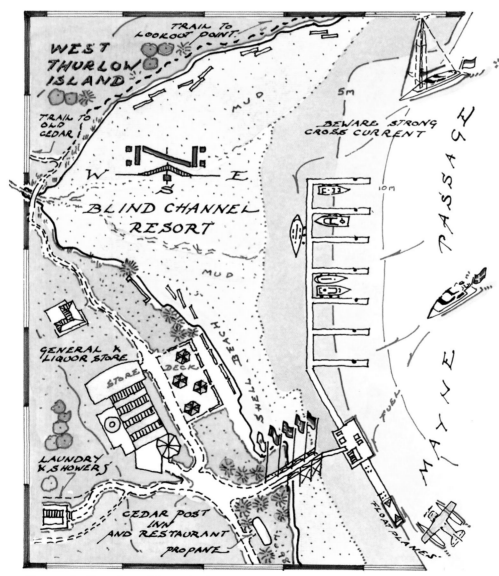

Not to scale. Not to be used for navigation.

Pristine docks, colourful artwork and terra cotta pots spilling over with flowers welcome you to the efficiently run BLIND CHANNEL RESORT. Owned and operated by three generations of the Richter family since 1970, this self-contained resort has a restaurant and patio, store, post office, BC Liquor Store outlet and waterside cottages with full facilities. Free moorage of two to three hours is given to boaters while they shop or dine at the restaurant. Clean shower and laundry facilities are available and they offer a garbage service with a commercial incinerator. The store sells delicious, freshly baked goods, picnic fare and fresh bread daily in high season. It also carries a variety of basic provisions, frozen meats and a selection of fresh produce. "Spring water ice" is produced on site. Pick up a hiking trail map and visit the 800-year-old cedar in the forest behind the resort.

Evidence of Annemarie Richter's artistic talents can be seen in the CEDAR POST RESTAURANT, which offers fine dining. In summer, reservations for both moorage and the restaurant are essential.

Note: The resort has scheduled float plane and water taxi service from Campbell River.

CHARTS 3543. 3312, page 24.

APPROACH: CHARLES BAY
From Mayne Passage at LW slack.

ANCHOR
Due N and W of Eclipse Islet, and swing in back eddies. Depths of 2–4 m (6.5–13 ft), holding good in mud.

Note: The bay, although open to Mayne Passage, lies in the wind shadow of W Thurlow Island and is therefore protected from the prevailing summer westerlies.

APPROACH: "BLIND CHANNEL RAPIDS"
On or near slack water.
Reference current station: Seymour Narrows
Direction of flood: N
Times of slack water as follows:
- Turn to flood:
  minus (–) 20 minutes
- Turn to ebb: minus (–) 1 hour

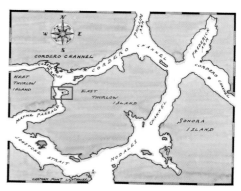

✱ 50° 25.2' N 125° 29.6' W

Good crabbing and a protected anchorage can be found across the way from BLIND CHANNEL RESORT (see page 134) in secluded Charles Bay. Sheltered from southeasterly and northwesterly winds and the effects of the Greene Point and "Blind Channel Rapids," this small haven offers peace. Beautiful Eclipse Islet, surrounded by clear water, provides an idyllic picnic spot. You can pick fresh sea asparagus, poke around the rocks or just relax on the colourful pebble beach watching boat traffic in Mayne Passage challenge the "Blind Channel Rapids."

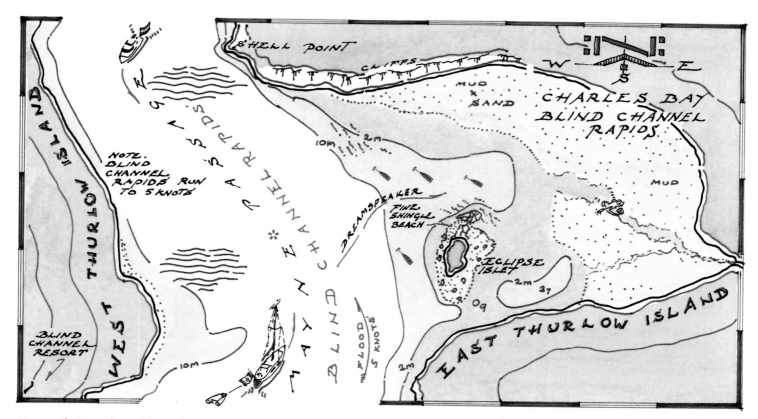

Not to scale. Not to be used for navigation.

10.9 THURSTON BAY MARINE PARK & CAMELEON HARBOUR, SONORA ISLAND

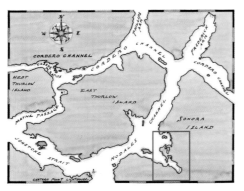

✳ 50° 22.1' N 125° 20.4' W

CHARTS 3543. 3312, page 25.

ANCHOR

THURSTON BAY: See 10.10 (page 137).
"ANCHORAGE LAGOON": Snug, all-weather protection, but the entrance is shallow, 0.6 m (2 ft), and requires careful navigation.
HANDFIELD BAY: See 10.11 (page 137).

CAMELEON HARBOUR: Anchorage is possible throughout the harbour. Depths vary, holding good in sticky mud. However, if a strong westerly is forecast for Johnstone Strait, the same wind will whistle through the harbour. When entering be sure to keep clear of Douglas Rock off Bruce Point, and avoid the rocky ledges that extend out from Greetham Point.

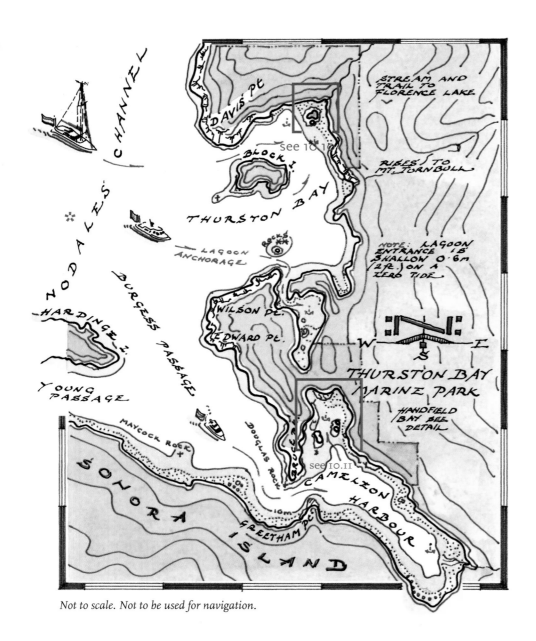

Not to scale. Not to be used for navigation.

Thurston Bay Marine Park is peaceful and undeveloped, although its middle section is private property. The northern section of the park is in Thurston Bay itself and offers partly protected, temporary anchorage behind Block Island, especially if you tuck into the western side of what we have dubbed "Hook Islets." Snug but very shallow and restricted anchorage can be found in "Anchorage Lagoon" at the southern end of the bay. Almost landlocked, it should be navigated with caution as submerged rocks guard the entrance. From the marshy southern portion of the lagoon, you can hike the overgrown trail leading to Handfield Bay (see page 137) and Cameleon Harbour.

Cameleon Harbour is a protected anchorage that also catches the last rays of the evening sun, so following local advice we dropped our hook in the southeast corner of the harbour. This secure and quiet spot overlooks a creek and the grassy foreshore of a long-deserted homestead. Wind can funnel down into the harbour, but the holding is excellent in sticky mud.

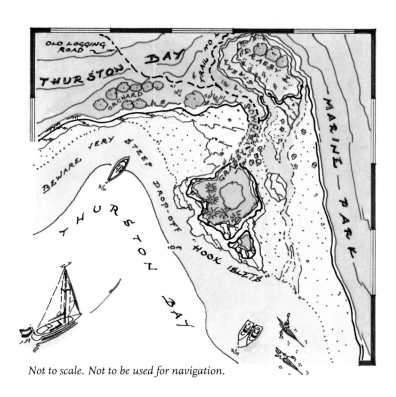

Not to scale. Not to be used for navigation.

APPROACH

A safe approach can be made either to the N or to the W of Block Island.

ANCHOR

Temporary anchorage can be found to the NW or S of "Hook Islets." Depths of 5–10 m (16–33 ft), holding good over sand and mud.

Note: If a strong westerly is forecast for Johnstone Strait, the wind will penetrate into the bay. Block Island gives no real protection.

Partly protected, temporary anchorage can be found behind Block Island and east or west of "Hook Islets," the larger islet being connected to Sonora Island by a narrow, grassy isthmus. The islets are fun to explore, and you can relax and dip your toes in the clear water from the comfortable sunbathing rocks. En route to the stream that flows down from Florence Lake, you can pick pears and blackberries in season, and the wild mint that grows along the trail makes a great addition to a "boater's salad."

Overgrown trails beside the stream and behind the bay take you to the old BC Forest Service Station site, which served for over 25 years as the regional marine headquarters, and to Florence Lake, 2.4 km (1.5 mi) inland.

HANDFIELD BAY 10.11

APPROACH

From the S out of Cameleon Harbour. Best approached at LW, when the rocks and drying foreshore are visible.

ANCHOR

All-weather protection, best with a stern line ashore. Depths of 2–4 m (6.5–13 ft), holding moderate over a mix of rock, shell and mud.

Quiet and solitude welcome you to this lovely pocket bay, where a few idle days can be spent digging clams, picnicking on Tully Island, swimming or exploring the rocky shoreline by dinghy or kayak. The bay's narrow entrance should be navigated with caution. An overgrown trail leads through the park forest, connecting Handfield Bay with "Anchorage Lagoon." A smooth sunbathing rock in the northeast corner of the bay fronts a mossy glen shaded by wild fruit trees, where signs of visiting deer and bears are evident. Any form of disturbance is frowned on in this secluded anchorage.

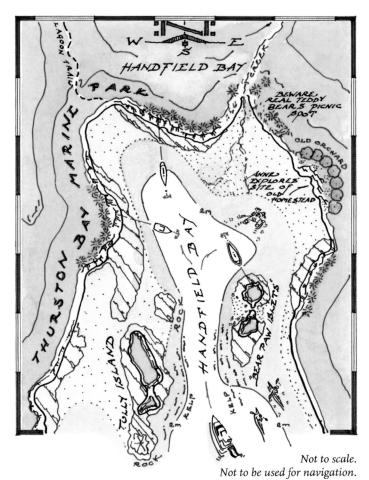

Not to scale.
Not to be used for navigation.

THE HEAD OF HEMMING BAY, EAST THURLOW ISLAND

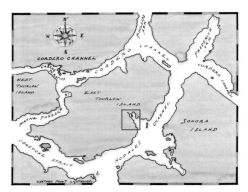

❊ 50° 23.6' N   125° 22.7' W

CHARTS 3543. 3312, page 25.

APPROACH
Leave the six rocky islets to port as you approach the head of the bay.

ANCHOR
There is all-weather protection for one or two boats W of the private buoy. An alternative anchorage more open to the S, but protected from the prevailing westerlies, lies N of the private buoy. Depth, holding and bottom condition vary.

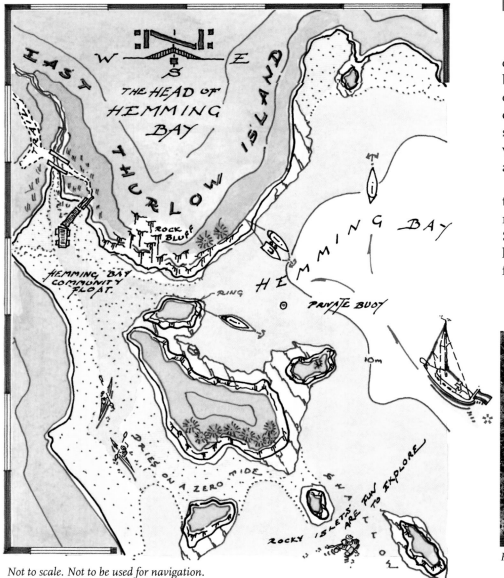

Not to scale. Not to be used for navigation.

The bay offers sheltered overnight anchorage with a stern line to the grassy islet or deeper anchorage at the head of the bay. The lagoon-like haven northwest of the islets is perfect for exploring by dinghy or kayak. It has a stunning, sheer rock face at its narrow northwest entrance, a freshwater stream and a sunset view through the gap.

A small private float, bridge and trail lead to the Hemming Bay Community Lodge and to Hemming Lake. Signs request that visitors respect the lodge's privacy and the community's freshwater supply.

Rock bluff, head of Hemming Bay.

Chapter II
NORTHERN
QUADRA
ISLAND

Anne and Tink explore Bodega Point.

Octopus Islands Marine Park.

Chapter 11
NorthernQuadraIsland

TIDES

Canadian Tide and Current Tables,
Volume 5
Reference Port: Point Atkinson
Secondary Port: Surge Narrows
Volume 6
Reference Ports: Campbell River
& Owen Bay
Secondary Port: Octopus Island
& Chatham Point

CURRENTS

Volume 5
Reference Station: Beazley Passage
Volume 6
Reference Stations: Hole in the Wall
(west end) & Seymour Narrows

Secondary Station: Okisollo Channel
(Upper Rapids)

WEATHER

Area: Johnstone Strait
Reporting Stations: Chatham Point,
Campbell River

Note: The strong westerly winds in
Johnstone Strait, which can reach
30–35 knots during summer evenings,
will continue, although with reduced
strength, through Discovery Passage
and into Kanish Bay. These winds are
also felt in Granite Bay and Hoskyn
Channel prior to diminishing overnight.

CAUTIONARY NOTES

Although the Surge Narrows–Okisollo
Channel route is considered less daunt-
ing than Seymour Narrows or the
Yucultas, all tidal rapids require diligent
use of the Canadian Tide and Current
Tables *and careful cruise planning.*

The currents in Beazley Passage,
Lower Rapids, Upper Rapids and Hole
in the Wall are extremely hazardous
and present a real danger to all craft.

This chapter takes you north to the head of Hoskyn Channel and through the Settlers Group of islands, via Beazley Passage, a route known locally as "Surge Narrows." It also includes Okisollo Channel with the Upper and Lower Rapids, Hole in the Wall and Northern Discovery Passage. Beginning with the quiet, historic anchorage in Village Bay on Quadra Island's eastern shore, the boater can choose from a good cross-section of quiet hide-away anchorages, scenic picnic stops and popular summer spots along the way.

A cozy refuge can be found in what we call "Boulton Bay" with its smooth picnic rocks and breathtaking views down to Rebecca Spit. The enchanting "Diamond Islets" (our name for them) in Okisollo Channel invite you to stay for a while and enjoy their tranquility. From here a mossy viewpoint looks over to the alluring Octopus Islands, where sheltered coves are neatly tucked into the northeast corner of Waiatt Bay. Although these islands are extremely popular in the summer months, they still provide you with the opportunity to take it easy and enjoy life's simpler pleasures. The spacious and protected waters of Waiatt Bay offer a less crowded alternative.

Protected anchorage can be found throughout Owen Bay and opposite the small public wharf. Backed by a wild apple orchard, this unassuming spot has a relaxed charm all its own. Although a good portion of Kanish Bay is occupied by fish farms, there's a lovely picnic anchorage behind Bodega Point. Historic Orchard Bay is backed by a grass-covered midden and an overgrown orchard laden with edible fruit in season. Sheltered Granite Bay once supported a thriving community of over 500 people, but today locals visit their rustic summer cabins to enjoy its out-of-the-way peace and solitude.

The all-weather anchorage found inside Small Inlet's restricted channel is surrounded by lush forest. Abundant with wildlife, it is ideal to explore by dinghy or kayak or by hiking the portage trail to the pebble beach at Waiatt Bay.

Protected from westerly winds and seemingly unaffected by the tidal turmoil in Discovery Passage, Otter Cove provides a convenient spot to stop and relax while you wait for slack water or calmer wind conditions in Johnstone Strait.

FEATURED DESTINATIONS

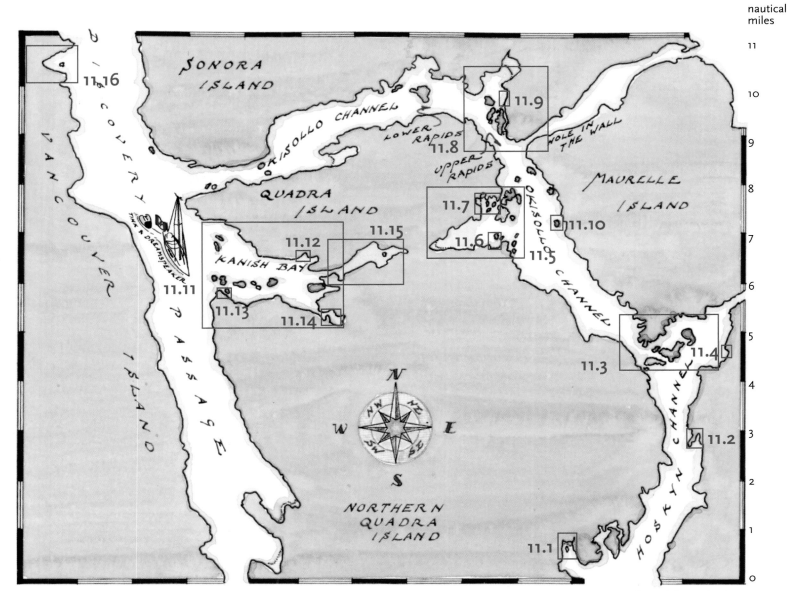

Not to be used for navigation.

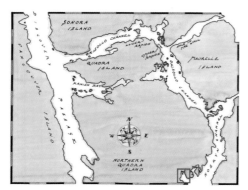

✽ 50° 9.5' N   125° 11.3' W

CHARTS 3539. 3312, page 19.

APPROACH

From the SE out of Hoskyn Channel.

ANCHOR

Temporary anchorage at the head of Village Bay on either side of the spot we call "Castle Islet." Exposed to the SE, although provides good protection from westerly and northwesterly winds. Depths of 4–6 m (13–19.5 ft), moderate holding in shingle and rock.

Village Bay, once a sizeable Native village.

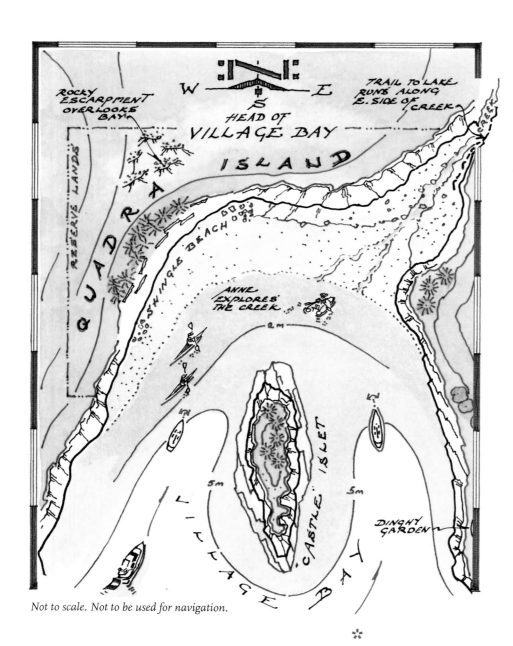

Not to scale. Not to be used for navigation.

"Castle Islet," at the northern end of this quiet hideaway, is covered with a medley of shrubs, grasses and windswept trees, and provides a great adventuring playground for those in need of a little exercise.

Village Bay was once the site of a sizeable Native village, and a log "flume" was constructed in the late 1800s to transport lumber from the southern end of Village Bay Lake downstream into the bay. A natural, warm-water swimming pool can be found a short distance up from the mouth of the creek. From here a shady trail meanders alongside the stream and ends above a grassy cliff, overlooking Village Bay Lake. Although the path is on private land, as of 1998 the owners have refrained from posting "No Trespassing" signs, and we urge boaters and kayakers to respect the property. Village Bay Lake joins with Main Lake, making this freshwater system the largest in the Gulf or Discovery Islands.

Access to the Shellaligan Pass Trail is possible from the southwest shoreline of Village Bay.

"BOULTON BAY," SHEER POINT, READ ISLAND 11.2

The sheer cliffs of "Boulton Bay."

CHARTS 3539. 3312, page 19.

APPROACH
From Hoskyn Channel by rounding Sheer Point.

ANCHOR
Temporary anchorage is possible at the head of the bay. Open to the S, but provides good protection from westerly and northwesterly winds. Depths of 6–12 m (19.5–39 ft), holding good in mud and shingle.

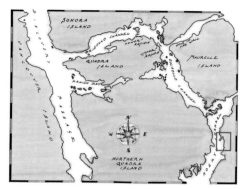

❀ 50° 11.8' N   125° 7.6' W

Steep cliffs on the western shore of what we have dubbed "Boulton Bay" form a spectacular backdrop to this quiet refuge. Open to the south but protected from northwesterly winds, it provides temporary anchorage for two or three boats. Kayakers can beach their craft and find some shelter at the head of the bay, although overnight camping on crown land is available farther north at "Freedom Point" (local name). A freshwater creek flows down to the log-strewn pebble beach, and a sign posted beyond the big tree stump reads "You are welcome to the water—take a rest—but beyond this point you are TRESPASSING."

There are smooth sun-basking rocks below a sign that reads "Shell-fish Lease—No Pickin' Please." The picnic rocks at what we call "Sunset Point" are ideal for catching the last rays of the setting sun while taking in the breathtaking views down to Rebecca Spit.

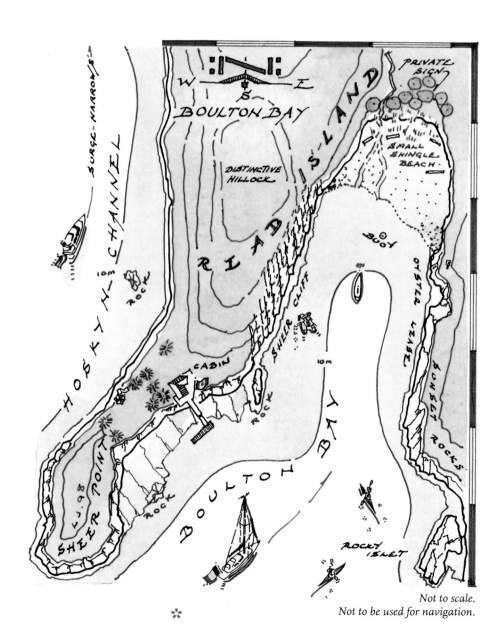

Not to scale.
Not to be used for navigation.

11.3   S U R G E   N A R R O W S

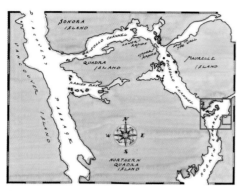

✴ 50° 13.4' N   125° 8.1' W

CHARTS 3537. 3312, page 20.

APPROACH

Beazley Passage on or near slack water. Beazley Passage is the only safe passage through or around the Settlers Group of islands.
Reference current station: Beazley Passage *(Volume 5)*
Direction of flood: SE
Slack water (turn): 5–11 minutes

ANCHOR

Anchorage in the vicinity of the Settlers Group of islands isn't recommended because of the strong tidal streams and poor holding.

Note: Beazley Passage is wider than it appears, 60 m (197 ft), but most craft file through one at a time in the centre channel. Beware of Tusko Rock, defined by a kelp bed when the rock is submerged.

The name "Surge Narrows" is applied locally to the entire route from Hoskyn Channel, through Beazley Passage, to Okisollo Channel. It has become the chosen scenic route north and is exceedingly popular with recreational boaters in the summer months. Because it's best to transit the narrows with the tidal turn to your advantage, be courteous and give priority to craft taking the last of a tide.

The southern tip of Maurelle Island, Peck and Goepel Islands in the Settlers Group and a small portion of Quadra Island are provincial parks, ideal for kayakers who practise low-impact camping.

Not to scale. Not to be used for navigation.

SURGE NARROWS PUBLIC WHARF, READ ISLAND

CHARTS 3537. 3312, page 20.

APPROACH

From the W out of Hoskyn Channel. Leave the port-hand (green) buoy to the N when approaching the public wharf and from the S if planning to anchor.

ANCHOR

Temporary anchorage in the one-boat bight as indicated, with the bow pointing W and a stern line ashore. Fair holding in gravel and kelp in depths of 4–8 m (13–26 ft).

PUBLIC WHARF

A small facility mainly used by locals, but visitors are always welcome.

Note: The Surge Narrows Store is closed—please tie up only at the public wharf. Take care while docking because strong back eddies swirl around the wharf.

Dreamspeaker *in the bight just north of the public wharf.*

Each Monday, Wednesday and Friday, mail is delivered to and collected from the dock post office, where a small book exchange offers some interesting titles. From here you can stretch your legs and walk to the island school and playground or hike to Evans Bay.

A small one-boat anchorage to the northwest of the public wharf offers protection from the southeast and is a good spot to wait for slack water in Beazley Passage if the dock is full. *Dreamspeaker* and crew spent a night anchored here with plans to hike to Read Island Provincial Park and take a refreshing swim in Rosen Lake (8 km/5 miles). The following morning gusty northwest winds buffeted the boat about, making it time to head west and take advantage of slack water at Beazley Passage.

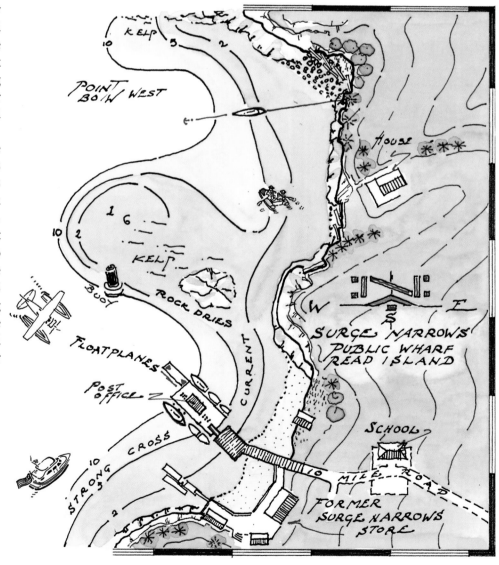

Not to scale. Not to be used for navigation.

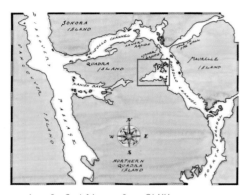

❋ 1) 50° 16.1' N   125° 12.8' W
❋ 2) 50° 17.1' N   125° 13.2' W

CHARTS 3537. 3312, page 21.

APPROACH

If you are approaching from the E, S of Octopus Islands, the entrance is best transited at LW when the rocks and reefs are visible. For an alternative approach from the N, see 11.7 (page 148).

ANCHOR

Protected anchorage can be found throughout the bay or in one of its numerous coves and nooks. Depth, holding and bottom condition vary, but holding is generally good in mud.

Note: To protect the portage trail's natural heritage and beauty, BC Parks is endeavouring to acquire the land between Waiatt Bay and Small Inlet. However, the majority of the southern shoreline in Waiatt Bay is now part of Octopus Islands Marine Park.

During summer months, the numerous nooks and crannies in spacious Waiatt Bay offer a peaceful alternative to the more popular anchorages in OCTOPUS ISLANDS MARINE PARK. The bay's waters are also a Parks Protected Area set aside for recreational use only.

A spot we named "Cabin Cove" on Waiatt Bay's northern shore offers good holding and accommodates five or six boats comfortably. The rock and pebble beach is backed by a grassy foreshore. Land beyond the high-water mark is private.

"Trail Cove" (also our name) at the head of the bay has a smooth pebble beach and plenty of room to swing. It's worth spending some extra time here to explore SMALL INLET MARINE PARK. A shaded portage trail (Small Inlet Provincial Park Protected Area) takes you on a leisurely half-mile ramble through tranquil, second-growth forest and concealed middens to the head of Small Inlet (see top inset chart page 147). From here you can take the path to Newton Lake for a refreshing, warm-water swim or a more energetic hike to Granite Bay (see page 156).

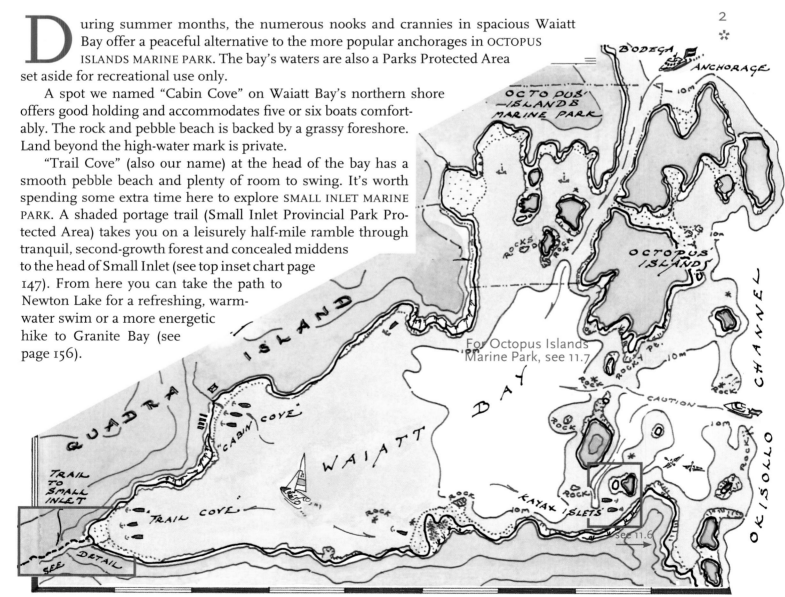

Not to scale. Not to be used for navigation.

"Kayak Islets," Waiatt Bay, 11.6
Octopus Islands marine Park

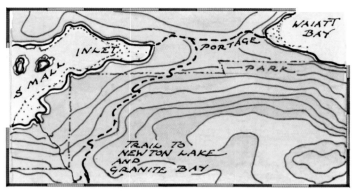

Inset detail: The portage trail between Waiatt Bay and Small Inlet.

CHARTS 3537. 3312, page 21.

APPROACH

See 11.5 (page 146), Waiatt Bay.

ANCHOR

Temporary anchorage, exposed to westerly winds. Depths of 3–6 m (10–19.5 ft), holding good in mud.

The exposed rocks we dubbed "Kayak Islets" are part of Octopus Islands Marine Park, and provide a peaceful haven for kayakers and boaters alike. They are best navigated at low water to avoid the numerous submerged rocks. Outboards and generators are definitely not welcome in this back-to-nature retreat populated by a variety of intriguing wildlife and the colourful tents of fellow campers. The flat sunbathing rocks on the southwest shore also provide a convenient ramp for beaching a kayak or dinghy. For the longest evening light, drop your hook in the small cove southeast of "Kayak Islets."

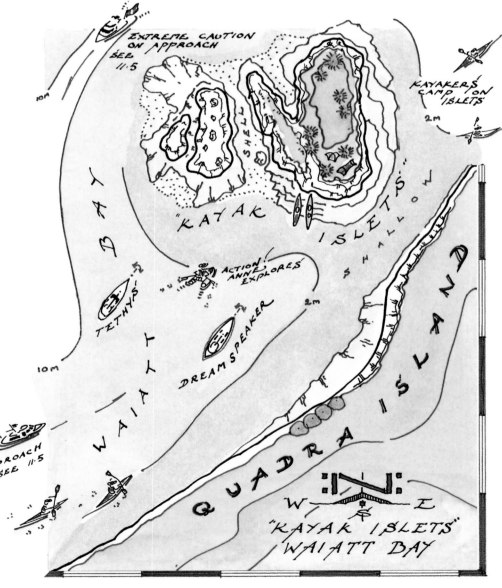

Not to scale. Not to be used for navigation.

A boat gets lucky in "Kayak Islets."

11.7 OCTOPUS ISLANDS MARINE PARK, QUADRA ISLAND

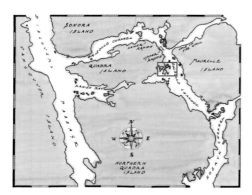

✻ 50° 17.1′ N   125° 13.2′ W

Find a nook, drop the hook and take a line ashore.

Looking over Waiatt Bay to the Octopus Islands.

The sheltered coves of OCTOPUS ISLANDS MARINE PARK are neatly tucked into the northeast corner of Waiatt Bay and offer the cruising boater refuge between the tidal passes and an opportunity to take it easy while enjoying life's simple pleasures.

Although extremely popular in the summer months, with boats rafted together and tied back to every available tree, the anchorages empty out rapidly each day as boaters on tight schedules move on to the next desirable location. If you have the time, stay awhile and explore the rocky islets by dinghy, kayak or paddle board. Most boaters try to avoid the use of noisy outboards and generators within the park, thereby making life quieter and wildlife-spotting far easier.

We named "Osprey Cove," the larger of the two coves, after a pair of local birds that performed an incredible diving routine. The cove can accommodate a good number of boats, especially when stern lines are used. Shoal-draft anchorage is possible in a cozy nook to the west, where drying mud flats, a freshwater creek and an open grassy area provide the perfect facilities for kayakers to set up camp. An alternative campsite with a view is concealed above the rocky point in a secluded mossy glen.

There is certainly no room to swing in what we call "Tentacle Cove," but there are many choice, snug spots to drop your anchor, and the rocky perimeter of the cove is backed by lush forest, which almost reaches into your cockpit. One of the most desirable stern-to anchorages can be found along the foreshore of a wooded islet lying between the two coves. Early arrival is advised if you plan to claim this spot.

Because there are no major trails through the park, it's fun to explore the scattered islets at low water by foot. An easy climb to the top of "Pinnacle Rock" (our name) rewards you with an excellent view over the islands, while the smooth, sloping boulders below are great for sunbathing and swimming. The two larger islands are private and fires are prohibited.

CHARTS 3537. 3312, page 21.

APPROACH

From the N out of Bodega Anchorage via a narrow passage W of the Octopus Islands. The centre channel of this passage is free of dangers, but numerous rocks fringe the passage and entrances to the anchorages. Dead-slow speed and a bow lookout are recommended.

ANCHOR

There is good shelter from the prevailing westerly and northwesterly summer winds. Stern lines ashore are recommended because swinging room is often limited. Depths of 2–4 m (6.5–13 ft), holding good over mud.

Note: For alternative southern approaches, see 11.5 (page 146).

Boats tuck into every nook and cranny.

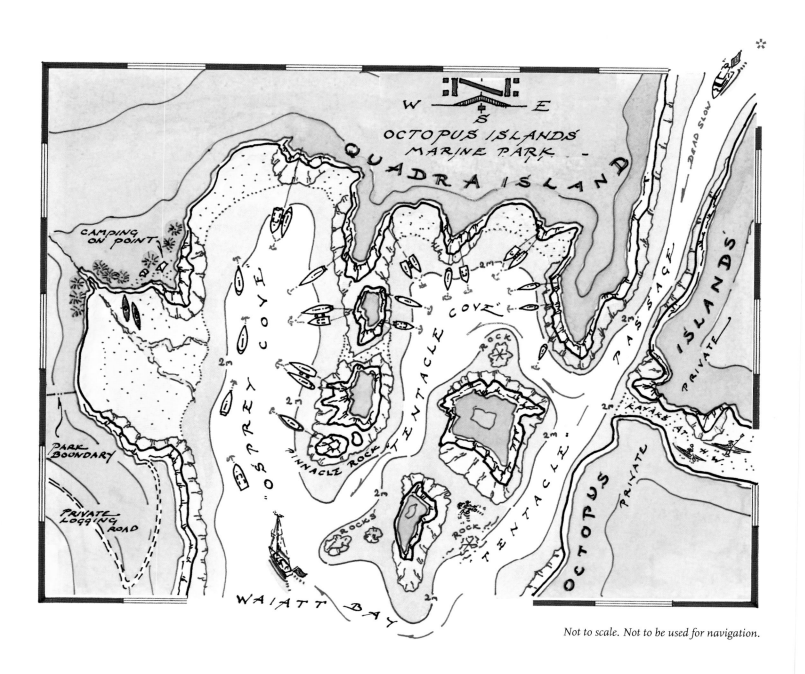

Not to scale. Not to be used for navigation.

11.8 HOLE IN THE WALL, UPPER RAPIDS & OWEN BAY

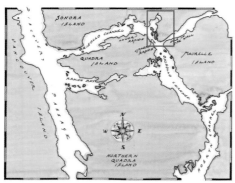

CHARTS 3537. 3312, page 21.

APPROACH OWEN BAY

From the SW, favouring Grant Island's western shoreline to avoid being swept by the currents onto the rocks off Walters Point.

ANCHOR

Sheltered anchorage is available throughout Owen Bay. Depths vary, but the holding is good in mud.

Approaching Hole in the Wall.

Snug in the NW corner of Owen Bay.

HOLE IN THE WALL

Hole in the Wall is literally that! A narrow passage, complete with rapids at the western end, links Okisollo to Calm Channel (Chapter 8). The secondary current station lies centre channel off the western end of Hole in the Wall (adjacent to the light shown on the chart), recording 12 knots flood and 10 knots ebb. Hole in the Wall should only be navigated at or near slack water. Duration of slack is less than 5 minutes.
Reference current station: Hole in the Wall
Direction of flood: NE

Note: Don't forget to add 1 hour in periods of daylight saving time. The eastern entrance experiences a tidal stream of up to 2 knots.

UPPER RAPIDS

The Upper Rapids lie E of Cooper Point and W of the numerous islands that shelter Owen Bay on Sonora Island. The secondary current station lies NW of Bentley Rock, which dries 1.0 m (3.3 ft) and is unmarked. Currents at both flood and ebb are recorded at 9 knots. The overfalls and eddies are extremely dangerous, and the rapids should only be navigated at or near slack water.
Reference current station: Seymour Narrows
Direction of flood: SE

OWEN BAY

Owen Bay offers a quiet retreat with ample anchorage and sheltered nooks and crannies to explore by dinghy or kayak. Legend has it that the spectacular sheer cliff on the NW shore was created by a wayward meteorite. The public wharf is usually filled with local boats; good anchorage is possible off the wharf.

Local residents welcome visitors, although they do request that due respect be paid to private property, as even the most tumbledown building has an owner!

Note: Beware of two unmarked rocks that dry NW of Francisco Island, S of Etta Point, Okisollo Channel.

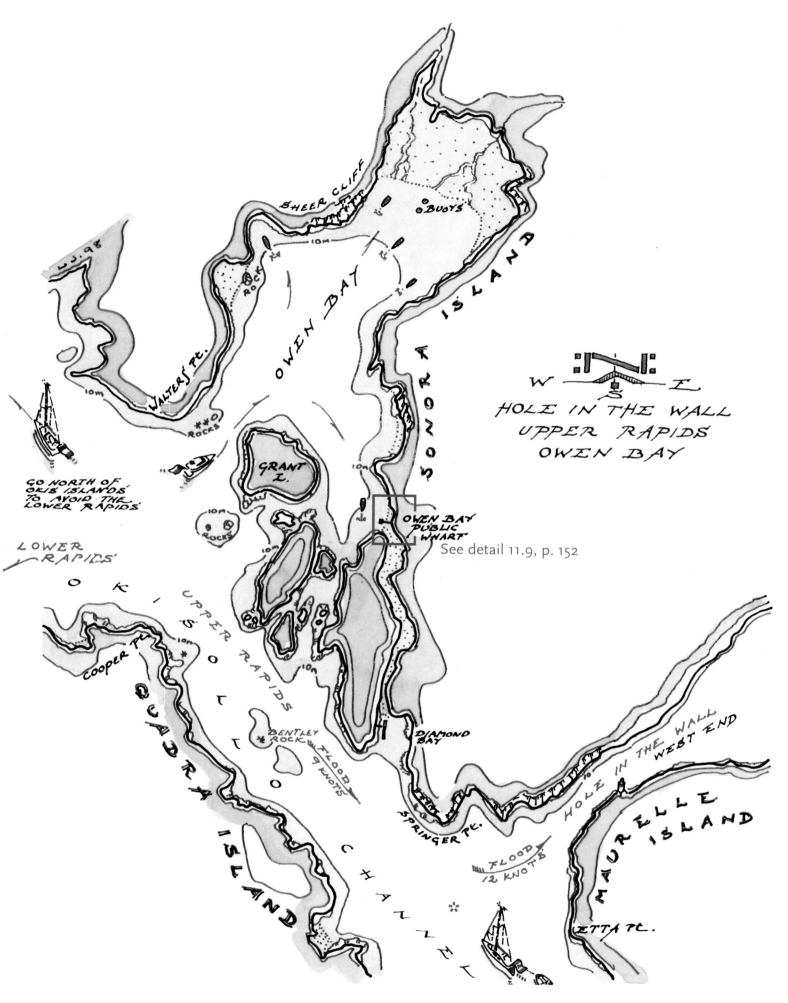

HOLE IN THE WALL
UPPER RAPIDS
OWEN BAY

W — S — E

SHEER CLIFF

BUOYS

OWEN BAY

10M

D.J.98

WALTERS PT.

ROCK

**O ROCKS

GO NORTH OF
OKIS ISLANDS
TO AVOID THE
LOWER RAPIDS

SONORA ISLAND

GRANT I.

10M ROCKS

10M

OWEN BAY
PUBLIC
WHARF

See detail 11.9, p. 152

LOWER
RAPIDS

O K I S O L O

UPPER RAPIDS

10M

10M

COOPER PT.

QUADRA ISLAND

BENTLEY
ROCK

FLOOD
9 KNOTS

DIAMOND
BAY

HOLE IN THE WALL WEST END

MAURELLE
ISLAND

SPRINGER PT.

FLOOD
12 KNOTS

C H A N N E L

ZETTA PT.

Not to scale. Not to be used for navigation.

11.9 OWEN BAY PUBLIC WHARF, SONORA ISLAND

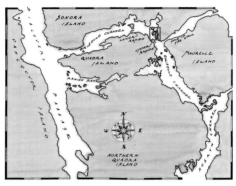

APPROACH

The Owen Bay public wharf lies in the SE corner of the bay.

ANCHOR

Good all-weather anchorage can be found NW of the public wharf. Depths of 4–8 m (13–26 ft), holding good in mud.

✿ 50° 18.7' N   125° 13.5' W

PUBLIC WHARF

A small facility, with moorage usually taken up by local craft.

Note: Exploration of the channels between the islands S of the public wharf by dinghy or kayak isn't recommended because the tidal currents rush between them at a remarkable speed.

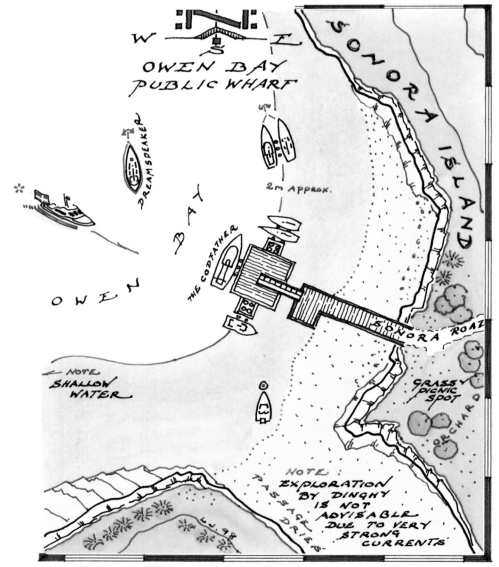

Not to scale. Not to be used for navigation.

Once home to a bustling community, Owen Bay was practically deserted by the early 1950s. A new generation of pioneers has now settled on the island, attracted by its peaceful lifestyle, beautiful surroundings and convenient location.

Although the Owen Bay public wharf needs repairs, it has a low-key charm and is usually filled with local boats. Good anchorage is possible off the wharf in a spot that holds the light well into the evening. The lovely wild apple orchard above the dock produces tasty fruit and leads to a trail that joins the main Sonora Road. An inviting, grassy picnic spot below the orchard is often a gathering place for islanders.

Owen Bay public wharf.

"DIAMOND ISLETS," OKISOLLO CHANNEL

CHARTS 3537. 3312, page 21.

APPROACH

From the SW out of Okisollo Channel. The Islets appear as a small oasis against the more rugged Maurelle Island shoreline.

ANCHOR

Temporary anchorage is possible in the bight between the southern islet and Maurelle Island. A stern line ashore is advisable. Depths of 2–4 m (6.5–13 ft), holding good in mud and shell.

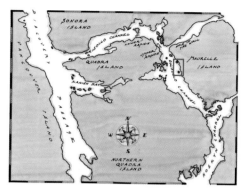

✳ 50° 16.3' N   125° 11.6' W

These enchanting islets we call "Diamond Islets" invite you to stay for a while and enjoy their tranquility. The tiny cove provides quiet, temporary anchorage and makes a perfect one-boat picnic stop. There are plenty of nooks and crannies to explore, and at low water it's fun to poke around the rocky pools formed between the three islets.

You can take a stern line back to one of the trees on the big islet. Its rocky shoreline offers smooth sunbathing boulders that gently slope down into the cool, clear water, and a short climb will take you up to the flat, mossy viewpoint that looks over Okisollo Channel to Waiatt Bay and the popular Octopus Islands.

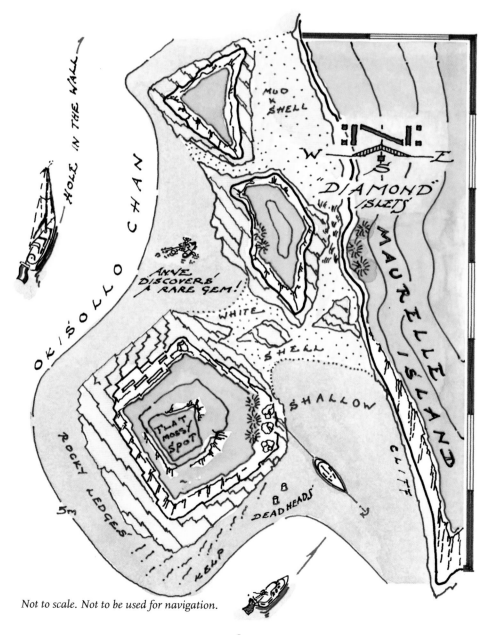

Not to scale. Not to be used for navigation.

Anne, Tink *and* Dreamspeaker *aglow in the filtered light.*

11.11 Kanish Bay, Quadra Island

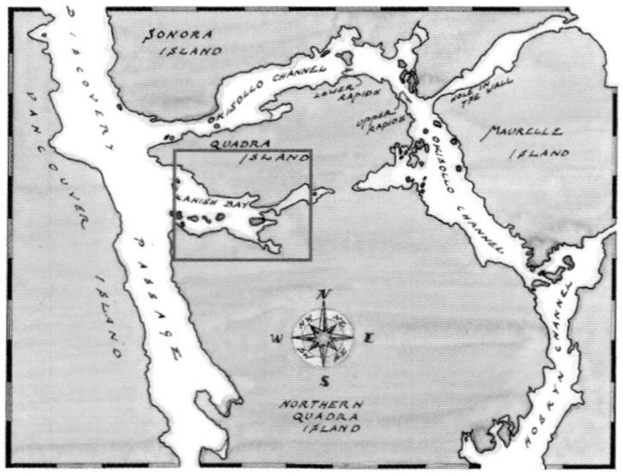

50° 15.6' N 125° 22.3' W

CHARTS 3539. 3312, page 23.

APPROACH

From the W out of Discovery Passage. The passage between Bodega Point and the Chained Islands is fringed by rocks and best navigated at low water, when the reef and rocks are clearly visible. The passage north of the Chained Islands is deep all the way into Kanish Bay and free of natural obstructions.

ANCHOR

There are numerous temporary anchorages within the bay. The tail end of westerly winds within Johnstone Strait often penetrates deep into the bay. Depth, holding and bottom conditions vary.

Although this large bay is open to the west, it offers shelter in several temporary anchorages that are well worth investigating. What we call "Canoe Rock," en route to Granite Bay, warrants a stop at low water because a white-shell beach is suddenly revealed. Numerous First Nations villages once occupied the head of Kanish Bay, and ancient kitchen middens can be found in the area.

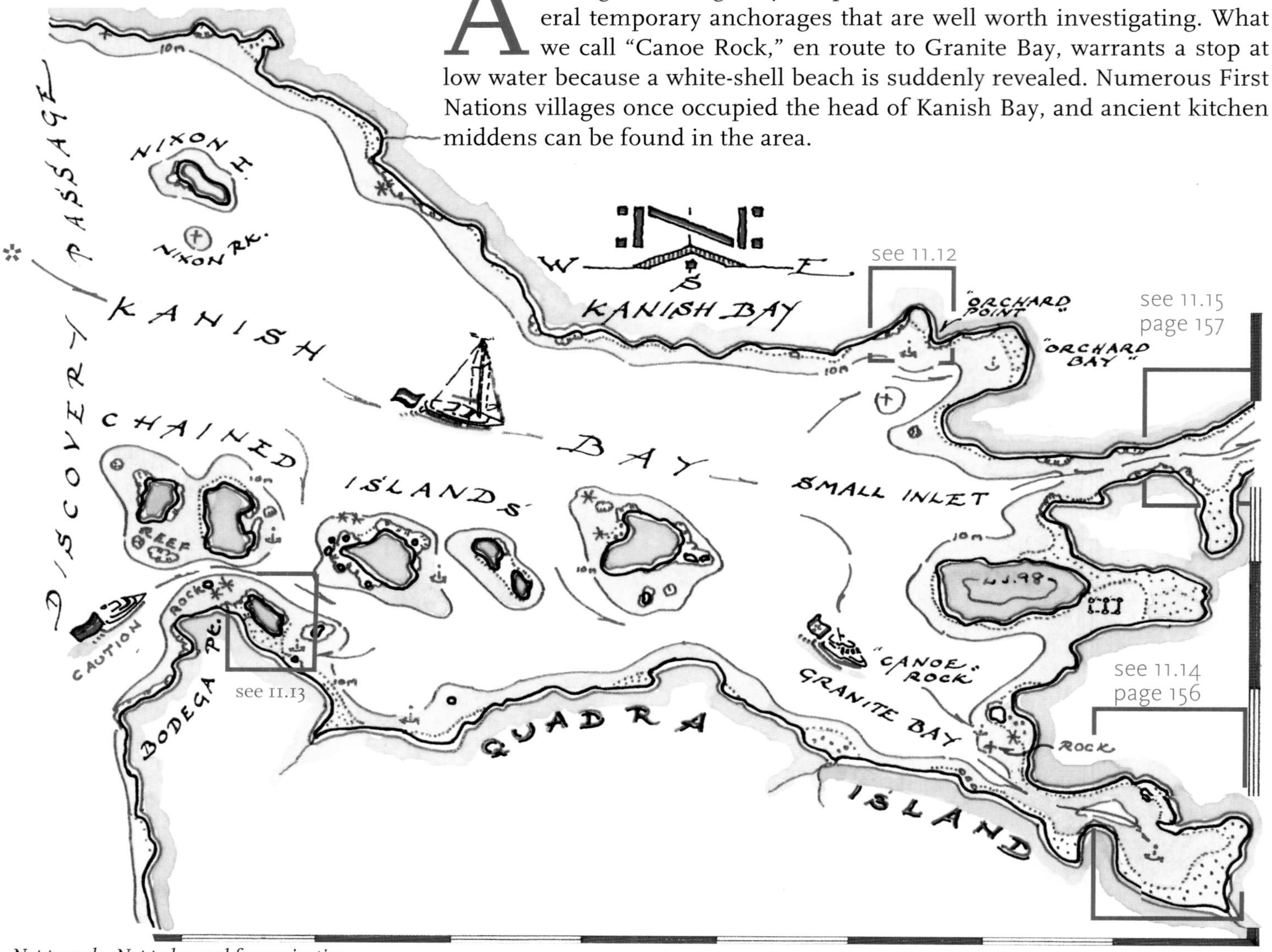

Not to scale. Not to be used for navigation.

"ORCHARD POINT," KANISH BAY

ANCHOR

Temporary picnic stop off the shell and mud beach. Depths of 6–8 m (19.5–26 ft), holding moderate in mud, rock and shell.

Tucked into the northeast corner of Kanish Bay, the place we call "Orchard Point" offers an idyllic picnic spot steeped in history. Once the site of a prosperous First Nations village, the ancient midden is now covered by an overgrown meadow and wild orchard, reminiscent of more recent pioneering history. The plum and apple trees are laden with fruit in season, and a small creek brings fresh water down to the shell and pebble beach, abundant with squirting clams at low water.

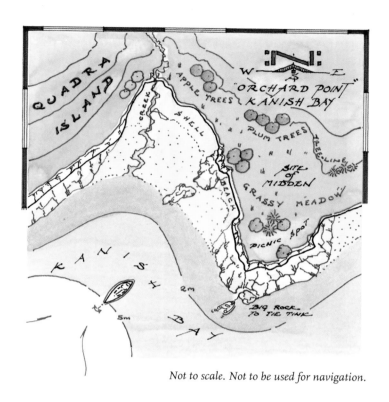

Not to scale. Not to be used for navigation.

"Canoe Rock" at low water.

BODEGA POINT, KANISH BAY

ANCHOR

To the E of the lagoon. This is an anchorage for one or two boats and offers fair protection from westerlies. Depths of 2–4 m (6.5–13 ft), holding moderate over rock and mud.

The anchorage behind Bodega Point, southeast of what we call "Link Islet," provides a pleasant temporary anchorage. Protected from westerly and northwesterly winds, you can relax and swing in the back eddies, pick fresh sea asparagus or walk along the grassy isthmus to enjoy an uninterrupted view across Discovery Channel.

Not to scale. Not to be used for navigation.

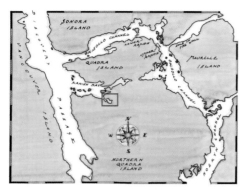

✳ 50° 14.6' N   125° 19.2' W

CHARTS 3539. 3312, page 23.

APPROACH

Granite Bay lies in the SE corner of Kanish Bay. A rock with less than 2 m (6 ft) of water over it lies N of the outer entrance. Stay in the centre channel of the passage because it is free of hazards.

ANCHOR

The anchorage is protected from the chop that sometimes forms in Kanish Bay. At times, though, the westerly winds responsible for the chop funnel into Granite Bay at speeds equal to those reported at Chatham Point Light. Depths of 4–8 m (13–26 ft), holding moderate to good in mud.

Note: The community float is reserved for local craft.

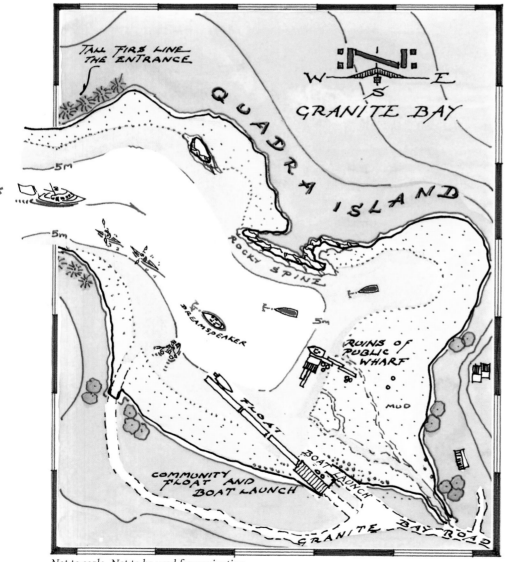

Not to scale. Not to be used for navigation.

As you enter the sheltered waters of Granite Bay, you may find it hard to imagine it as a thriving community of over 500 people in the early 1900s. Neglected remains of an old public wharf give the bay a bit of a desolate air, but the friendly locals, who own many of the rustic summer cabins, enjoy its peace and solitude.

There is a kayak and small-boat launch at the end of the road that links Granite Bay with Southern Quadra Island, giving public access to the road and trail to Granite Lake. Peaceful overnight anchorage can be found in the centre of the bay.

Ruins of the public wharf in Granite Bay.

SMALL INLET, QUADRA ISLAND

CHARTS 3539. 3312, page 23.

APPROACH

The narrow entrance to Small Inlet lies in the NE portion of Kanish Bay and has a minimum depth of 4 m (13 ft). Kelp lines the entrance passage on either side, and although it appears to block the channel in places, safe entry is possible with careful navigation in the centre of the channel. There is no significant current here.

ANCHOR

Good all-weather protection can be found throughout the inlet. Depths vary, and holding is good in mud and shingle. Entrance to the inner basin is best attempted at LW, when the rocks are visible.

CAUTIONARY NOTE

A strong NW wind in Johnstone Strait will funnel into and through the inlet. The southern nook and inner basin offer the best protection.

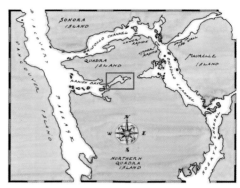

✿ 50° 15.2' N   125° 19.0' W

Once you have successfully navigated Small Inlet's restricted channel, the bay opens up to reveal the tranquil waters of a sizeable all-weather anchorage. Surrounded by lush forest and with abundant wildlife, it is ideal territory to explore by kayak or dinghy. An early First Nations portage trail, found at the head of the inlet, takes you through dappled second-growth forest and past ancient middens to a lovely pebble beach in Waiatt Bay (see page 146). A hand-carved driftwood sign also leads you to Newton Lake, a pleasant 1.6 km (1 mi) hike and the possibility of a refreshing warm-water swim. Granite Bay is a more energetic 5 km (3 mi) trip but worth the effort if you've been boat-bound for a few days (see page 156).

View to Waiatt Bay, end of Portage Trail.

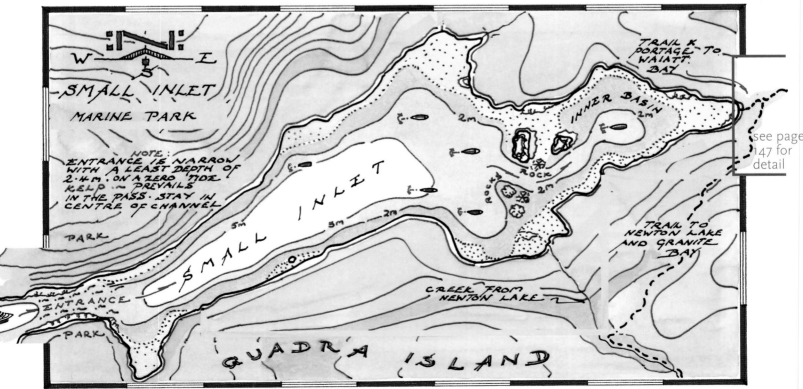

see page 147 for detail

Not to scale. Not to be used for navigation.

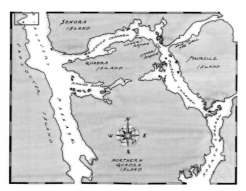

✤ 50° 19.5' N   125° 26.4' W

CHARTS 3539. 3312, page 24.

APPROACH

Otter Cove anchorage from the E, out of Discovery Passage, N of Limestone Island.

ANCHOR

At the head of the cove. Good shelter from the westerlies that rocket down Johnstone Strait and the currents that prevail in Discovery Passage. Depths of 4–10 m (13–33 ft), holding good in mud, sand and shell.

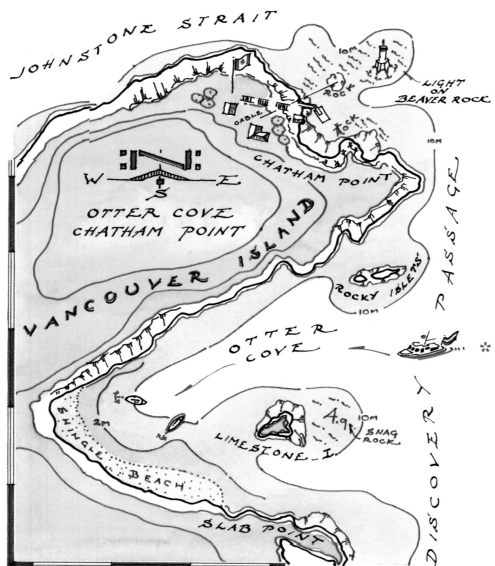

Not to scale. Not to be used for navigation.

Well protected from westerly winds, Otter Cove provides a convenient spot to stop and relax while waiting for the turn of the tide or calmer wind conditions in Johnstone Strait. The anchorage is apparently unaffected by the strong currents and tidal turmoil outside its entrance, which is best navigated between the Rocky Islets and Limestone Island.

Although an extended visit here may not be part of your itinerary, it's a pleasant spot to wait and take stock before continuing on your trip.

While the land surrounding Otter Cove is private, the cove itself is part of Rock Bay Marine Park.

Looking north up Johnstone Strait.

SEYMOUR NARROWS

Seymour Narrows looking north from Maud Island.

Maud Island anchorage.

Chapter 12
SEYMOUR NARROWS

TIDES

Canadian Tide and Current Tables, Volume 6
Reference Port: Owen Bay
Secondary Ports: Bloedel, Seymour Narrows, Brown Bay

CURRENTS

Reference Station: Seymour Narrows

WEATHER

Area: Johnstone Strait
Reporting Stations: Chatham Point, Campbell River, Cape Mudge

CAUTIONARY NOTE

The strong westerly winds in Johnstone Strait penetrate S into Seymour Narrows. Strong southeasterlies in the summer are less common, but if forecast these winds intensify in strength within the confines of the narrows. Fog, although rare in summer, may drift down from Johnstone Strait and blanket the narrows in the morning hours.

CAUTIONARY NOTES

If you've miscalculated slack and the flood is literally taking you S, try to steer the boat between what's left of Ripple Rock and the Maud Island shore, where less turbulent water can be found.

When trying to power against a counter-current, boaters run the risk of overheating their engines.

Seymour Narrows lies midway between Cape Mudge and Chatham Point in Discovery Passage, the primary route to the northern coastal waters of British Columbia and Alaska. The narrows create a tidal pass where slack water is a timekeeper for even the largest commercial vessels.

Since the removal of Ripple Rock (see page 162), Seymour Narrows is now relatively deep and without obstructions. However, perpetual tidal currents, dangerous whirlpools, overfalls and turbulent waters still exist. With up to 16 knots of current on the flood and 14 knots on the ebb (flooding S and ebbing N), it still ranks as one of the most dangerous tidal passes in the world.

Recreational boaters are advised to be as wise as commercial skippers to the time of slack water in Seymour Narrows. Keep in mind that cruise ship captains time their passage north from Vancouver and south from Alaska on slack water at the narrows.

SLACK WATER

The reference current station is mid-channel between Maud Island and Wilfred Point, under the hydro lines. This is the narrows proper, where you should be at slack water if the tide is turning in your favour. Slack water lasts for only 12–15 minutes, and the narrows are eight nautical miles north from the Campbell River Public Wharf and eight nautical miles south from the entrance to Kanish Bay. (At 5 knots, your journey will take 12 minutes for a mile; at 6 knots, it will take 10 minutes, so timing your arrival at slack water is everything!)

Missing the slack and trying to power against the current creates one of the real hazards of this pass, because it accommodates a heavy flow of commercial traffic, and it is common to see vessels come to a standstill. If you are attempting a northbound transit and have missed slack at the pass, convenient anchorage at Maud Island is a good spot to wait out the tide. This is also the dive site of the HMCS *Columbia*. BROWN'S BAY MARINA (see 12.2, page 164) presents a similar opportunity for southbound boaters. Moor at one of the new floats and then enjoy a meal at the floating restaurant and a peaceful night before tackling the famous Seymour Narrows.

FEATURED DESTINATIONS

NORTHBOUND

It is advisable to stay overnight in the Campbell River vicinity, where good moorage and anchorage can be found (see 13.1, page 168). Proceed on the last hour of the flood so that you arrive at the narrows at slack water, with the turn to the ebb helping your journey north. If you are taking the last of the ebb north, time slack water at Brown Bay and you should get past Separation Head before the flood has time to build.

SOUTHBOUND

Good overnight anchorage can be found in Small Inlet, Quadra Island (see 11.15, page 157). It's best to proceed during the last hour of the ebb so that you arrive at the narrows at slack water, with the turn to the flood helping your journey south. If you are taking the last of the flood south, time slack water at Race Point and you should get to a safe moorage or anchorage in the Campbell River vicinity before the ebb has time to build.

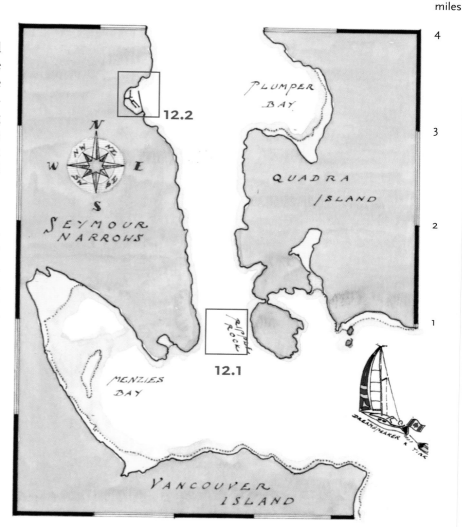

nautical miles

Not to be used for navigation.

12.1   RIPPLE ROCK—THE HISTORY

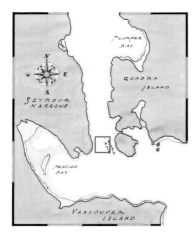

50° 7.9' N   125° 21.2' W

9:31 a.m., April 5, 1958. PHOTOGRAPH COURTESY OF THE CANADIAN HYDROGRAPHIC SERVICE.

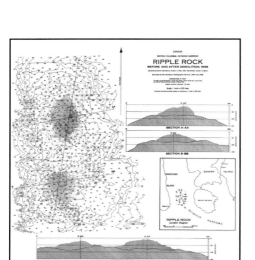

Ripple Rock before and after demolition.
COURTESY OF THE CANADIAN HYDROGRAPHIC
SERVICE.

R ipple Rock, which, prior to 1958, lay just nine feet below chart datum, was once the scourge of Seymour Narrows. Together with ferocious currents, overfalls and boat-swallowing whirlpools on all sides, it has claimed 114 lives and sunk or badly damaged at least 100 small craft and more than 20 large ships, many of them American vessels.

Determined to remove this costly shipping hazard and encouraged by the US government, the Canadian government began extensive research, and several plans for removal were considered over the years. The first attempt, in 1942, ended in tragedy when a workboat anchored over the rock was sucked into a whirlpool and all nine men aboard drowned.

Finally, in 1953, a proposal previously shelved due to expense was renewed. The twin heads of Ripple Rock had to be removed forever. In 1955, Canada's Department of Public Works, together with a team of CHS surveyors, set out to build a tunnel from Maud Island, under the narrows, to the dangerous rock. Three years later, Seymour Narrows made international news: at 9:31 a.m. on April 5, 1958, the world's largest non-nuclear explosion, using 1,400 tons of explosives, blasted rock over 300 metres (1,000 ft) into the air and briefly emptied nearby Menzies Bay of most of its water. Spectators included curious scientists from around the world and apprehensive local residents who feared that an aftermath of tidal waves and earthquakes would destroy their homes, but their fears were never realized. The "big blast" was over in minutes, wave action and rubble settled, the air cleared and a charted depth of 13 m (45 ft) replaced menacing Ripple Rock.

Schematic drawing showing the mining of Ripple Rock. COURTESY OF THE CANADIAN HYDROGRAPHIC SERVICE.

The "big blast" at Ripple Rock in 1958 was the largest non-nuclear human-made explosion in history. PHOTOGRAPH
COURTESY OF THE CANADIAN HYDROGRAPHIC SERVICE

12.2　BROWN'S BAY MARINA

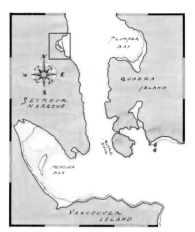

✳ 50° 9.8' N　125° 22.2' W

CHARTS 3539 (inset). 3312, page 23.

APPROACH
From the E. A floating breakwater of former oil barrels protects the marina. Enter N of the breakwater.

MARINA
Brown's Bay Marina, 250-286-3135, has extensive visitor moorage for boats up to 100 feet and monitors VHF 66A. Power, water and free Wi-Fi on the docks.

FUEL
Fuel barge at the marina; gasoline, diesel, ice, bait, fishing tackle, licences, marine supplies, snacks and ice cream.

BOAT LAUNCH
Private, at the marina.

CAUTIONARY NOTE
When approaching the fuel barge or a designated moorage, exercise caution because strong tidal currents sweep through the bay.

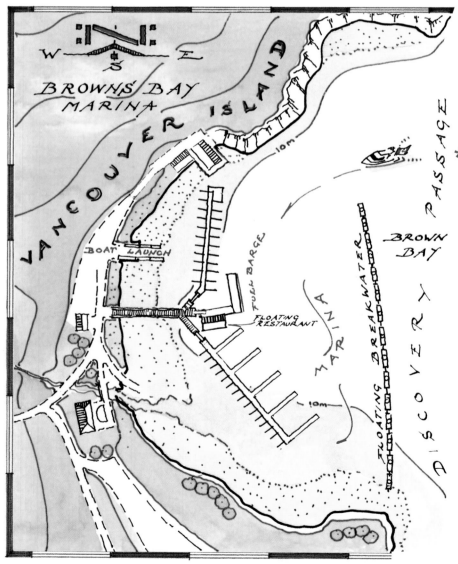

Not to scale. Not to be used for navigation.

Entrance to marina from Discovery Passage.

Located just north of Seymour Narrows in sheltered Brown Bay, the efficiently run BROWN'S BAY MARINA is conveniently situated for boaters transiting Discovery Passage or waiting for slack water in Seymour Narrows. The marina offers comfortable moorage for boats of all sizes. Shower and laundry facilities are available and the tackle shop sells live bait, fishing licences and marine supplies. If you have time, take a break from the galley and enjoy fresh Dungeness crab or fish and chips in the floating restaurant overlooking Discovery Passage.

Chapter 13

CAMPBELL RIVER & SOUTHERN QUADRA ISLAND

*Boats anchoring at the tip of Rebecca Spit with
the* Cortes Queen *steaming to Whaletown.*

Rebecca Spit Marine Park.

Chapter 13
CAMPBELL RIVER
& SOUTHERN QUADRA ISLAND

TIDES

Canadian Tide and Current Tables, Volume 6
Reference Port: Campbell River
Secondary Ports: Quathiaski Cove, Gowlland Harbour

CURRENTS

Reference Station: Seymour Narrows

Note: Currents in Discovery Passage, S of Seymour Narrows, reach 6–7 knots off Campbell River and 7–9 knots off Cape Mudge. The flood tidal stream sets S and the ebb N through Discovery Passage.

WEATHER

AREA: Johnstone Strait, Northern Strait of Georgia
REPORTING STATIONS: Chatham Point, Campbell River, Cape Mudge

Note: The strong westerly winds in Johnstone Strait penetrate S into Discovery Passage. Strong southeasterlies (less common in summer) intensify within the confines of Discovery Passage. Fog, although rare in summer, usually blankets Discovery Passage in the morning but dissipates by early afternoon.

CAUTIONARY NOTE

Cape Mudge should be approached with caution because Wilby Shoals extends a considerable distance S from Quadra Island. Even in light southeasterly winds and against a flooding current, dangerous seas can be generated over the shoals and right across the entrance to Discovery Passage. These conditions present an extreme hazard to all craft.

C onveniently located and well serviced by land, sea and air, Campbell River has fast become a major rendezvous and provisioning stop for cruising boaters and yacht-charter companies that view it as a gateway to the Discovery Islands and Desolation Sound.

Quadra Island, the largest of the Discovery Islands, lies at the northwestern end of the Strait of Georgia. Cape Mudge Lighthouse, perched above the 61-metre (200-foot) cliffs on the island's southern tip, affords stunning vistas and has witnessed the sinking of numerous ships off Wilby Shoals.

The hazards of Cape Mudge aside, the shoreline of Southern Quadra Island is a delight to explore, enticing the cruising boater with a selection of excellent marinas, provisioning stops and anchorages, with magical Rebecca Spit Marine Park being the jewel in the crown. To best enjoy all that this lovely island has to offer, go all out and rent a bike, join a sunset kayaking expedition or pick up a map and hike the many scenic trails that criss-cross the island from Cape Mudge Lighthouse in the south to Newton Lake in the north.

On the island's western shoreline, peaceful Gowlland Harbour offers sheltered anchorage, pockets of wilderness and a quiet moment to enjoy the fascinating seal population. Comfortable overnight moorage, numerous lodge amenities and fine dining are available at the renowned APRIL POINT RESORT AND MARINA, and Quathiaski Cove, a short ferry ride from Campbell River, is a charming provisioning stop with all the amenities, including an excellent bakery, supermarket and colourful farmers' market in the summer months. The HERIOT BAY INN AND MARINA, on Quadra's eastern shore, has a charm all its own and is a favourite rendezvous for locals and ferry passengers en route to Cortes Island. Juicy blackberries in season and free delivery to your boat are included when provisioning at the nearby HERIOT BAY TRU VALUE FOODS.

Rebecca Spit Marine Park, celebrated as one of our oldest and most loved marine parks, entices the cruising boater year after year to its sheltered waters, picnic meadows, sandy beaches and groomed trails. From here you can pop over to Open Bay for some warm-water swimming or to Moulds Bay for a peaceful picnic. With Heriot Bay and its amenities close by, this is the perfect spot to begin or end a voyage cruising the Discovery Islands and Desolation Sound.

FEATURED DESTINATIONS

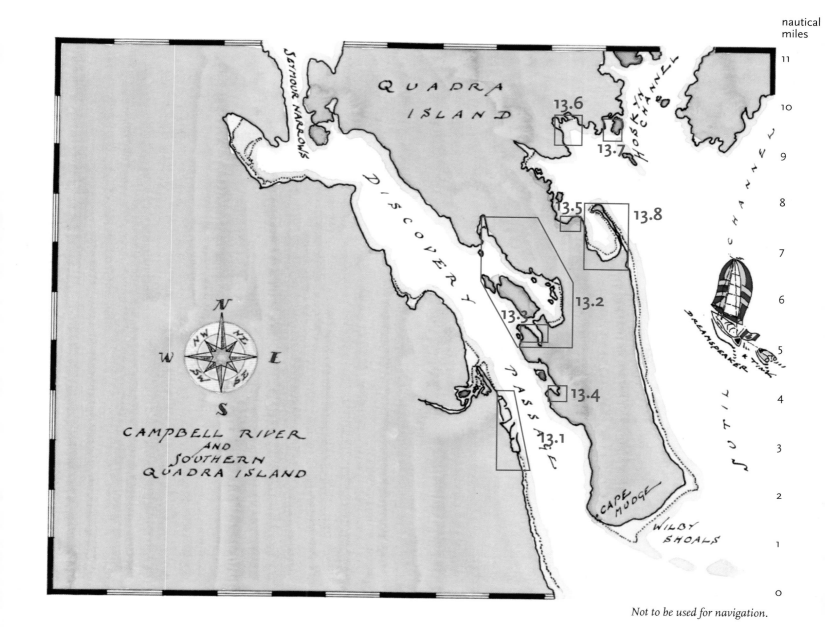

Not to be used for navigation.

13.1 Downtown Campbell River

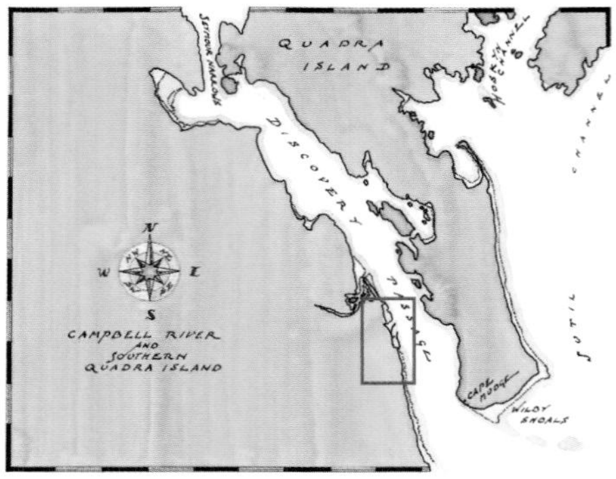

✲ 50° 1.3' N 125° 13.9' W

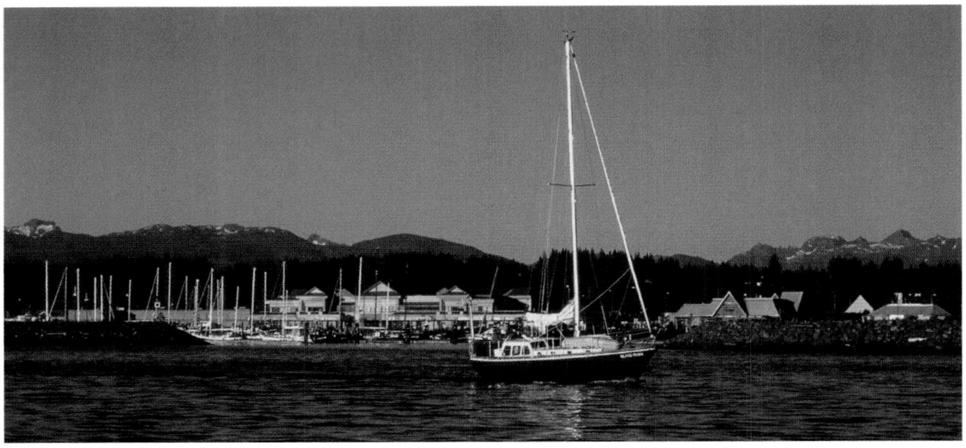

Sailboat departing Discovery Harbour Marina.

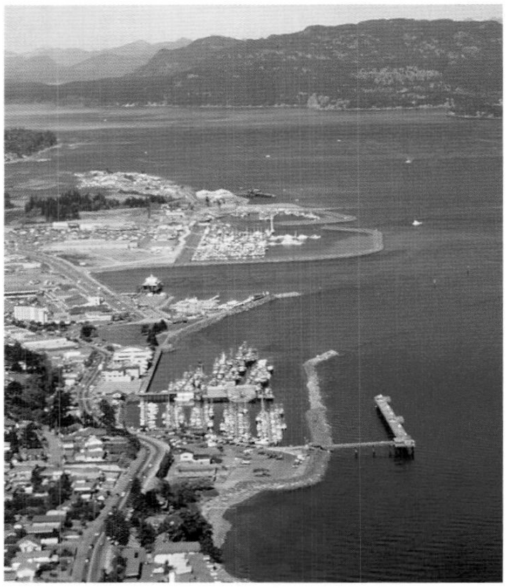

Downtown Campbell River from the north.

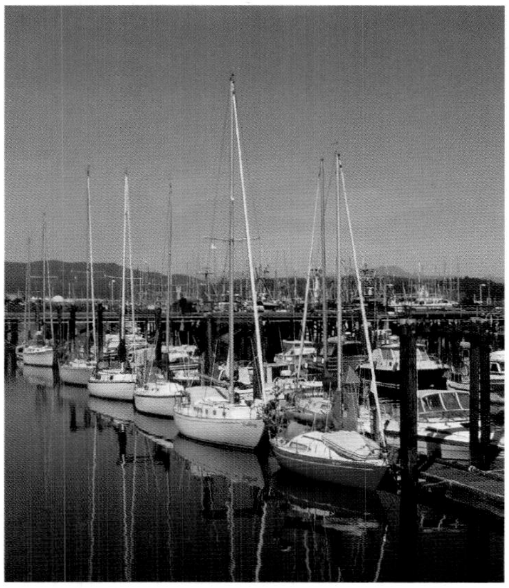

Visitors at the public wharf.

Although Campbell River built its reputation over the years as a centre for excellent sport fishing, it is now recognized as a gateway to the popular Discovery Islands and Desolation Sound. Known locally as "The River," Campbell River, easily accessible by land, sea and air, provides excellent provisioning facilities and offers three diverse marinas to choose from—one being the welcoming public wharf, just south of the downtown core. Sheltered by a substantial breakwater and the longest fishing pier in Canada, the wharf provides shower and laundry facilities and the opportunity to buy fresh-caught fish from the local fishermen. DICK'S FISH & CHIPS, across from Fisherman's Wharf, is highly recommended. A visit to the nearby MUSEUM AT CAMPBELL RIVER, which has an excellent display of hand-carved First Nations masks, is certainly worthwhile. It offers special summer events and guided historical and nature tours.

The COAST MARINA offers full facilities and is situated adjacent to the Quadra Island Ferry Terminal and the Robert V. Ostler (Foreshore) Park. Just across the road is the TYEE PLAZA & SHOPPERS ROW. Here you'll find a variety of bookstores, shops and cafés, including a large supermarket, pharmacy, post office, cold-beer-and-wine store and an excellent laundromat. The VISITOR INFORMATION CENTRE, CAMPBELL RIVER ART GALLERY and historic TIDEMARK THEATRE are also located here. All community buses service the plaza and the DISCOVERY HARBOUR SHOPPING CENTRE.

The large DISCOVERY HARBOUR MARINA with full facilities is backed by the DISCOVERY HARBOUR SHOPPING CENTRE, a vast complex complete with waterfront restaurants, gift stores and banks. The complex includes THE REAL CANADIAN SUPERSTORE, CANADIAN TIRE and METRO LIQUOR STORE. Don't miss the WEI WAI KUM HOUSE OF TREASURES, a gallery and store featuring original art from First Nations artists on Vancouver Island. The marina, developed by the Wei Wai Kum First Nation, is busiest in July and August, especially on weekends. The RIPTIDE, just up from the docks, offers a waterfront pub, restaurant, Wi-Fi, ice, a liquor store and shower and laundry facilities.

OCEAN PACIFIC MARINE SUPPLY provides a fully stocked marine store and excellent boat yard with a 110-ton Travelift. They are also able to perform repairs on boats in the water using their 200 feet of working dock space. Call 250-286-1011.

Note: Campbell River is a Canada Customs port of entry. Customs offices are located at the Coast Marina and Discovery Harbour Marina.

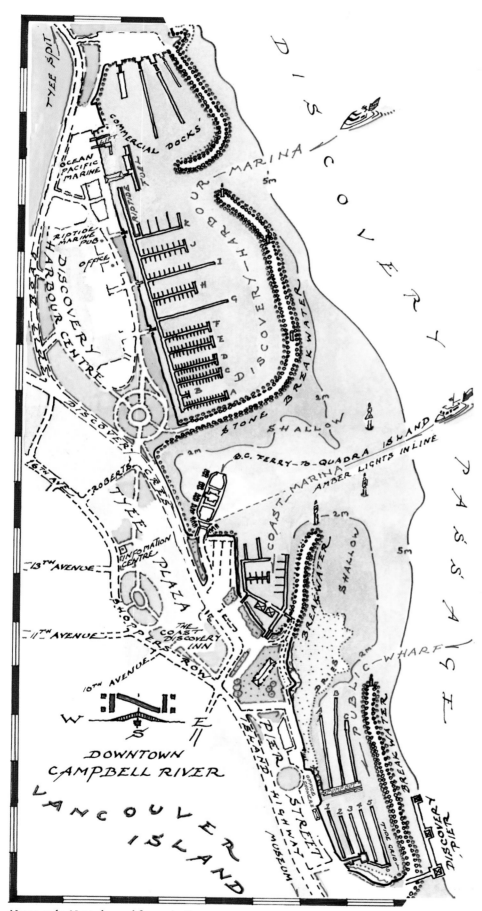

Not to scale. Not to be used for navigation.

CHARTS 3540. 3312, page 18.

APPROACH

At or near slack water for all the downtown marine facilities. At any other time, allow ample sea room to counter the S-flowing flood or N-flowing ebb tide.

PUBLIC WHARF

Fisherman's Wharf is managed by Campbell River Harbour Authority, 250-287-7931, VHF 66A—call when outside the breakwater to be assigned a slip. Open year-round. Usually ample visitor moorage; rafting permitted. Water and power up to 50 amps (one 100 amp) and Wi-Fi on the docks. Pump-out facility on "C" dock. Good shower and laundry facilities and garbage drop-off. Tide grid available.

MARINAS

The Coast Marina, 250-287-7455, VHF 66A. Open year-round. Reservations recommended. Keep a careful lookout for the ferry arriving or departing. The two amber lights that come into line at 245° true are the range lights for the ferry. They can be used as a navigational aid by cruising boaters. Moorage for boats up to 180 ft. Water and power up to 100 amps and Wi-Fi on the docks. Showers in the marina office building. Laundry facilities at Tyee Plaza. Moorage open to NW winds.

The Discovery Harbour Marina, 250-287-2614, VHF 66A. Open year-round. Has extensive visitor moorage and can accommodate boats up to 200 ft. Reservations essential during July and August. Water, Wi-Fi and power up to 50 amps on the docks. If 100 amp single-phase and three-phase power is required, please request in advance. Shower and laundry facilities and garbage drop-off available.

FUEL

At Discovery Harbour Fuel Sales, 250-287-3456, VHF 66A. Open year-round. Gasoline, diesel, oil and filters, marine parts, guides, ice and convenience items.

Notes: An extensive float plane and helicopter terminus is located just N of Discovery Harbour marina, behind Tyee Spit. The only two lift facilities in the area covered in this guide are at Ocean Pacific Marine and Jack's Boat Yard (see page 49) in Lund.

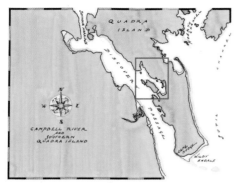

❀ 1) 50° 5.1' N   125° 15.2' W
❀ 2) 50° 3.9' N   125° 14.4' W

CHARTS 3540. 3312, page 18.

APPROACH

From the W, entering N of the Vigilant Islets. Favour the Vigilant Islets side because the shallows off Entrance Rock and Entrance Bank lie to the N.

ANCHOR

Reasonable all-weather anchorage can be found in the harbour and is a favourite with large yachts. Depths vary, holding good in mud.

MARINAS

Gowlland Harbour Resort, 250-830-8179. Breakfast and dinner by reservation. Moorage available while visiting or staying at the lodge. Spa includes sauna, hot tub and small gym.

Seascape Waterfront Resort. At the time of writing, the resort, with its moorage, was up for sale.

Sheltered by Gowlland Island, the peaceful anchorage in Gowlland Harbour offers you refuge and the opportunity to discover five lovely islets protected as provincial park reserves. Vigilant, Wren, Crow, Fawn and Mouse Islets are ideal for exploration by kayak, canoe or dinghy, providing visitors with individual pockets of wilderness and a quiet moment to commune with the fascinating seal population.

Boaters can anchor behind Vigilant Islets and between Crow and Fawn Islets. Less quiet anchorage, but protected from southerly winds, can be found in the southern portion of the harbour. The navigable boat passage nearby is used by small speedboats taking a shortcut to April Point, but it shouldn't be attempted without thorough local knowledge because of the strong tidal currents, mid-channel rocks and shallow depths.

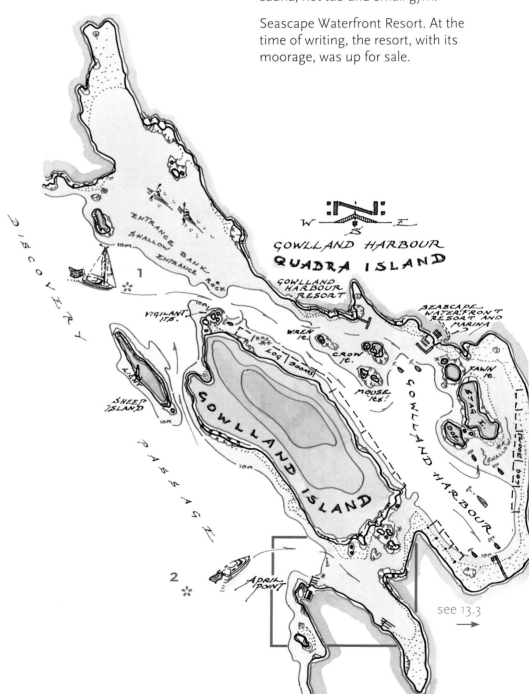

Not to scale. Not to be used for navigation.

see 13.3 →

APRIL POINT RESORT & MARINA, QUADRA ISLAND

CHARTS 3540. 3312, page 18.

APPROACH

From the W, leaving the starboard-hand (red) buoy to the S.

ANCHOR

Good anchorage with fair shelter can be found N of the marina. Depths of 4–6 m (13–19.5 ft), holding good in mud.

MARINA

April Point Marina, 250-285-2222, VHF 66A. Full-service marina with visitor moorage, power (up to 100 amps), water and Wi-Fi on the docks; the airy laundry room is the best spot for Wi-Fi reception. Complimentary showers and cube-ice machine. Scheduled float plane service by Kenmore air.

Note: There's a shallow sandbar S of the starboard-hand (red) buoy. Float plane operations are frequent in the busy summer months.

Totem pole at April Point Resort.

The original APRIL POINT RESORT AND MARINA was founded by the Peterson family in 1945. The resort is just a short walk from the marina and overnight moorage includes the use of all resort and spa amenities.

With a magnificent view of Discovery Passage, the resort and its surrounding cottages offer rustic luxury that includes hot tubs, Jacuzzi baths and cozy fireplaces. Although sport fishing is one of the key activities, kayaking and ecotours are also offered. The meals are as impressive as the surroundings and feature favourite classics with a West Coast twist. Lunch and dinner guests can tie up at the visitors' dock adjacent to the main lodge. Step into the sensory bliss of the AVEDA SPA set amidst manicured gardens and centred on a tranquil pool. The spa is housed in a Japanese-inspired studio with open views across Discovery Passage.

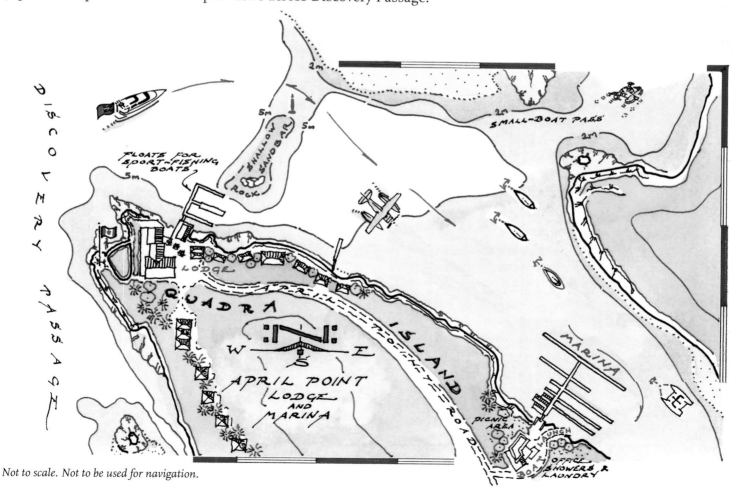

Not to scale. Not to be used for navigation.

13.4 QUATHIASKI COVE, QUADRA ISLAND

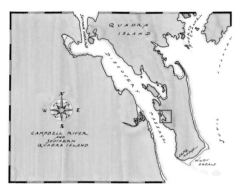

✳ 50° 2.6' N   125° 13.4' W

The public wharf looking north from Whiskey Point Resort.

The public wharf is primarily for commercial vessels, but there's room if you're prepared to raft.

Known locally as "Q. Cove" and only a 15-minute ferry ride from Campbell River, Quathiaski Cove has a charming island plaza that provides a pleasant alternative to shopping in the big city. The island's main road also connects the cove to Heriot Bay and the Cortes Island ferry.

Space for local and visiting boats is possible at the welcoming public wharf although rafting is the norm. Q-BEANS COFFEE KIOSK, at the ferry landing, specializes in good coffee to go, and THE LANDING PUB offers great food, local beer and a cozy meeting place for visitors and locals waiting for ferry connections. ORCA LAUNDRY provides clean and airy laundry facilities and is located at the plaza.

THE PLAZA and COVE CENTRE are just a short walk up the hill from the public wharf and house a variety of shops, gift stores, two quite diverse health product stores, a post office and a credit union with an ATM; pick up an informative Quadra Island trail map from the VISITOR INFORMATION booth opposite.

The LOVIN' OVEN PIZZERIA AND CAFÉ bakes heavenly loaves of bread that stay fresh for days, and its delicious, thick-crust pizza comes with unusual toppings. TRU VALUE FOODS, open 7 days a week, has a BC LIQUOR STORE outlet and carries bulk foods, specialty and organic produce. Pop into BOOK BONANZA, an excellent bookstore that stocks a diverse selection of local and international books and cards. Enjoy good food, including great salads and a cordial atmosphere on the small patio of the locally owned KAMELEON restaurant. A colourful outdoor farmers' market takes place at the COVE CENTRE every Saturday between May and September (10 a.m.–2 p.m.) and offers a selection of local preserves, baking and crafts.

Biking around beautiful Quadra Island is a lot of fun, and ISLAND CYCLE specializes in custom tours of the island—call 250-285-3627. Its "cultural excursion" tour stops at local artisan studios and the impressive NUYUMBALEES CULTURAL CENTRE. The "pedal and paddle" tour includes a day of cycling and kayaking and ends with a sunset barbecue.

CHARTS 3540. 3312, page 18.

APPROACH
From the W, keeping a sharp lookout for the ferry arriving or departing, because boaters are often taken by surprise when it rounds "Whiskey Point" en route to Campbell River.

ANCHOR
Anchorage is possible in the channel between Grouse Island and Quadra Island, but the holding is only moderate over a rocky bottom and varying depths. Alternative anchorage can be found at the mouth of Unkak Cove, north of Quathiaski Cove.

PUBLIC WHARF
Managed by Quadra Island Harbour Authority, 250-285-3622. This is a busy commercial facility. Be prepared to raft up. The wharf is subject to ferry wash and wake from passing boats. Water, power up to 50 amps and Wi-Fi available on the docks. Shower facilities in the office building. Good for a quick trip into the village.

BOAT LAUNCH
Public, adjacent to the wharf.

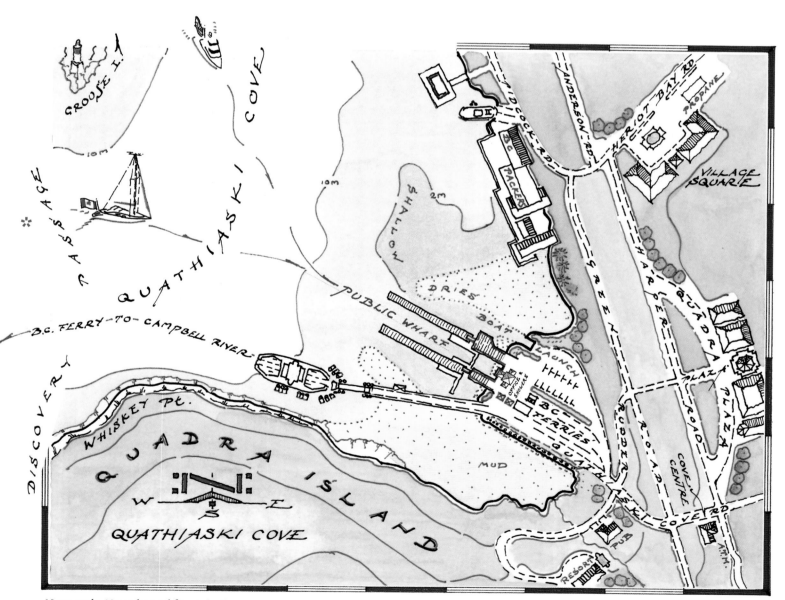

Not to scale. Not to be used for navigation.

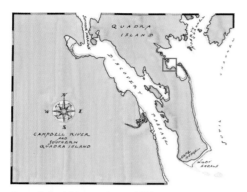

✳ 50° 6.5' N 125° 12.5' W

A sailboat and ferry cross paths in Heriot Bay.

Dreamspeaker at Heriot Bay Inn Marina.

Watching the ferry activity from the inn's lawn.

With a charm all its own, the HERIOT BAY INN AND MARINA provides a convenient stop to fuel, provision and enjoy the resort pub and restaurant. The delights of REBECCA SPIT MARINE PARK are just across the bay in Drew Harbour, and the Cortes Island ferry makes scheduled departures to Whaletown on Cortes Island from here. A short taxi ride will take you to Quathiaski Cove (see 13.4, page 172) to connect with the Campbell River ferry. The public wharf and the surrounding anchorage are often filled with local craft, but this is a good spot to tie up or anchor if space is available.

The marina has ample moorage for visiting boats, friendly staff, power and water on the docks (for drinking only) and shower and laundry facilities at the resort. Garbage drop-off is for a fee, although recycling is complimentary; propane is also available. The Heriot Bay Inn and pub is a popular rendezvous for locals, visitors and ferry passengers. Inviting HERONS restaurant has a large waterfront patio and serves breakfast, lunch and supper. Their West Coast-inspired menu includes fresh seafood specials and scrumptious oyster burgers. The resort gift store carries ice, books, guides and locally crafted gifts. Ocean-view cottages and a large RV campground are also part of this diverse complex. Quadra's hiking trails are extensive and well maintained and a detailed trail map is available at the inn store.

A short walk up the hill from the Heriot Bay Inn will take you to the HERIOT BAY TRU VALUE FOODS, complete with an in-house bakery, BC Liquor Store outlet and post office—the store offers a complimentary delivery service to the marina. WORKS OF H'ART, a gallery and gift store, showcases the work of over seventy local artists, artisans and craftspeople. The CONSIGNMENT SHOP across the way carries some marine supplies and a fascinating variety of new and used paraphernalia that will keep you amused for hours. To rent a bike or book a cycling tour that visits local artisan studios and the impressive NUYUMBALEES CULTURAL CENTRE, visit ISLAND CYCLE on Taku Road.

CHARTS 3539. 3312, pages 18 & 19.

APPROACH

From the NE, leaving the port-hand (green) buoy to the S. The ferry terminal, marina and public wharf are all close to one another.

ANCHOR

Moderately sheltered anchorage can be found among the local boats at anchor and on mooring buoys. Less congested and better protected anchorage is possible in the NW corner of the bay, in the lee of Heriot Island. Depths, holding and bottom condition unrecorded.

PUBLIC WHARF

Managed by Quadra Island Harbour Authority, 250-285-3555. Frequented by local craft. Be prepared to raft up. Water, power up to 50 amps and Wi-Fi available on the docks.

MARINA

The Heriot Bay Inn & Marina, 250-285-3322 or 1-888-605-4545, VHF 66A. Extensive visitor moorage, 50 amp power, water and Wi-Fi on the docks. Shower and laundry facilities at the inn. Reservations recommended.

BOAT LAUNCH

Public, adjacent to the public wharf.

FUEL

At the marina. Gasoline, diesel and propane available. Ice available at the inn store.

Note: Watch for the ferry manoeuvring adjacent to the marina. The afternoon northwesterly wind causes quite a chop in the bay, making moorage on the outside of the marina and public wharf rather bumpy.

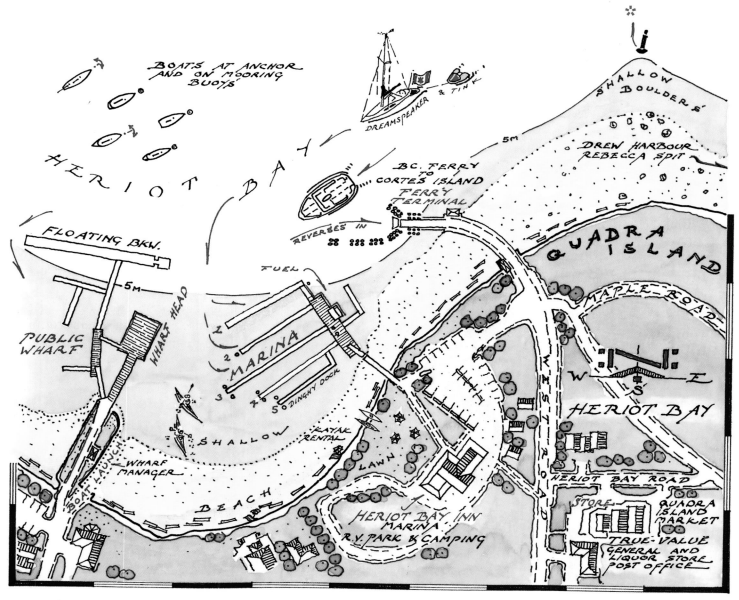

Not to scale. Not to be used for navigation.

13.6 Open Bay, Quadra Island

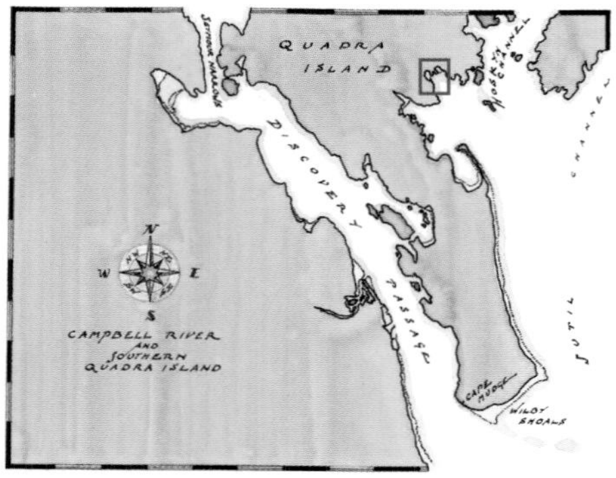

✲ 50° 8.0' N 125° 12.6' W

CHARTS 3539. 3312, page 19.

APPROACH
From the SE.

ANCHOR
Temporary anchorage, although sheltered from the W and NW, is totally exposed to the S. Depths of 4–8 m (13–26 ft), holding good over a sand and gravel bottom.

Note: Rather idyllic on a fine summer day but treacherous if the wind switches to the SE.

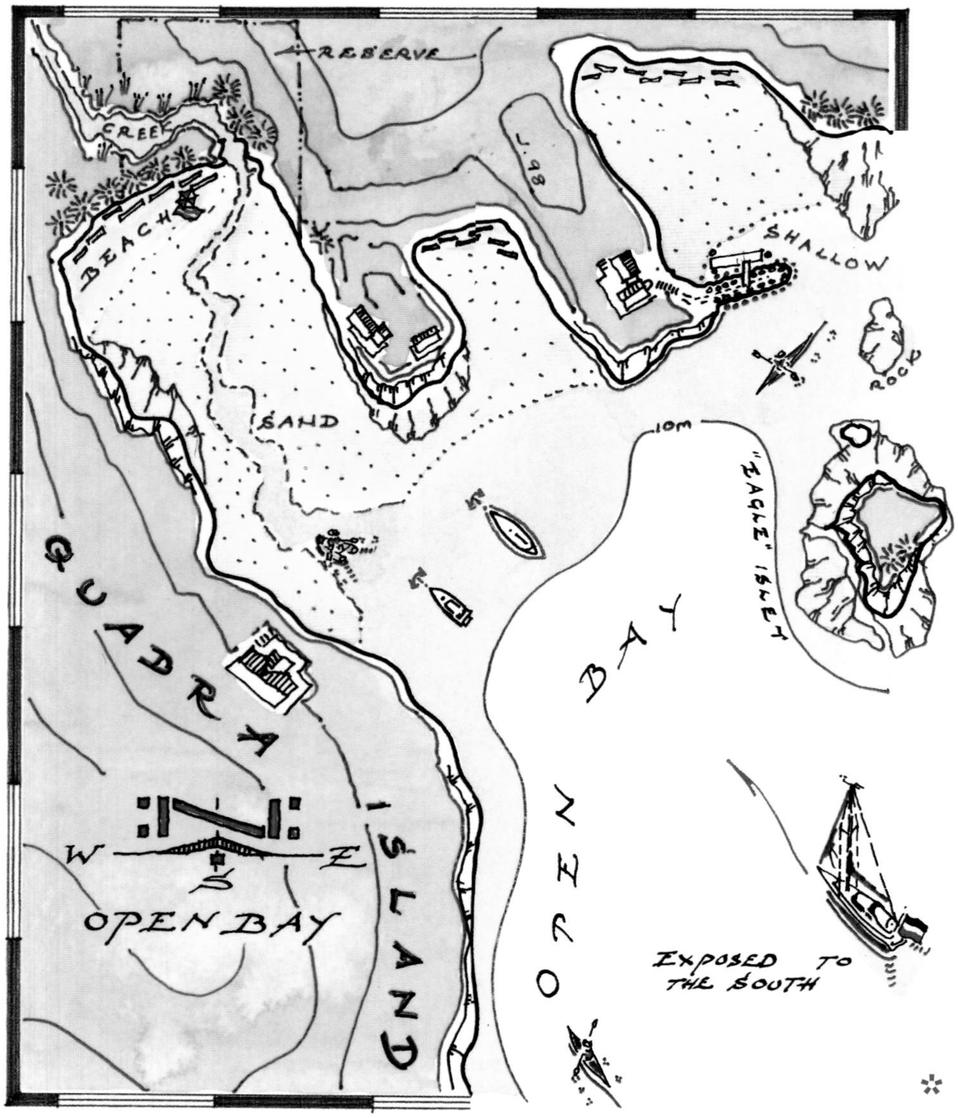

Not to scale. Not to be used for navigation.

On a sunny day when the tide begins to cover the exposed stretch of sand, Open Bay offers fine warm-water swimming. It is a glorious picnic stop for boaters and kayakers, with a freshwater estuary sheltering plants and wildlife and a stream flowing down onto the beach. At low tide, it's fun to explore the pools teeming with small fish, crabs and other fascinating sea life. There are rocks for climbing and weathered logs to sit on, and what we call "Eagle Islet" is great to explore by dinghy, but don't forget your binoculars.

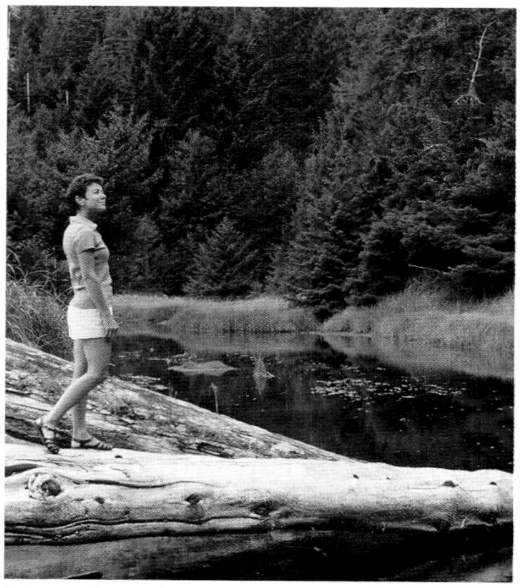

The creek north of Open Bay beach.

CHARTS 3539. 3312, page 19.

APPROACH

From the S, W of the Breton Islands. The passage to Hoskyn Channel has a minimum depth of 7.9 m (26 ft) mid-channel.

ANCHOR

Temporary anchorage, sheltered from all quarters except the S. Depths of 6–12 m (19.5–39 ft), holding moderate over a rock and shingle bottom.

Note: Although the Breton Islands provide some protection from southeasterly winds, chop still enters the bay.

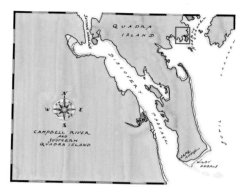

✳ 50° 8.0' N   125° 11.4' W

A small, perfectly serene tea or lunch stop awaits you in Moulds Bay, and the most wonderful rock formations criss-crossed with colourful fissures can be found while you explore the northeast corner by dinghy or kayak. A log-strewn pebble beach is backed by private property, with a blue-roofed cabin tucked away in the tall trees. Kayakers exploring the nearby Breton Islands and boaters looking for a peaceful spot often pop into this quiet, unassuming bay. Private boundaries should be respected.

Kayaks transit Moulds Bay.

Not to scale. Not to be used for navigation.

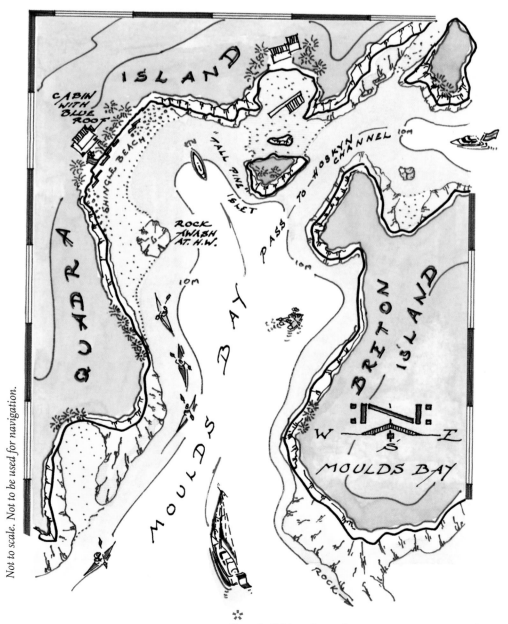

13.8 REBECCA SPIT MARINE PARK, DREW HARBOUR, QUADRA ISLAND

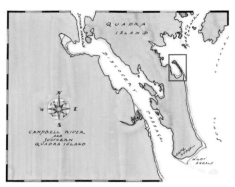

✽ 50° 6.6' N   125° 12.0' W

CHARTS 3539. 3312, pages 18 & 19.

APPROACH

From the NE out of Sutil Channel, giving the tip of the spit a wide berth, especially at HW. Maintain a wake-free speed after clearing the tip.

ANCHOR

The spit offers moderately sheltered anchorage along its western side. Drew Harbour affords ample swinging room for larger craft in the S and protection from SE winds. Anchor in depths of 6–12 m (19.5–39 ft). Holding good over a sand/mud and gravel bottom.

MARINA

The Taku Resort (250-285-3031 or 1-877-285-8258, VHF 66A) has sturdy docks, visitor moorage and the use of all resort facilities. Water, power up to 50 amps and Wi-Fi on the docks—reservations recommended. Shower and laundry facilities at the resort.

BOAT LAUNCH

Public in the marine park. Private at Taku Resort.

Note: In a strong northwesterly wind, a chop will often build W of Rebecca Spit's tip. For the best protection tuck in E of the tip and take a stern line ashore.

Our friends aboard Squib, *anchoring off Rebecca Spit.*

A sunset stroll on the spit.

Magical Rebecca Spit creates a natural breakwater on Drew Harbour's eastern side and is celebrated as one of British Columbia's oldest and most loved marine parks. Year after year, it continues to entice boaters to its sheltered waters, picnic meadows, shaded trails and gently sloping beaches. With Heriot Bay and its amenities close at hand (see 13.5, page 174), this is the perfect spot to begin or end a voyage while cruising the Discovery Islands and Desolation Sound.

A favourite of Quadra Island residents, the park provides maintained trails for running, cycling, walking the dog or just taking a leisurely stroll, and suitably placed benches welcome you to relax and enjoy the breathtaking view. The sand and shingle beaches on either side of the spit are wonderful to explore, and they offer safe warm-water swimming on the inside and a log-strewn beachcombing paradise on the outside.

Its history as a First Nations fortress between the 16th and 18th centuries, and its survival after an earthquake in the 1940s, make Rebecca Spit an intriguing though fragile landmark. To protect the spit from additional erosion today, the park has been designed for day use only. Picnic tables and fire pits are provided for comfortable family get-togethers, pit toilets are placed at convenient intervals and water is available from a hand pump located near the park's information shelter.

The park has also become a popular kayaking destination, and overnight camping facilities are available at the nearby WE WAI KAI CAMPSITE. Shower and laundry facilities are available and a small convenience store sells ice, pop and snacks.

The TAKU RESORT AND MARINA on Drew Harbour's western shoreline provides moorage, sturdy docks, tenting sites for kayakers, self-catering cottages and shower and laundry facilities. Moorage includes all the resort amenities. If at anchor, dinghy over to the beach south of the resort; it's just a short walk from the beach up Taku Road to provision at the HERIOT BAY TRU VALUE.

To enjoy one of the best spots in Drew Harbour, tuck into the northwest tip of the spit, take a line ashore, adjust your watch to "island time" and then sit back and enjoy a glorious view out to the islands and beyond.

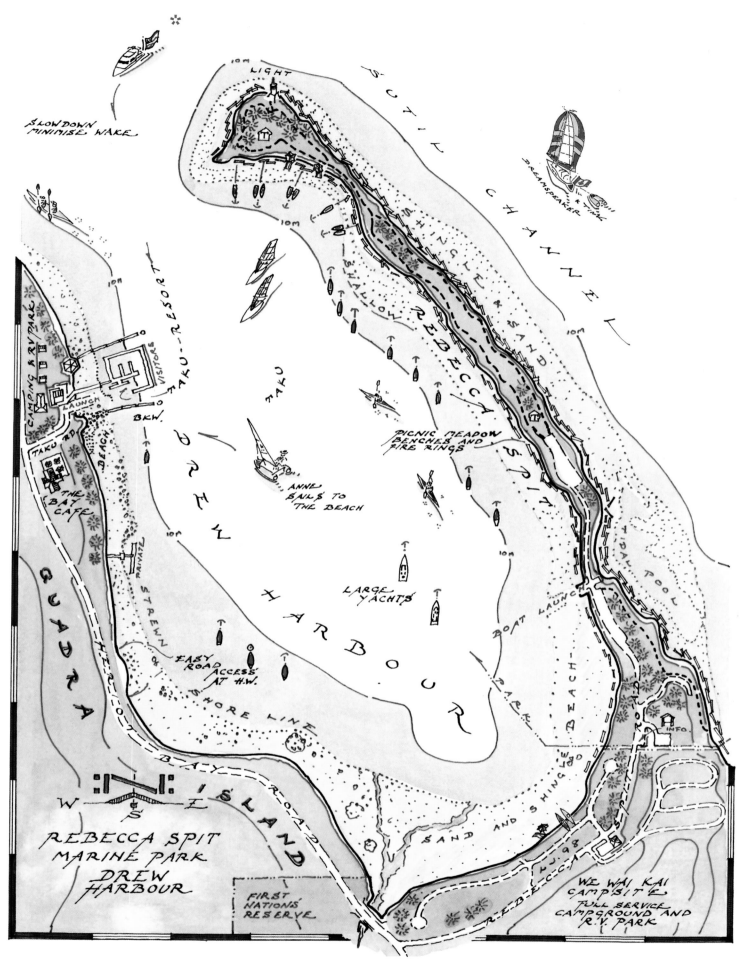

SLOWDOWN
MINIMISE WAKE

SCOTLAND CHANNEL

LIGHT

10M

10M

SHINGLE & SAND

SHALLOW

REBECCA

DREAMSPEAKER & TIME

CAMPING & RV PARK

VISITORS RESORT

TAKU RD

LAUNCH

BKW.

BEACH

TAKU

THE BAY CAFE

PRIVATE

STREWN

10M

DREW

TAKU

ANNE SAILS TO THE BEACH

PICNIC MEADOW
BENCHES AND
FIRE RINGS

10M

LARGE
YACHTS

SPIT

TIDAL POOL

BOAT LAUNCH

PARK

SAND AND SHINGLE BEACH

EASY
ROAD
ACCESS
AT H.W.

HARBOUR

SHORE LINE

QUADRA

HERIOT BAY ROAD

ISLAND

W   E
S

REBECCA SPIT
MARINE PARK
DREW
HARBOUR

FIRST NATIONS
RESERVE

INFO

SAND AND SHINGLE SPIT

REBECCA

WE WAI KAI
CAMPSITE
FULL SERVICE
CAMPGROUND AND
R.V. PARK

Not to scale. Not to be used for navigation.

SELECTED READING

Barber, James. *One Pot Wonders: James Barber's Recipes for Land and Sea*. Madeira Park, BC: Harbour Publishing, 2006.

_____. *The Genius of James Barber: His Best Recipes*. Madeira Park, BC: Harbour Publishing, 2008.

Baron, Nancy, and John Acorn. *Birds of Coastal British Columbia*. Edmonton: Lone Pine Publishing, 1997.

Blanchet, M. Wylie. *The Curve of Time*. Sidney, BC: Gray's Publishing, 1968.

Bunzel, Mark (ed), 2016 *Waggoner Cruising Guide*, Burrows Bay Associates, 2016 (published annually).

Clark, Lewis J. *Wild Flowers of British Columbia*. Madeira Park, BC: Harbour Publishing, 1998.

Clarkston, Bridgette. *A Field Guide to Seaweeds of the Pacific Northwest* (pamphlet). Madeira Park, BC: Harbour Publishing, 2015.

Eathorne, Alison Malone, Hilary Malone and Lorna Malone. *Sea Salt: Recipes from the West Coast Galley*. Madeira Park, BC: Harbour Publishing, 2013.

Emery, Maud. *Seagull's Cry*. Surrey, BC: Nunaga Publishing, 1975.

Harbo, Rick M. *A Field Guide to Seashells and Shellfish of the Pacific* (pamphlet). Madeira Park, BC: Harbour Publishing, 2009.

Harbord, Heather. *Desolation Sound: A History*. Madeira Park, BC: Harbour Publishing, 2007.

Hill, Beth. *Guide to Indian Rock Carvings of the Pacific Northwest Coast*. Surrey, BC: Hancock House Publishers, 1984.

_____. *Upcoast Summers*. Ganges, BC: Horsdal and Schubart, 1985.

Hudson, Phillipa. *A Field Guide to Coastal Flowers of the Pacific Northwest* (pamphlet). Madeira Park, BC: Harbour Publishing, 2011.

Jebda, Richard J. *A Field Guide to Edible Fruits and Berries of the Pacific Northwest* (pamphlet). Madeira Park, BC: Harbour Publishing, 2014.

Lawrence, Grant. *Adventures in Solitude: What Not to Wear to a Nude Potluck and Other Stories from Desolation Sound*. Madeira Park, BC: Harbour Publishing, 2010.

McDaniel, Neil. *A Field Guide to Sea Stars of the Pacific Northwest* (pamphlet). Madeira Park, BC: Harbour Publishing, 2009.

McKervill, Hugh. *The Salmon People*. Sidney, BC: Gray's Publishing, 1967.

The Museum at Campbell River. *The Raincoast Kitchen: Coastal Cuisine with a Dash of History*. Madeira Park, BC: Harbour Publishing, 1996.

Nelson, Michelle. *Field Guide to Foraging for Wild Greens and Flowers* (pamphlet). Madeira Park, BC: Harbour Publishing, 2015.

Obee, Bruce. *Coastal Wildlife of British Columbia*. Vancouver: Whitecap Books, 1991.

Pacific Yachting's Marina Guide and Boaters Blue Pages: The Complete Guide to B.C. Marinas and Marine Services. Magazine supplement (January issue), updated and published annually by *Pacific Yachting*.

Pinkerton, Kathrene. *Three's a Crew*. Ganges, BC: Horsdal and Schubart, 1940.

Scott, Andrew. *The Encyclopedia of Raincoast Place Names: A Complete Reference to Coastal British Columbia*. Madeira Park, BC: Harbour Publishing, 2009.

Snively, Gloria. *Exploring the Seashore in British Columbia, Washington, and Oregon: A Guide to Shorebirds and Intertidal Plants and Animals*. Vancouver: Gordon Soules Book Publishers, 1978.

Stewart, Hilary. *Looking at Indian Art of the Northwest Coast*. Vancouver: Douglas & McIntyre, 1979.

_____. *On Island Time*. Vancouver: Douglas & McIntyre, 1998.

Taylor, Jeanette. *The Quadra Story: A History of Quadra Island*. Madeira Park, BC: Harbour Publishing, 2009.

_____. *Tidal Passages: A History of the Discovery Islands*. Madeira Park, BC: Harbour Publishing, 2008.

_____. *River City: A History of Campbell River and the Discovery Islands*. Madeira Park, BC: Harbour Publishing, 1999.

Thommasen, Harvey, and Kevin Hutchings. *Birds of the Raincoast*. Madeira Park, BC: Harbour Publishing, 2004.

Turner, Nancy J. *Food Plants of Coastal First Peoples*. Vancouver: UBC Press, 1995.

Van der Flier-Keller, Eileen. *A Field Guide to the Identification of Pebbles* (pamphlet). Madeira Park, BC: Harbour Publishing, 2006.

Vassilopoulos, Peter. *Cruising to Desolation Sound, the Sunshine Coast & the Discovery Islands of BC*. Delta, BC: Pacific Marine Publishing, 2017.

_____. *Docks and Destinations*, Delta, BC: Pacific Marine Publishing, 2017.

_____. *Anchorages and Marine Parks*. Delta, BC: Pacific Marine Publishing, 2013.

Vipond, Anne and William Kelly. *Best Anchorages of the Inside Passage*, 2nd edition. Point Roberts, WA: Ocean Cruise Guides, 2015.

White, Howard, and Jim Spilsbury. *The Accidental Airline: Spilsbury's QCA*. Madeira Park, BC: Harbour Publishing, 1988.

_____. *Spilsbury's Coast*. Madeira Park, BC: Harbour Publishing, 1988.

Williams, Judith. *Clam Gardens: Aboriginal Mariculture on Canada's West Coast*. Vancouver, BC: New Star Books, 2006.

_____. *High Slack: Waddington's Gold Road and the Bute Inlet Massacre of 1864*. Vancouver, BC: New Star Books, 1996.

Winkler, Daniel. *A Field Guide to Edible Mushrooms of the Pacific Northwest* (pamphlet). Madeira Park, BC: Harbour Publishing, 2011.

INDEX

OTHER DREAMSPEAKER PRODUCTS

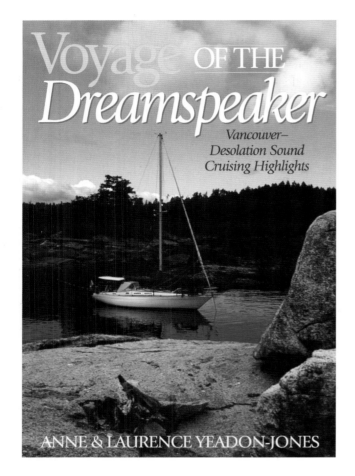

VOYAGE OF THE DREAMSPEAKER
Anne & Laurence Yeadon-Jones

Voyage of the Dreamspeaker is a personal record of three magical and balmy months from early July to late September when Anne and Laurence cruised the beautiful coast of BC aboard their sailboat *Dreamspeaker*, with *Tink,* their faithful dinghy, in tow. Their voyage took them from the cosmopolitan city of Vancouver to the laid-back anchorages of Howe Sound, the delights of the Sunshine Coast, warm-water swimming in the lakes of Desolation Sound and the majesty of Toba Inlet. The authors had always dreamed of taking an unhurried journey with their Dreamspeaker guides in hand to revisit favourite haunts that they had discovered during their fifteen years of adventuring and recording. This personal cruising companion will also give readers a special insight into a number of new experiences that Anne has smoothly interwoven with stories and discoveries from earlier journeys among the islands and along a coastline that they have grown to love. This coast has won their hearts.

Voyage of the Dreamspeaker is published by Harbour Publishing at www.harbourpublishing.com and distributed in the US by Fine Edge www.fineedge.com. Personalized books and guides are also available from the authors' website at www.dreamspeaker.ca.

COASTAL MAGIC
A DREAMSPEAKER DESTINATIONS DVD
Anne & Laurence Yeadon-Jones

Dreamspeaker Cruising Guide authors Anne and Laurence Yeadon-Jones have added *A Dreamspeaker Destinations DVD* titled *Coastal Magic* to their series of colourful and informative guides.

With Anne and Laurence as your hosts, this scenic DVD takes you on a 5-day dream cruise from the city of Vancouver, up the Sunshine Coast to Jervis Inlet and magical Princess Louisa Marine Park, backed by the powerful beauty of Chatterbox Falls.

The cruising itinerary includes the authors' favourite anchorages and marinas en route to Princess Louisa Inlet: Snug Cove on Bowen Island, colourful Gibsons Landing, Halfmoon Bay, Simson Marine Park and the white sand beaches of Buccaneer Bay, popular Smuggler Cove Marine Park, Secret Cove and historic Pender Harbour.

Coastal Magic is available worldwide at www.dreamspeaker.ca.

PASSAGE PLANNING CHARTS
Hand-drawn and watercoloured by Laurence Yeadon-Jones

Following requests from numerous boaters, Laurence Yeadon-Jones spent over two years developing six handy Passage Planning Charts to complement he and Anne's Dreamspeaker Cruising Guide series. His practical approach was to build a set of workable charts layered from current chart mapping data that included NOAA, CHS and Admiralty Charts. Initially hand-drawn at a scale of 1:200,000, each chart was reduced equally to ensure that the final products were of equal scale and, when overlapped, created a consistent representation of the Inside Passage from Puget Sound, WA, to the Broughtons in BC.

Sized at 12 x 17 inches and sold individually or as a set of six, these Passage Planning Charts are available online at www.dreamspeaker.ca.

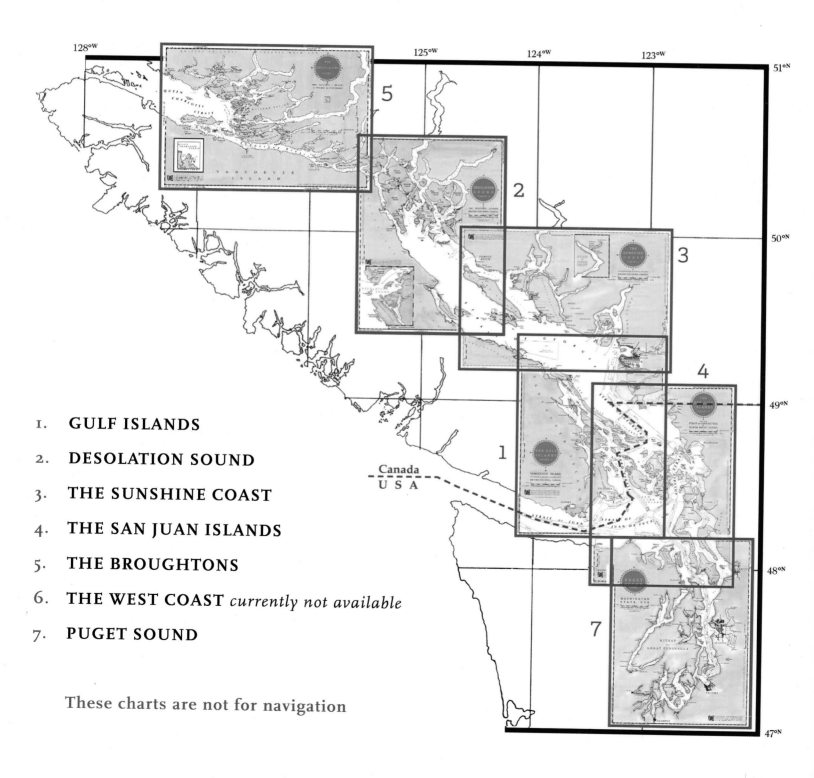

1. **GULF ISLANDS**

2. **DESOLATION SOUND**

3. **THE SUNSHINE COAST**

4. **THE SAN JUAN ISLANDS**

5. **THE BROUGHTONS**

6. **THE WEST COAST** *currently not available*

7. **PUGET SOUND**

These charts are not for navigation

THE DREAMSPEAKER SERIES
BY ANNE & LAURENCE YEADON-JONES

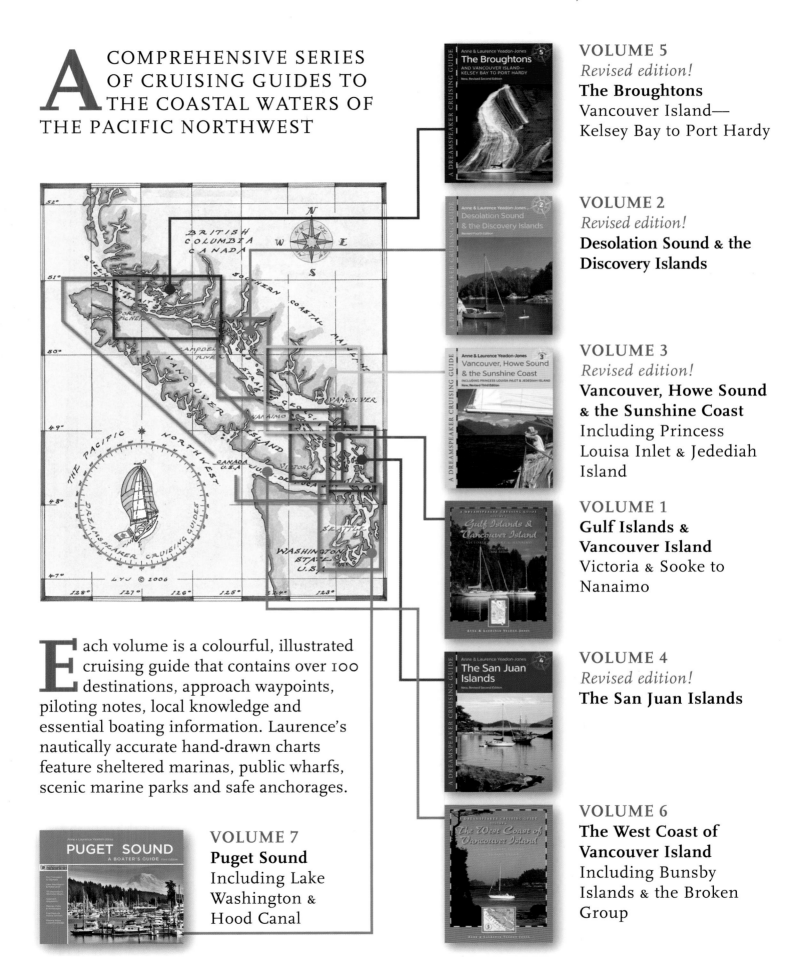

A COMPREHENSIVE SERIES OF CRUISING GUIDES TO THE COASTAL WATERS OF THE PACIFIC NORTHWEST

VOLUME 5
Revised edition!
The Broughtons
Vancouver Island—
Kelsey Bay to Port Hardy

VOLUME 2
Revised edition!
Desolation Sound & the Discovery Islands

VOLUME 3
Revised edition!
Vancouver, Howe Sound & the Sunshine Coast
Including Princess Louisa Inlet & Jedediah Island

VOLUME 1
Gulf Islands & Vancouver Island
Victoria & Sooke to Nanaimo

Each volume is a colourful, illustrated cruising guide that contains over 100 destinations, approach waypoints, piloting notes, local knowledge and essential boating information. Laurence's nautically accurate hand-drawn charts feature sheltered marinas, public wharfs, scenic marine parks and safe anchorages.

VOLUME 4
Revised edition!
The San Juan Islands

VOLUME 7
Puget Sound
Including Lake Washington & Hood Canal

VOLUME 6
The West Coast of Vancouver Island
Including Bunsby Islands & the Broken Group